WS 600

MEDICAL LIBRARY
ROYAL HAMPSHIRE COUNTY HOSPITAL
WINCHESTER

To be renewed or returned on or before the date marked below:

10. JAN. 1973 7th Feb. 1973	21. FEB. 1975 8. SEP. 1975	24. MAY 1978 23. JUN. 1978
15 NOV 1973 13. DEC. 1973 27. MAR. 1974 -1 MAY 1974 25. JUN. 1974	22. MAR. 1976 -2 DEC. 1976 -5 JUL. 1977 23. AUG. 1977 12·10·77 11.11.77 24.3.78	10. NOV. 1980 12. FEB. 1981

WITHDRAWN FROM STOCK
ROYAL HAMPSHIRE COUNTY HOSPITAL, WINCHESTER DISTRICT LIBRARY

PLEASE ENTER ON LOAN SLIP:

AUTHOR: KIRMAN, B.H.

TITLE: The mentally handicapped child.

ACCESSION NO: **1965**

The mentally handicapped child

Dr Brian H Kirman
Psychiatrist at Queen Mary's Hospital for Children, Carshalton, Surrey

The mentally handicapped child

Nelson

Thomas Nelson and Sons Ltd
36 Park Street London W1Y 4DE

PO Box 18123 Nairobi Kenya

Thomas Nelson (Australia) Ltd
597 Little Collins Street Melbourne 3000

Thomas Nelson and Sons (Canada) Ltd
81 Curlew Drive Don Mills Ontario

Thomas Nelson (Nigeria) Ltd
PO Box 336 Apapa Lagos

Thomas Nelson and Sons (South Africa) (Proprietary) Ltd
51 Commissioner Street Johannesburg

© Brian H. Kirman 1972

First published 1972

SBN 0 17 138054 1

Printed in Great Britain by Northumberland Press Ltd Gateshead

Contents

1 The size of the problem. What is mental handicap? 9
2 The pathology of mental retardation 28
3 The history of mental handicap 47
4 The cultural, social and economic background of mental handicap 64
5 Assessment 84
6 Causation 101
7 The services 118
8 Care: some parental problems 136
9 Education 154
10 Growing up 171
11 Employment 186
12 Research 203
   Bibliography 221
   Glossary 224
   Appendix 1: Speech development 231
   Appendix 2: Functional assessment record 232
   Index of authors 234
   Index of subjects 236

Acknowledgements

It gives me pleasure to acknowledge the help which I have received from my colleagues and friends in the Fountain and Carshalton Hospital Group, who have kindly read and improved this little book with their constructive criticism. I am indebted to the team of which I am a member for their collective wisdom. I am also grateful to Professor Tizard, Dr O'Connor, Professor Clarke and many other friends from whose work I have freely quoted. I would particularly like to thank the staff of the Department of Health and Social Security for permission to quote certain statistics which they kindly provided. My gratitude is due to Miss Phyllis Wolf who typed this book, to Mr LaPage for kindly preparing the figures, and to my wife for her forbearance.

Chapter 1
The size of the problem.
What is mental handicap?

Many people are today aware of mental handicap. Some families themselves have a mentally handicapped child; others will have watched television programmes dealing with different aspects of backwardness. Recent scandals concerning difficulties at particular hospitals have caused much public concern and made many people who perhaps were previously unaware that such institutions existed realize that this is a matter for common concern. I suppose that most of us remember from our school days some unfortunate boy or girl who just could not do sums and always got on badly with school work. Such children were mocked in the past and were literally put in a corner and compelled to wear the dunce's cap. In my own time at school I well remember one poor lad who was regularly caned every week because of his bad marks. It did not seem to occur to anyone that his marks did not improve with this treatment!

Others may have had some acquaintance with more severe degrees of mental handicap. Some will remember, as I do, the traditional 'village idiot' in their own village. Others will have read the books of Thomas Hardy or other literature which touches on the problem. In recent years the work of the National Society for Mentally Handicapped Children and the National Association for Mental Health has done a great deal to inform the public of the needs of those less well endowed than themselves. With the growth of special provision since the Second World War, there has been an increasing number of people employed in schools for the educationally subnormal, in junior and senior training centres, in play-groups and in providing a social service for the mentally handicapped in each locality. Through them and their families there is now more awareness of the special needs of the dull and backward child and his family. Most of us have probably seen a group of backward children waiting to go to their centre, or an individual backward child with his parents. Although we have seen such things the matter is not often brought home to us emotionally and we may not pay much attention until we are directly and personally involved. Backwardness is no respecter of social class and cases occur in families at all economic levels. The work of research and social provision for mental handicap has benefited directly from the fact that leading families in the United States, France, Italy and Holland have been so afflicted.

Frequency

It is not possible to give a straight answer to any question about the frequency of mental handicap. It is sometimes said by those who wish to arouse the public to awareness of the problem that 3 per cent of the population are affected, a figure obtained by counting all those who do badly on a standard test of intelligence. The precise proportion would depend on the nature of the test, but if we counted all those scoring less than an intelligence quotient (I.Q.) of 75 on some tests, this would be about 3 per cent of the whole population, or about a million and a half people in a fifty million population or six million individuals in a country like the United States. These figures may help to show that mental handicap is widespread, but they are of limited practical value. In fact most of these people get by as ordinary citizens without too much in the way of special help. As will be discussed later, however, changes now taking place in our society may in the future focus more attention on this intellectually deprived section.

Relative nature of intelligence

Tests of intelligence are what we make them and some of the questions used in the Terman-Merrill type of test, much employed in schools, are really tests of school knowledge. Porteus, who developed a system of mazes as a test of intelligence was concerned at one time with trying to assess the mental ability of Australian aborigines who had had no schooling. All notions of intelligence are relative and the attempt to measure ability, as this is usually done nowadays, derives from the work of Binet and Simon in France at the beginning of this century. They noticed that people varied greatly in their intellectual capacity and tried to compare them one to another. The scientific basis for such comparisons is now usually derived from taking a large sample of children of a given age and finding suitable problems which, on average, they can manage to solve. This process of standardization will result in a test battery which is right for a particular population at a particular time, but we still know very little about what takes place in the long term. We do not know, for instance, if people are getting more or less clever as time goes by, though there is some evidence from two surveys of Scottish school children that there is no rapid decline, but perhaps even a slight improvement.

It should also be emphasized that a test standardized on one population is not necessarily suitable for another. A standard American test is not appropriate for Spanish speaking people in California.

It is now generally recognized that there is no such quality as abstract intelligence, but rather that individuals have a variety of different abilities which are said to correlate with one another. Thus, a person who is good at arithmetic is also likely to be quite good at solving problems involving shape as well as at tasks involving manual skill. There are, however, many exceptions to this general rule. For this reason the *Wechsler* type of test is more informative than one which gives only a mental age or an I.Q. The Wechsler scale divides up into verbal items and performance items, and these are further sub-divided. It thus becomes possible to see that an individual child may be of good intelligence in some ways but may be failing on speech. This then raises the question as to whether he is deaf or has a speech defect.

If we take thirty children in one classroom we can get them to stand in order according to height. This is not difficult. It is also possible to rank people according to other measures, such as the amount of haemoglobin in their blood. In considering height we could divide the class into those who are 'tall' and those who are 'short'. But we would then have to decide what we meant by these terms. We can do something similar with intelligence, and if we put the result in the form of a graph we get something like the curve in Figure 1. Intelligence is much more difficult to measure than height, and different tests measure different things though there is usually fairly good agreement. As with height, children may change position compared with other children. Some grow faster at one time than at another in both height and intelligence. It will be seen from the curve in the Figure that there is no sharp difference between people who are 'normal' and people who are 'mentally retarded'. It is all a question of degree.

Is mental retardation becoming commoner?
If we accept that intelligence is relative, then our opinion of what constitutes mental retardation may change. It is all a question of why we should want to measure intelligence and what we are looking for. The extremely retarded are obvious, and it was always evident that the 'village idiot' could not look after himself but had to be looked after by the community or his family. There would be no advantage today in passing a law which compelled anyone scoring less than an I.Q. of 70 on a particular test to be entered on a special register. This might involve a million or so people in Britain, most

12 The Mentally Handicapped Child

of whom are looked upon as ordinary citizens, attending school or working or looking after their homes.

The fact that so much more has been heard about mental retardation lately does not necessarily imply that backwardness is commoner than it was. One way in which the problem arises has been as a result of conscription for military service. In the nineteenth century, Morel became worried about the poor level of the soldiers recruited into Louis Napoleon's army in France. In the First World War Yerkes in

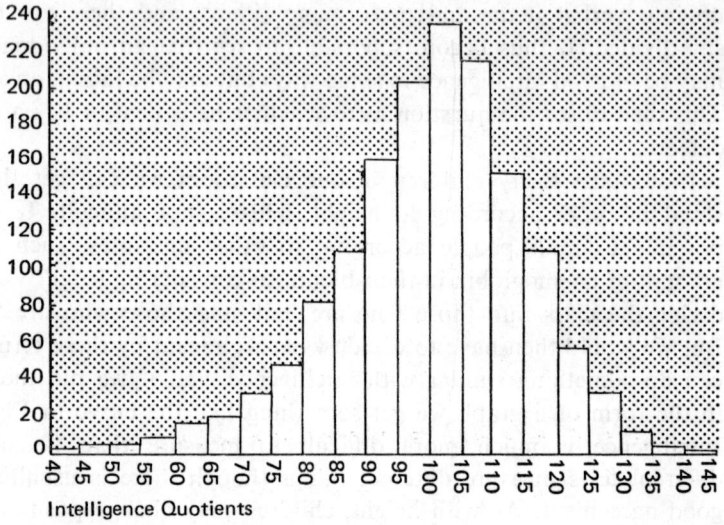

Fig. 1 Intelligence Quotients
Distribution of intelligence. (Reproduced from Wechsler, D. *The Measurement and Appraisal of Adult Intelligence* (1958))

America showed a similar concern, and developed routine methods of testing the intelligence of soldiers. He found that the measured intelligence in different states was very different, and also that, on average, Negroes did less well on the tests of intelligence than did whites. Since then, workers have pointed out that a higher proportion of the Negro population is in the poor states, and that the level of intelligence can be related to the amount spent in each state on education per head.

So conscription and war have been one of the ways in which attention has been drawn to the great variation in intelligence and to the large numbers of those who, in technically advanced countries such as the United States, seem to have received little benefit from their schooling. We are now inclined to take schooling for granted, but compulsory general education in Britain has really only been fully effective since the end of the nineteenth century. The writer's mother attended one of the original 'Board' schools at which she solemnly had to pay one penny per week. One effect of the right of all children to schooling has been to draw attention to the difficulty which many have with formal education. There are still numbers of children leaving school in both Britain and the United States who are virtually illiterate. The recognition of these difficulties has led to the creation of special schools and special classes. At one time these were classed as 'M.D.' schools in local authority case papers, but they are now regarded as schools for the educationally subnormal, and it is recognized that they cater for a wide range of children with difficulties in learning.

Professor Penrose and others have pointed out that there seem to be more retarded children proportionately than adults. It is true that very young, very retarded children do die more easily than ordinary children: but the difference between the figures for children of school age and adults is not really due to this. What happens is that there are many children who are not very good at sums and spelling and other schoolwork. When they leave school they often find a job which they can do well enough and are not much bothered about scholarship until perhaps they occasionally have a problem in filling in a form.

Administrative prevalence

This brings us to the conclusion that mental handicap is not really a thing in itself but involves the notion of how society reacts to its less able citizens. In an underdeveloped country, very few people are listed as being mentally handicapped; there may be little opportunity for schooling and much of the population may be doing unskilled work. In a developed country where most parents have great expectations for their children, they seek, expect and indeed demand special advice, facilities and help for those children who seem to be less gifted than others. Table 1 shows the growth in schools for the educationally subnormal which are part of the recognition accorded to the problem of mental handicap.

Until recently there has been a sharp division between the more and the less severely handicapped. At one time, in the Mental Deficiency Act 1913 the terms in use for the severely handicapped were 'idiot' and 'imbecile'. It was agreed in the international classification of diseases that these terms could be interpreted in terms of intelligence quotient, so that an idiot had an I.Q. of less than 20, whereas imbeciles occupied the range from 20 to 30. This meant that those in these two

Table 1 Growth of provision of places for educationally subnormal children in schools in England and Wales, 1952-69

1950	15,173	1962	36,276
1952	18,700	1963	37,822
1953	19,459	1964	40,921
1955	22,644	1965	42,670
1959	30,656	1966	44,699
1960	32,815	1967	46,347
1961	34,347	1968	50,036
		1969	52,849

grades were functioning less than half as well as a normal child on measures of intelligence. In other words, such a child, if aged fourteen would do less well than the average seven-year-old. The Mental Health Act 1959 introduced the unfortunate term 'severely subnormal' for such children, and the Department of Health is now using the term 'mental handicap' for all degrees of mental retardation. The present international agreement is to describe children with an I.Q. below 50 as moderately, severely and profoundly handicapped in descending order thus:

Degree of mental handicap

Contemporary term	Intelligence quotient	Other terms
Mild retardation	50-70	Educationally subnormal; Feebleminded; Moron; Subnormal
Moderate retardation	35-49	Imbecile trainable; Severely subnormal
Severe retardation	20-34	
Profound retardation	0-19	Idiot

More seriously retarded children and adults are much more likely to become known to various authorities than are the less severely handicapped. Fortunately they are less numerous. As mentioned, from 2 to 3 per cent of the population may score less than I.Q. 70, depending on the test used. For those with I.Q. below 50, the proportion at seven years of age is about 0·4 per cent or 4 per 1,000. It is, of course, not possible to assess a newborn baby in terms of intelligence, but it seems likely that about 1 per cent of the newborn have such a defect or abnormality in their brains that they would function in the range below I.Q. 50 if they lived. In fact, nowadays with a low infantile death rate the greater number of deaths among young babies is due to developmental abnormalities, including those of the brain. For this reason, there is a reduction of the figure to about 4 per 1,000 at school age. Incidentally, it is not until the age of about seven years that a reasonable reliable estimate of intelligence can be made. However, in the case of the more seriously handicapped, it is possible to say with fair confidence that they are indeed severely retarded at a much earlier age.

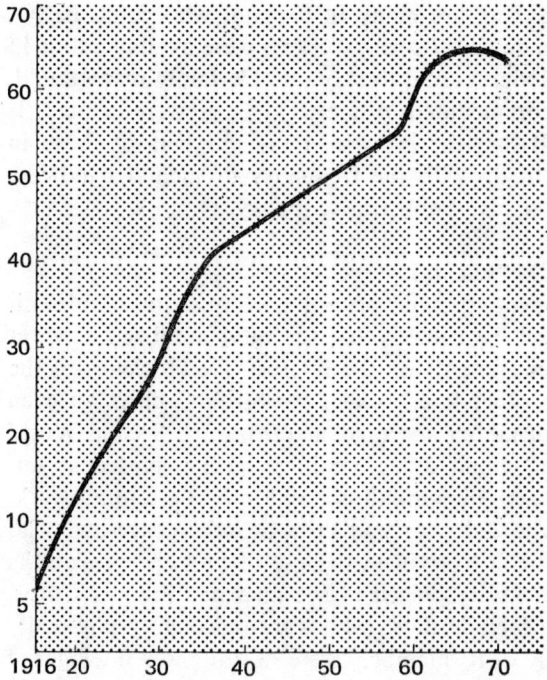

Fig. 2
Growth of hospital population of mentally handicapped in England and Wales, 1916-69 (in thousands)

In the earlier years of this century the emphasis was on providing institutional care for the mentally handicapped. This was partly because those who then concerned themselves with eugenics believed that such a policy would reduce the numbers of the 'unfit'. It was also due to the fact that there was little social provision in the community for the more handicapped members. Figure 2 shows the growth in the institutional population for the mentally retarded. This curve has now levelled off, and it was suggested by the Chief Medical Officer some years ago that this was due to better provision in the community. This may be so, but cynics may argue that it is simply because there are no places in the hospitals. There is certainly a big waiting list. In fact, we are uncertain about the real need, since if there is no possibility of admission then names are not added to a meaningless waiting list which never moves. In many institutions, perhaps in most, the only prospect of long-term admission is to fill a death vacancy, while at the same time, the expectation of life for people in these institutions has increased along with that of the general population. It may, of course, be argued that there are many in hospital who could be got out if the effort were made and if social workers were available to help them to find jobs and lodgings and to stay out. Certainly many could, with advantage, be accommodated in hostels if these were created. It should not be assumed that the growth in the numbers of those in hospital has anything to do with the frequency of mental handicap. It is simply a reflection of administrative policy.

The 'ineducable' and the 'unemployable'
If the numbers of the mentally handicapped are a question of administrative procedure, it will be evident that the total number known at any one time will depend in part on the interest and efficiency of the social services. On the other hand, social background plays an even greater part. In times of labour shortage, as during the Second World War, many people who might otherwise have been regarded as unemployable were engaged in agriculture and other essential work. Those army recruits who did poorly at tests of intelligence and who were thought to be difficult to train in the use of firearms or at tasks such as that of signaller, were placed in the unarmed Pioneer Corps. This corps was only to include those who were reasonably physically fit, but, given this, many of its members were of quite low intelligence but were able to carry out much necessary 'pick and shovel' work. Similar considerations apply during peace time depending on level of employment, degrees of automation and, most of all, on the attitudes of employers.

At about the level of I.Q. 50 there seems to be a sharp change in the likelihood that a person will find a job. Some people, remarkably, find and hold useful jobs despite an I.Q. below this level. But they are the exceptions, and most with an intelligence in this range find it difficult to fit into open employment because they take longer to train than the employer is willing to allow, or require more supervision than is available or have poor work discipline, or, more usually, fail to make ordinary social adjustments. There is no absolute reason why this should be so, and much of what is done in the way of contract work in sheltered employment could be carried out within the framework of industry if arrangements could be agreed. In other words, there might be some advantage in having handicapped workers go to a special shop or fit into the general pattern of a factory rather than having work brought to them in an adult training centre or hospital industrial department. This would help in the process of assimilation into the general community which is the present official policy.

In the meantime, local authorities provide a certain number of adult training centres, which are attended daily by the more seriously mentally handicapped living at home, and so provide an alternative to hospital care. Such provision is at present inadequate and as it develops the pressure on the hospitals will presumably be eased. It should be remembered, however, that at this level of intelligence a degree of care and help is usually required in quite simple matters such as cooking, laundry, achieving a presentable appearance and so forth. These duties may be willingly undertaken by parents (who often err on the side of overprotection), but as the handicapped individuals become older their parents may die or become incapable of carrying this burden. This is one reason for such a great pressure for hospital beds. It has recently been suggested by Professor McKeown and Dr Albert Kushlick that there is no particular need for many of these people to be in hospital and that they could be more suitably accommodated in hostels from which they could continue to attend their senior training centre or other place of employment as they had done from their own homes.

The biggest and most solid contribution made by local health authorities to the well-being of the more seriously handicapped has been the provision of junior training centres. There was very little such provision before the Second World War, and Figure 3 shows how development has proceeded since that time. The numbers of children attending these junior training centres is some indication of the total of seriously mentally handicapped children in the area, since adequate provision is now made in most regions for the school-age group. Figures for nurseries and play-groups, if available, would not indicate the number of affected children under five, nor would figures for adult training centres give the size of the adult handicapped population since, unfortunately, there are nothing like enough places in these establishments. The knowledge that local authority health and social service departments have of the numbers of younger retarded

18 The Mentally Handicapped Child

children in their locality will vary very considerably, depending on the resources and the provision which they have for this task. If they have sufficient mental health workers or other social workers or health visitors concerned with this task, and if they have a good provision of nurseries and play-groups, they will probably know most of the pre-school retarded children in the locality. Regrettably, few authorities are in this happy position.

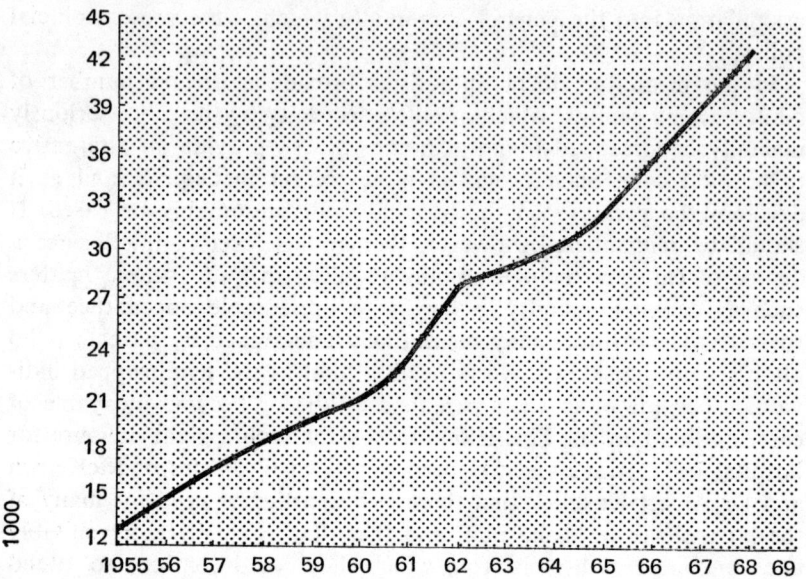

Fig. 3
Growth of places in local authority training centres for mentally handicapped

As from 1 April 1971 local education authorities have been responsible for the education of all children. Until now, some children—those with approximately an I.Q. below 50—have been regarded as 'unsuitable for education at school'. These included the children attending junior training centres, which will now be classified as schools and staffed by fully trained teachers, having previously been run either by hospitals or, for the most part, by local authority health departments.

Recognition of mental handicap

To collect facts and figures about the mentally handicapped, it is necessary to have definite criteria or standards by which the disability can be recognized. It will be realized in the light of what has been written above that this is very difficult. At one time, before the 1959 Mental Health Act, local health authorities had a statutory duty to 'ascertain' mental defectives, and kept registers for this purpose. The new Act dropped this provision, probably because it was recognized that the only reason for ascertainment is to supply a service. If no service can, in fact, be supplied, then there is little advantage in ascertainment, except for future planning.

There are even some circumstances in which a child or adult may be worse off if he is 'ascertained'. In the past, questions of civil liberty often arose, and this occasionally still happens; so that someone who is formally and legally regarded as mentally handicapped may be detained against his wishes if he is, for example, found guilty of a minor offence. This then swells the numbers of those in hospital. If the question of mental handicap had not been raised, then the offender would probably have been put on probation and have continued to live at home. It may to some extent be a matter of chance whether or not a court treats such a person as mentally handicapped. Similarly, a mentally handicapped person may be eligible for inclusion in the Register of Handicapped Persons. However, it has been our experience that this is sometimes a disadvantage, and that it is sometimes easier for an employer to accept the person of rather low intelligence if he or she is not specially labelled. He may then feel that the new employee is not very different from many other workers in the same place of employment.

On the other hand, there are many advantages in knowing about a handicap when services are provided. If a child of school age is accepted as educationally subnormal, this may mean his transfer to a school where teachers may be specially qualified in teaching slow learners and with classes less than twenty instead of, perhaps, being as many as forty. The numbers recognized as mentally handicapped tend, therefore, to increase as services are provided. It is significant that throughout the period of the existence of schools for the educationally subnormal, there have been long waiting lists, and there is little sign of these diminishing. As to care in institutions, there is still a considerable waiting list for places and although this may now be seen as not the best way of providing residential care, the waiting list shows something of the unsatisfied demand.

People who are only mildly retarded will not be noticed in a crowd of ordinary people. The more seriously handicapped are different. Physically they often *look* different—if, for example, they have Down's syndrome (mongolism), a small head (microcephaly) or a big head (hydrocephalus), or cerebral palsy (spasticity in most cases). Even if the seriously retarded child looks fairly ordinary, physically his behaviour may soon draw attention. He may grind his teeth or dribble saliva at an age when other children have long ceased to do so.

Some conditions associated with severe mental retardation are recognizable at birth. The best known of these is Down's syndrome, or 'mongolism' as it is commonly, though incorrectly, known, since it has nothing to do with Mongols! The characteristic facial appearance and many other features make it easy even for those who have little experience of the condition to know it again when they see it. Babies with very small heads are obviously abnormal at birth, though careful measurement of the head circumference is helpful in recognizing borderline cases of microcephaly. Hydrocephalus, or 'water on the brain', is not usually present at birth but may develop soon afterwards, when the head becomes obviously bigger and the 'soft spot', or fontanelle, begins to bulge. This is a common complication of spina bifida, or open spine, and may lead to mental retardation in babies with this condition. Open spine occurs in about one baby in every 300, though it varies from one part of the country to another and in different parts of the world. Down's syndrome is found in one in 600 babies, more among children of older mothers, and does not seem to vary very much in frequency in different countries. Other conditions which can be recognized at birth are less common. For example, a hereditary chemical disorder known as phenylketonuria happens in about one in 10,000 babies, though it seems to be commoner than this in Ireland and areas like Glasgow and Liverpool.

In the conditions mentioned above there is little doubt that the baby will be much less able than a normal child, though the exact amount of backwardness will only become known when the child is older. In many other types of cases, however, the child is in danger of being backward, though this is not certain. Local health authorities now make use of an 'at risk' register for such babies, though the scheme does not seem to have been very successful so far. The objective is for the health visitor and child specialist to keep a special eye on those babies who may not develop normally. Such babies might be those with a very low birth weight, with a history of a very difficult delivery, or who were difficult to start breathing after birth, or who were in poor shape when they were born, or babies who were jaundiced or who suffered from meningitis or encephalitis (inflammation of the brain) in early life. Others would include those who, at an early age, show signs of cerebral palsy, stiffness, limited movement or

The size of the problem. What is mental handicap? 21

disordered reflexes. After the new-born period the baby may cause anxiety by failure to thrive, by not gaining weight, perhaps by being constipated, perhaps by vomiting, being difficult to feed or having fits, either with or without fever. Investigation may strengthen the suspicion that something is wrong, providing evidence such as abnormal brain waves (electroencephalogram) or abnormal substances in the urine or the blood; or, in the case of cretinism, a low level of iodine in the blood.

Recognition at a later age
As a general rule the less profound the retardation the later it is likely to be recognized. However, this depends on circumstances such as the experience and expectations of parents and grandparents, and the attitude of the health visitor and others who may be concerned. Many children who later prove to be very backward indeed leave the hospital where they have been born without any suspicion that anything is wrong. At a later stage, they may be slow in taking notice, in sitting up, in standing, walking or becoming clean in their habits. However, a number of my colleagues and myself recently studied the age at which backward children walk. We found, as expected, that on average they walk later than ordinary children. But there are some children who are amongst the most backward in speech and in most other ways, but who walk early. So early walking does not rule out the possibility of backwardness in other ways.

In another study we found that children whose backwardness was only recognized at about the age of two, because of a failure to talk, were more likely to be disturbed. Such a child may seem acceptable up to that time, though on questioning the mother may admit that her child never seems to have had really warm and good contact with her. He always seemed to have been cold, distant and aloof. Some children who are conspicuous because they fail to talk are among those who may be described as *autistic*. At a later age, such a child may come into a room where there are a number of adults. Typically, he pays no attention to them but begins to investigate the room, looks out of the window, turns on the taps if there are any, switches on the lights or other electrical equipment, plugging it in if it is not connected. In other words, he shows some apparently intelligent behaviour with things but seems to have little use for people. While such a child may not seem to be noticing people, in some cases it is apparent that he does, because he immediately takes avoiding action when he realizes that someone has come to take him away from an interesting situation. Sometimes these children appear to be deaf, but it becomes clear that they are not, because while at first they take no notice, when they are told to do something, if the command is given several times, they reluctantly obey.

If we wish to know whether a child can hear and understand speech it is always important to try him with words alone. Parents and many professional people make the mistake of using gestures as well, pointing or looking at the thing which is to be brought and in other ways allowing the child to guess what is expected of him. Some children who behave in this way are, of course, truly deaf, and it may be very difficult to distinguish them from other children who do not talk, so-called 'non-communicating children'. Most ordinary young children can be persuaded to co-operate with a bit of coaxing, and can be tested to a range of sounds of different strengths and frequencies so that it becomes possible to plot an 'audiogram' comparing their hearing with that of average children. With disturbed children, on the other hand, especially those who are withdrawn and aloof, this cannot effectively be done by ordinary means. We have to observe and try to play with them over a long period to get to know and understand them well. We can then begin in a 'free field' situation, that is, by observing them whilst they are free to move about and play, to assess their hearing for speech and for a variety of sounds at different pitches, distances and strengths.

Autism

Autistic children may be mentioned at this point because they have been better recognized of recent years. A good deal has been written and said about them. The subject is fashionable, and many parents with a backward child ask if he is autistic. Perhaps it seems better, or less of a slur, to have a child who is autistic than one who is 'subnormal'. Parents may also think that if a child is autistic, it is more like an illness and he can somehow be made well again, whilst once a child is backward or 'subnormal' he will always be so. This distinction is not correct. A child who is backward but friendly and co-operative may be greatly improved by patient education and training. It is true that some autistic children do well but, unfortunately, these are a minority. Many of them always need care and will be unable to take up gainful employment. Some children who are classed as autistic are obviously intelligent; others may be thought to be intelligent, but cannot be proved to be so. In fact, the best test of whether a child who is thought to be autistic can do well is how he does on an ordinary intelligence test. We may think that he could do better if he tried, and this may be true, but the hard facts are that if he does badly on such a test now he will probably not do well at school or work. This does not mean that we should not create special units for autistic children, or try to understand them better, to find out why they live in a world of their own and what has made them like that. If we try hard enough, we may become better at helping them. Meanwhile it is useful to remember that a proportion of backward children are also disturbed, behaving oddly and failing to make contact. Some of these will be regarded as autistic, but there is no sharp line dividing autistic children from others. It is very much a matter of opinion whether or not a child is autistic. Different psychiatrists may classify the same children differently, and there is no way of saying who is right or wrong at our present stage of understanding. It is really best to think of intelligence and behaviour pattern separately, so that a child who may show both poor intelligence and peculiar behaviour is seen as both backward and autistic. On the other hand, most backward children have the kind of behaviour we would expect for their level of intelligence and from the way in which they have been brought up. A child of ten with an I.Q. of 50 may behave very much like an ordinary five-year-old and be friendly and affectionate, just like a younger boy or girl.

School entry
Most children do not go to school until they are five. Quite a few who have been well accepted by their parents up to that time are found on entry to have great difficulty with lessons and with keeping up with other children. There is now a better understanding of the difficulties of such children, and more effort to help them. Some education authorities are fortunate in having observation and opportunity classes for those new entrants who are doing badly but who seem to need more observation. There is an increasing use of psychologists in the field of education, contrasting with the often clumsy and insensitive attitudes of the past. The writer remembers an incident from his own village school when a little girl attending on her first day, and not seeming to respond to the teacher, was brought before the whole school whilst the headmaster in a loud voice questioned the elder brother, asking among other things, 'Is she stupid?' Because of the extra attention that children get at this age, and because of the demands of the school, the numbers who are looked upon as backward at this stage increase and continue to do so, reaching a maximum perhaps by about the age of fourteen.

Surveys
There have been various surveys of the problem of mental handicap.

These surveys are very difficult to do, involving a great deal of work by different people who have to agree between themselves on what exactly they are looking for. One of these was carried out by Professor Jack Tizard in Middlesex, who confined his attention to the more severely handicapped, those children who used to be called idiots or imbeciles, and who would now be described as moderately, severely or profoundly handicapped, or having an I.Q. below 50. He did this deliberately because these children are easier to find and to recognize and there is less likely to be disagreement about their classification. In a way, the mildly handicapped are more important, if only because there are more of them and more can be done for them educationally. But this makes it all the more important to find out how many seriously handicapped there are, so that we can see the size of the problem and think how best to help parents with such children and, in the long term, to find out whether there are ways in which such cases could be prevented.

The Middlesex survey showed that for every 1,000 children aged 0–4 years, there was almost one seriously retarded child. At age 5–9 years the figure was almost exactly 3 per 1,000, and at 10–14 the result was 3·61 per 1,000. As Professor Tizard points out, and for the reasons mentioned above, these figures are not complete, though they fit in with a rough estimate of 4 per 1,000 seriously retarded children of school age. It seems likely that these results are valid for the country as a whole, since another survey carried out by Professor Tizard in London, an analysis of findings in Salford by Dr Kushlick, as well as his more intensive study of the Wessex hospital region, all tie in with these findings, if account is taken of the nature and depth of the survey in each case.

For the mildly retarded, the size of the problem as seen and reported by the authorities will depend very much on the kinds of school and other facilities they have available. The more trouble they take, the bigger the problem will seem to be. For London, Tizard found only 0·29 mildly retarded people of all ages per 1,000 population, but this was just the people known to the authority as needing help or presenting a problem. The figure was highest at age fifteen, when it was 0·56 per 1,000. To put it another way, one in 2,000 young teenagers was seen to be needing special help on account of mental retardation. It is clear, by any reckoning, that this is only a small part of the total. It is also, perhaps, some indication of the extent to which young people of limited intelligence do manage without a great deal of special help. The total figures of those known to the authorities in Salford as being mentally retarded is similar, as is the case in Wessex.

It is interesting that of those mildly retarded people known to the authority in London, half were in institutions.

Mortality

Part of the anxiety felt by members of the Eugenics Society at the time of its foundation in 1909 about the future of national intelligence was due to a somewhat naïve belief in the 'law of the jungle', the survival of the fittest. It is naïve to apply this concept to human society because it is difficult to be sure who is fit, and for what. Many famous figures who have made big contributions to science, art and humanity in general have been conspicuously unfit in many ways. This applies, for example, to Darwin himself, who pioneered understanding of the laws of natural selection. This simple notion put about by some of those who popularized fear of an impending catastrophe in regard to mental handicap was that, if left to nature, the 'unfit' would perish. If they were protected by society, they would survive, and would produce many more of their own kind, thus undermining national 'fitness'. There are many faults in this argument. In fact most seriously retarded children have quite normal parents.

It is usually said that in Sparta parents exposed infants on hillsides so that those who were not 'fit' died. In more recent times, another military state, Nazi Germany, undertook the systematic extermination of the 'unfit'. In some poor or primitive societies at present there seems to be a similar attitude to malformed or abnormal infants, though such infanticide may be rationalized as due to fear of the devil or his works. The opposite attitude may be summarized in a traditional French phrase describing the mentally handicapped as 'les enfants du bon Dieu'. Pearl Buck's account of her handicapped child may be read in this connection, and Colonel Ireland in the nineteenth century gave an account of the care and collection of microcephalic children in Amritsar, where they were regarded as being under the special protection of the gods, were described as 'Shah Daula' rats', and were maintained at the shrine.

In fact, the more severely handicapped seldom have children, partly because they are usually cared for and partly because they are not acceptable mates. Some of them may not be biologically fertile. It is true that the prevalence in Britain of certain conditions such as Down's syndrome has increased. This is not because it happens more frequently. While we have no evidence about this, we do know that more children with the condition survive longer. Carter and Evans concluded in one study that there had been perhaps a fourfold increase in survivors with this condition over a period of twenty years.

Such children are still very delicate. Some have faults in the heart, and others are very liable to inflammation of the lungs. Like other backward babies, they are more prone to inhale food into the lungs. For these and other reasons, about half of them die before reaching the age of five. At the other end of their life span, they remain less robust than normal people of the same age, and few survive beyond fifty though exceptional cases may reach seventy.

A degree of 'natural selection' does take place before birth. Some spontaneous miscarriages may be due to illness or abnormality in the mother, or to poor living conditions. Others are due to abnormality in the unborn baby. A study of the products of such abortions, when they are obtainable, shows that many of them are malformed. Recent improvements in the study of chromosomes—the structures in the nucleus of the cell carrying genetic information—have permitted a study of such abortuses using this technique. Many of them have chromosome abnormalities. The incidence of Down's syndrome at conception is far greater than that at birth. It is now technically possible in some conditions to find out early in pregnancy whether the baby is suffering from that condition. This applies to Down's syndrome. The technique is known as 'amniotic puncture', and involves obtaining a specimen of the fluid which surrounds the baby in the womb.

The notion that national intelligence must decline was based on belief that heredity was the chief cause of mental handicap. At one time the importance of environment, or surroundings, was overlooked, but poverty, lack of food, low income and disease are now known to be associated with frequency of mild mental retardation. In addition, there have been a number of dramatic discoveries showing how severe mental retardation can be caused by disease and adverse circumstances. The rubella story is very well known, and we are now within sight of a situation where German measles may cease to be a cause of mental handicap, thanks to the development of an efficient vaccine. This is, at present, not a rare cause of damage to the brain and intellect. Recent epidemics in the United States and elsewhere must have resulted in thousands of brain-damaged babies.

It is over a hundred years since Little declared that some cases of severe brain damage were due to the 'want of a few breathings' at the time immediately after birth. His name has been given to 'Little's disease', a term which has been used to cover a number of children who are spastic and often have small heads. Nowadays we recognize that there are probably many different causes in such cases. However, a recent enquiry into perinatal mortality and morbidity in Britain lends support to the view that events at about the time of birth may well cause permanent damage to the brain in a large number of babies.

It is therefore possible to argue that improvements in the health of mother and child will reduce the number of children born with brain damage and mental backwardness. On the other hand, it is undeniable that, in some cases, in our present state of knowledge, the fall in infant mortality will have the effect of sparing the lives of some children with abnormal brains—for example, those with Down's syndrome—who might otherwise have died. It seems possibly true that, with very low birth-weight babies, the saving of life may outweigh the prevention of brain damage, so allowing more abnormal infants to survive. This is by no means certain, and further studies would be needed to establish this point. Be this as it may, there is good ground for optimism towards quite a few conditions known to cause mental backwardness. Perhaps the most reassuring factor is the likelihood that anything which improves the general standard of nutrition and maternal health will reduce the total of mental handicap, especially the milder forms. An important argument in favour of this view is the considerable difference of frequency of mental handicap, by social class, by region and by country. All the evidence suggests that poverty and hardship increase the incidence. Many of these effects are at a psychological level, and concern the child's educational opportunities. There is considerable evidence, however, much of which has been ably summarized by Herbert Birch, that malnutrition may of itself impair the function of the human brain. There is much experimental evidence to show that this is true of rats and other animals. It seems to be true in human cases of extreme deprivation of food such as causes kwashiorkor in areas of poverty. It may well be true for babies in areas where the deprivation is not so extreme.

In summary, mental handicap is very common. We recognize it best in developed countries where education and techniques are at high levels. But, until recently, few attempts have been made to measure the size of the problem or to provide services. It seems likely that, with appropriate measures, especially those designed to remedy poverty, malnutrition and a poor environment, fewer mentally handicapped children will be born. More research is urgently needed into the epidemiology of mental handicap. Perhaps, like other epidemics —such as those of smallpox or cholera—it can be checked.

Chapter 2
The pathology of mental retardation

One of the things which attracted the present writer to mental retardation was the fact that we know so little about it. It has always been an unpopular subject, and remains so. Many 'don't want to know' about mental handicap. They do not like to talk about the subject, or to be reminded of the existence of very backward children, let alone adults. The siting of St Lawrence's Hospital, Leavesden, and other such institutions at a considerable distance from the city at their foundation was doubtless due in part to a wish to keep such places at a proper distance from citizens who might be distressed by their nearness.

The situation is changing rapidly, and we are now beginning to learn quite a lot about some causes of abnormality of the brain and the way in which they work. But it is probably still true that it is much easier to get money and workers for many other popular forms of research. This is so in regard to some surgical advances which have recently received much publicity. Important though these are, their application seems likely to be confined to a limited number of people. What is needed, however, is not a redistribution of effort among different forms of medical research, but a proper appreciation of the economic as well as the humanitarian importance of mental handicap. Some people are impressed by the burden which society has to carry in caring for those seriously mentally handicapped who are in hospital, even though much less may be spent on them per head than on any other hospital patients. It is true that a high proportion of them are there for life, though a very much more important economic consideration is the enormous loss to society caused by the very limited endowment of such a considerable proportion of the population. In countries such as the United States and Britain there is a shortage of skilled workers and a great deal of unemployment among the unskilled.

There is now little argument about the immediate cause of the severe forms of mental handicap. Work reported by Dr Crome shows that, of children with very marked backwardness who die, the great majority have something obviously wrong with the brain. In some cases the head itself is small (microcephaly). There are all degrees of smallness of the head and some people of good or high intelligence have a small hat size; but the more extreme cases of smallheadedness are always associated with low intelligence. Reduction in brain size may be found, when the head is not very small. Smallness of the brain is the most obvious and commonest finding in severe mental handicap. Another common factor is hardening or scarring of the brain. The cells primarily responsible for memory and mental activity are the neurones. In most cases of marked mental handicap the number of these is greatly reduced, and they are replaced in part by glia, the supporting cells. These glial cells fill in much as scarring takes place in other parts of the body. Many such brains, when removed for examination, are found to be hard and shrunken. The gyri, the folds on the surface of the brain, are no longer smooth and round but narrow and distorted. Findings such as these are frequent, but give little clue in themselves as to the original cause of the abnormality. In a minority of cases there is some indication as to the stage at which things went wrong. Essential parts of the brain, such as the cerebellum, or small brain, may be missing, or other parts not properly formed, suggesting that something untoward happened early on in pregnancy. This also applies to some cases of hydrocephalus, where the passages inside the brain which allow the free flow of the cerebrospinal fluid are too narrow or end in a blind alley.

Specific findings
While it is relatively easy to detect loss of brain weight or disappearance of brain cells, if the loss is sufficiently large, it is more difficult to find out exactly what caused these changes or how things went wrong with the development of the brain. It is, however, possible to do this in a minority of instances. Some cases show a disease which is due to hereditary causes. In others, the trouble may be due to infection or some other outside agent. With the gradual improvement in technique of brain study it has become possible to recognize a number of fairly typical pathological pictures. There are, it is true, a number of diseases described which are little better than names, but there are many others which seem to be linked with a fairly specific process and cause of abnormality.

Some hereditary conditions can be recognized by the expert in a post-mortem examination of the brain without too much difficulty. Most methods depend on staining of very thin slices of brain with different agents which may show a loss of neurones or an overgrowth of the glial cells or a loss of white matter from the inner parts of the brain and a disappearance of the myelin sheaths which normally surround the nerve fibres in developed brains. Certain diseases have a very striking effect on the brain, and this applies to the 'lipidoses', hereditary diseases in which there is too much of a fatty type of substance in the brain. This accumulates in the neurones, which become quite blown up, losing their proper shape and becoming larger and globular. The lipid in the cells can itself be stained. There are several different kinds of lipid which may be found in excess in the brain cells, and other organs of the body may be involved as well. On the basis of these chemical differences, it is gradually becoming possible to distinguish a number of different diseases in this group. One form of this condition affecting mainly young infants has been much studied in New York and is known as Tay-Sachs disease. It is usually thought to be commoner in Jews originating from the Russian-Polish border area, but Crome has pointed out some reasons why this difference may have been artificially exaggerated.

Most children with severe degrees of backwardness are born with something wrong with the brain, or develop an abnormality early in life. Once brain damage has been caused, it does not usually get worse; the lesion, that is the damage, is static rather than progressive. Tay-Sachs disease and other lipidoses are exceptions to this general rule. They do get worse. Affected children usually appear normal at birth, but at some time during infancy they fall ill and lose the ground they have gained. For example, if they have learned clean toilet habits they become doubly incontinent again. They go slowly downhill and eventually die. At an early stage, they may become blind owing to the involvement of the retina at the back of the eye, which is developmentally part of the brain. The brain cells affected by the lipidosis gradually atrophy and die, until the stage is reached when the brain can no longer function. At this final phase, if the electric waves of the brain are recorded, an almost completely flat record may result, showing that the brain's activity is nearly extinct.

In Tay-Sachs disease and similar conditions we have an example of the operation of Mendel's law affecting recessive inheritance. Both parents are carriers of the disease and on average one in four children shows the condition which affects both boys and girls. The inheritance is indirect, for the parents are themselves clinically normal, but a brother or sister of the patient may be affected, and there may be a history of a similar case in other members of the family, perhaps an uncle or aunt. In such rare diseases, there is a greater frequency of consanguineous marriages among the parents. That is, the parents are related to each other, being perhaps first cousins. The disease is caused by an abnormal gene (the unit of hereditary material out of which the chromosomes are built). One abnormal recessive gene seems to be relatively harmless in itself. But a person who has one such abnormal gene is a carrier of the disease. If he is unlucky enough to marry another carrier, affected children may result. Cousin marriages are more at risk in this way, since two people from the same family are more likely to be carriers of the same genetic abnormality.

Other genetic abnormalities of the brain
Another very distinctive group of conditions is known as Schilder's disease which involve a gradual loss of the inner white matter of the brain. Again, as with the lipidoses, we do not know exactly what happens. The probability is that in all these conditions there is a hereditary fault in the brain chemistry. We assume that a faulty gene results in the formation of a faulty enzyme, and that this causes a breakdown in the normal function of the brain. Children with Schilder's disease, like those with lipidosis, are usually normal at birth. Then they gradually lose the ground they have gained, and eventually die, usually becoming blind in the process. In most cases, there is little abnormal to be seen at the back of the eye. The blindness is due to a loss of function in those brain fibres which carry messages from the sensitive retina in the eye to the back of the brain. Schilder's disease also runs in the family, and like the lipidoses it is handed on in a recessive manner, that is, by indirect inheritance. The parents must both be carriers, though without having the disease themselves.

'Gargoylism'
Like 'mongolism', 'gargoylism' is a bad term. The trouble is that while quite a few people know this name, there is no other simple term to put in its place. The group of conditions described by it is known technically as the *mucopolysaccharidoses*, which may sound a little daunting to the non-technical reader. These are a group of conditions in which the brain may be affected, and in which, again as with the lipidoses, there is a storage of material in the affected cells. The most likely reason is that the enzyme which normally deals with the accumulated material is absent or faulty. The situation might be compared to that in a factory where a key machine has broken down and supplies of raw material continue to arrive but cannot be used. The term 'gargoyle' was initially used to describe the faces of children afflicted with one of these conditions. They tend to look rather like each other, and are distinctly different from their normal brothers and sisters. Their features are coarser, perhaps a little more

hairy; the head is a little bigger because of an extra thickness of the skull; the mouth is big and the bones of the face and skull seem rather more prominent than usual. Vision and hearing may be affected, and, in some cases, joints may also be abnormal. The substances which are accumulated in the brain cells in this group of conditions are different from the lipids.

These diseases are only very slowly progressive, so that some affected children reach adult life. They are hereditary, and once again the abnormality is handed on indirectly, so that both parents usually are carriers. One important consideration is that if either partner marries again, the new spouse is very unlikely to be a carrier and therefore children of the second marriage should not be affected. On the other hand, there is one particular form where the condition is sex-linked: only boys are affected, but the condition is handed on

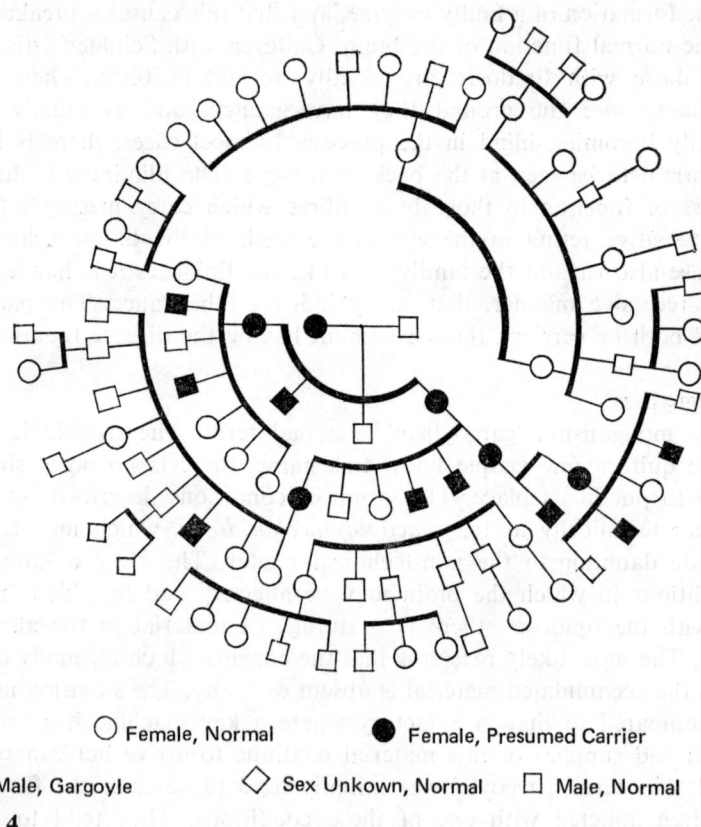

○ Female, Normal ● Female, Presumed Carrier
■ Male, Gargoyle ◇ Sex Unkown, Normal □ Male, Normal

Fig. 4
Pedigree of sex-linkage in mucopolysaccharidosis. (Taken from Beebe and Formel (1954))

by mothers, not by fathers. If the family has this variant then even if the mother marries again her children still have a 25 per cent risk of being affected, and half her daughters could be carriers. Figure 4 shows the pedigree of an affected family.

The appearance and staining properties of the brain cells under the microscope are characteristic, though in all these progressive hereditary diseases it should now be possible to make the diagnosis during life. It is, however, most important that brain studies should continue to be done to check the accuracy of diagnosis. There is usually no difficulty in diagnosing typical and straightforward examples of these diseases but examination of the brain may reveal other, less typical examples where the diagnosis has been missed. Although at present there is no treatment for any of the conditions so far mentioned, it seems theoretically possible that at some time replacement therapy with the missing enzyme may become practicable. Diagnosis is also of the greatest importance for those families who wish to have genetic counselling.

In this connection it is perhaps obvious that direct examination of the brain as a whole is only possible with the co-operation of those unfortunate parents whose children have died. Yet in agreeing to an examination of their child's body they are making a significant contribution to our knowledge and understanding which may ultimately pave the way to treatment, and which certainly clarifies the issue for genetic counselling.

Phenylketonuria

Many of those who have taken a passing interest in mental retardation will know about phenylketonuria. This disease has attracted a great deal of attention because it can be treated. It is not the first example of a condition giving rise to brain damage which can be improved by treatment. We have long known that cretinism can be treated with thyroid extract, and that many children derive benefit from this treatment, including, in some cases, an improvement in their mental state. But cretinism is rare in Britain at present. At the time of writing, there are no cases in any of the hospitals regularly visited by the writer, whereas there are perhaps a dozen cases of phenylketonuria. It seems to be commoner as a cause of mental handicap than the conditions mentioned above, partly because it is not progressive once the damage to the brain has been done, and affected children have a near-normal expectation of life, even without treatment. This means that cases accumulate in hospitals for the mentally handicapped. On the other hand, children with lipidoses or with

Schilder's disease may remain in children's hospitals or departments until their death, and may never be transferred to a psychiatric hospital.

Despite the relatively good outlook for life of children with phenylketonuria, some brains have come to autopsy and definite abnormalities have been found. It is now well recognized that the brain abnormality in these children is due to an interference with chemical function. However, if this functional change persists over a long period, then permanent and irreversible damage will be done to the brain's structure. This fact is of the utmost importance in considering management and treatment. If the special diet, which is the current form of treatment, is to do any good, then the condition must be diagnosed within the first few weeks of life and the special diet started right away. If there is too much delay, then the child may never reach full mental development. Furthermore, the treatment must be continuous during the first years of life to protect the developing brain from the ill effects of an abnormal accumulation of chemical substances.

Using the special techniques for staining the white matter of the brain it has been possible for Dr Crome and others to show that there is a definite loss of white matter in some long-standing cases of phenylketonuria. Dr Crome points out that the staining and microscopic techniques now in use for study of the brain are relatively crude, despite the tremendous improvements which have taken place. It follows, therefore, that for damage to be demonstrated by these methods it must be gross. He considers that it would be necessary for a cell loss of about 20 per cent to occur before it could be detected with confidence. Doubtless the same applies to loss of white matter. Like most of the conditions mentioned above, phenylketonuria is transmitted in an autosomal manner. That is, the parents are not affected but brothers or sisters may be. The term 'autosomal' implies that it is not confined to boys and is not carried on the X or female sex chromosome.

The example of phenylketonuria typifies the situation in regard to brain damage. Once this occurs, it is likely to be permanent. Some recovery does take place and it seems likely that cells and fibres which are temporarily out of action may recover. However, any damage which can be seen under the microscope is likely to be serious enough to lead to some permanent loss of intellect, if the damage is diffuse. The brain is different from many other organs in that its powers of recovery are limited. It is in general unable to grow new neurones to replace those which are lost. This fact has led to a rather pessimistic attitude towards mental handicap by the medical profession, since there is usually nothing which lends itself to specific medical treatment or cure. On the other hand, the brain is also unique in the extent to which it can compensate for injury, and it may therefore be regarded as having a considerable reserve of function. However, in many of the more severe cases of mental handicap which we see, the damage is so severe and extensive that even patient education may achieve relatively little. In the particular case of phenylketonuria, it appears that damage done to the brain cannot be reversed after the first six months of life. In any event, children who are not put on the special diet until this age do very poorly in comparison with those who are treated early, and they do not seem to derive any special benefit from the diet. The brain continues to grow actively especially during the six months after birth and is probably most likely to be damaged at that time or before birth.

One of the ways in which phenylketonuria can affect children is unusual, but is very important as an example of how dependent the baby's development is on the mother's state of health during the pregnancy. One of our patients was backward and had a small head. We could find no cause for the condition, and the child died. Our enquiries into the family met with some difficulty, as we were not able to contact the mother, but we eventually established that she had six other children, one of them by a different partner, and that all these children were likewise very backward and with small heads. We then found that the mother herself had phenylketonuria. It is sometimes the case that people with this disease may be of fairly good intelligence, although they have not had the special treatment. In this family, it seemed that the chemical abnormality in the mother had interfered with the baby's development in each successive pregnancy causing the severe backwardness and the small head. It seems likely that, in many other ways, unsatisfactory maternal health may have a bad effect on the baby. In this particular example, if we had known about the mother's chemical peculiarity she could have been put on a special diet during the pregnancies and presumably the children would have been normal.

Tuberous sclerosis
This disease is sometimes known as 'epiloia'. Like most conditions causing mental retardation, it has a wide range of effect on brain function. Some people with the condition are of normal intelligence; others are profoundly retarded; and all intermediate grades are possible. In this condition, as in others which may result in mental handi-

cap, a knowledge of the diagnosis in terms of disease is no great help to the teacher or parent. It is still necessary to take into account the individual child's mental ability, his temperament, the frequency of any fits that he may have and his social background. The disease is usually recognized by the appearance of a rash on either side of the nose in the third or fourth year. It may sometimes be possible to diagnose it earlier by the presence of small white areas of leaf shape on the skin associated with infantile spasms and sometimes with high voltage waves (hypsarrythmia) revealed by an electroencephalogram.

People who have tuberous sclerosis often suffer from epileptic fits. In babies these may be small fits which only last a short time and which are known as infantile spasms. In older children and adults, they may usually take the form of major attacks (*grand mal*) which last longer and in which the sufferer may fall to the ground if there is no warning. The frequency and severity of fits is very variable, as in other cases of backward children with epilepsy. Some individuals with the condition may have only one fit in several years, while in others with epilepsy there may be a series of fits, and the child may become very ill with loss of consciousness and a high temperature. This is often a reason for admission to a children's ward. The condition may be alarming to the parents—and is, indeed, sometimes fatal —but on the whole the disease is not usually progressive. The backwardness and the fits are both due to maldevelopment of the brain, and the abnormalities are present at birth. In older patients they can be seen in a simple X-ray picture of the skull because they have taken up a certain amount of calcium. In some cases there are many of these abnormalities and they take up a great deal of space and replace much of the brain. In others, there are fewer abnormalities and more of the normal brain is spared. This is presumably why some people can have the disease and yet be of normal intelligence.

Tuberous sclerosis is another disease where the copying mechanism of the cell goes wrong and it can be passed on by heredity. Here the heredity is direct, and an affected parent may have an affected child. This is known as dominant inheritance, and is another example of Mendel's laws. In conditions transmitted in this way, the risk of an affected parent having an affected child is high, in fact 50 per cent or 1 : 1; that is, an even chance. Most of the cases of this disease seen in hospitals are very retarded, and they are most unlikely to have children. It is the parents with mild forms who are at risk for affected children, and it does not follow that because the disease is mild in the parent it will necessarily be so in the child. We see a number of examples where the contrary is true. Incidentally, in speaking about genetic risks it may be thought that if parents have already had, say, two affected children, then they are more likely to be lucky next time. This is not true any more than it would be in a game of chance such as roulette. In cases of Mendelian inheritance, the risk is the same with each pregnancy, irrespective of whether or not previous children were affected.

In tuberous sclerosis most cases are not born to affected parents but result from a new mutation. This is to say, a change has occurred in one of the parent's reproductive cells to cause the condition in the child. The parent as such is not affected, so far as we understand the situation, but only one of his or her cells. If this is so, there is no good reason why another child born to the same parents should have the condition. If, therefore, we carefully examine the parents and find them quite free of any evidence of the disease, and there are no other cases in the family, we can safely reassure them and say that they have no greater risk of having another child with this condition than the ordinary parent. On the other hand, if one of the parents does have a mild form of tuberous sclerosis, then the disease has an even chance of being passed on to all the children of that parent, either by the present union or by another spouse.

This disease offers a good example of how easily parents may be incorrectly informed about genetic risks, and it demonstrates the need for expert counselling by those who know about genetic principles and also particular conditions associated with mental handicap. It could, for example, easily be concluded that because parents have had a child with tuberous sclerosis, and since this is known to be a 'dominant' condition, they should be advised not to have further children because of the heavy risk. This advice would overlook the fact that the majority of cases result from new mutations and might well lead to very unfortunate psychological consequences for the parents. With this disease, we know that the brain and the skin are affected, and sometimes other parts of the body, such as the heart or kidneys. So far, no reliable general test has been discovered which might enable us to diagnose the condition from the blood or from a small amount of tissue (biopsy). If this can be achieved in the future, it might enable a diagnosis to be made early in pregnancy by amniotic puncture. This would then enable those parents who were very anxious to have a healthy child to do so by terminating those pregnancies in which the foetus is affected. This is at the moment at the level of fiction, but with the speed of development in human biology, even with the present limited resources, it is something which might be realizable within the next few years.

Down's syndrome ('Mongolism')

Down's syndrome, like other errors affecting whole chromosomes or large parts of them, is an upset of the hereditary mechanism. In most cases only one member of the family is affected but there are exceptions. Any disturbance in the chromosome pattern is likely to affect the development of the brain as well as other parts of the body. It seems that if there is something wrong with those chromosomes which determine sex—the X and the Y chromosomes—a child is less likely to be mentally retarded. But any abnormality of any other of the remaining twenty-two pairs of chromosomes (the autosomes) will almost certainly result in definite brain abnormality. By far the most common of these abnormalities is the condition described by Langdon Down a hundred years ago, and now known to be due to the presence in the human cell of an extra chromosome 21, one of the smallest chromosomes which we have. Although small, it is obviously of great importance for bodily development, since the presence of an extra chromosome 21 upsets the whole development of the body. There are reasons for believing that its absence will lead to cell death, so that individuals short of one chromosome 21 are unlikely to be born, except perhaps in a 'mosaic' where not all the cells are affected.

The brain in Down's syndrome can be recognized by an expert at sight as having come from such a child. It is smaller than usual, and weighs less than average. It is rounded, and the frontal lobes do not project forward as much as usual. It seems to be a little 'simplified'. The area particularly concerned with hearing is less well developed, while a striking finding is the reduction in size of the brain stem and the cerebellum. These faults in brain development must date basically from a very early stage in pregnancy, and, indeed, the presence of the extra chromosome at the time of conception pre-determines the abnormal pattern of brain development. This is presumably the main reason why children affected achieve on average only about one third of the usual level of intellectual development. It is true that there are a few individuals who do relatively well, but a maximum I.Q. of 70 on standard tests is usually all that can be expected, even from those relatively gifted. There are also a few people who are 'mosaics' and who have a proportion of normal cells without the extra chromosome (see p. 110). Such people may be at any level of intelligence.

Children with Down's syndrome are more commonly born to older mothers, but the age of the father is not in itself usually important. From work carried out in Australia, it seems that infectious jaundice can sometimes cause the fault in the egg cell which leads to the syndrome. Another ingenious, but perhaps not very probable, theory has also recently been advanced. Each month when the egg cell is ripe it is discharged from the ovary and finds its way in the Fallopian tube, where it awaits fertilization. If it is not fertilized within a certain time, it will perish. It is now suggested that Down's syndrome, or perhaps other chromosome faults, are more likely to happen in those cases where the egg cell has waited too long for fertilization and has therefore already begun to deteriorate. The suggestion is that in older people intercourse is not so frequent and this is therefore more likely to happen. This would also tie in with the fact that, on one particular Scottish island, where most of the men are frequently away fishing, Down's syndrome is especially frequent. Attractive though this theory is, it is not generally accepted. The ova or egg cells are present in the female child before birth, and, unlike the sperms, are not renewed. It seems likely that the older they are, the greater the risk of some unfavourable change.

Other chromosome errors
The anatomy of the brain in other forms of visible chromosome abnormality has been less adequately studied than Down's syndrome. This is chiefly because such errors other than those of the sex chromosomes are less common. The two best established are those named after Patau and Edwards and are also due to the presence of one extra chromosome. There are normally in humans forty-six chromosomes which are divisible into twenty-three pairs. While Down's syndrome is due to the presence of a third member with the 21 pair, making three of these tiny chromosomes, both Patau's and Edwards's syndromes involve larger chromosomes. In all three conditions the disease may be described as a 'trisomy' in that there are three of a sort where there should be two apparently identical chromosomes. The mechanism is presumably the same in all three conditions. The process is known as non-disjunction. When a cell is dividing to form a sex cell, then half the chromosomes should go to one pole of the dividing cell and half to the other. This results in egg cells and sperms with half the usual number of chromosomes, that is twenty-three. When fertilization takes place an ovum and a sperm unite, bringing the number back to the original forty-six. In division, each pair of chromosomes of the same size and shape separates if the process is normal, one member going to each pole. If things go wrong for some reason which we fail to understand at present, then a pair may stick together and go together to one pole. This results in unequal division, with one cell having twenty-four chromosomes and one ovum

twenty-two. The one with the reduced number usually, so far as we know, perishes.

Presumably because Patau's and Edwards's trisomies involve bigger chromosomes, there is a greater upset of the copying process. The individual formed in this way is even less like ordinary humans than a child with Down's syndrome, and is also less viable. The greater number of such babies die early. Their external appearance may be very abnormal. In Patau's syndrome, or trisomy D, in which one of the middle-sized chromosome pairs number 13 to 15 has an extra member, the brain is strikingly abnormal. The technical terms *prosencephaly* and *arhinencephaly* are used, here. The latter meaning absence of the 'smell brain' which is so important in fishes and mammals; while in prosencephaly, the forebrain, which is essential for the elaboration of behaviour in higher mammals, is missing or very much foreshortened. Infants with these trisomies who are not still-born and who do not die in the early newborn period are usually very backward indeed.

There are a great many other things which can go wrong with the 'autosomes'. One of these has been referred to as the *'cri du chat'* syndrome because the infant makes a noise like the mewing of a cat. It is not possible for babies to survive with one of the big chromosomes missing, but in this condition the loss is confined to part of a chromosome, a bit of the short arm of one of the number 5 pairs. Even this loss has a very damaging effect on the development of the baby, and such children are usually very retarded.

Abnormalities of the sex chromosomes
Direct information about the brain in mental retardation is, as we have seen, gained from the study of those patients who die, though some conclusions can be drawn during life from clinical neurology, from the electroencephalogram, or from other evidence, such as the occurrence of fits or defects of vision, hearing or muscular activity. Children born with a defect in their sex chromosomes, although more delicate than normal, have a good chance of living to a considerable age, and there is therefore less information about the anatomy of their brains. In some cases an error in the sex chromosomes may have little obvious effect. Attention recently has been drawn to the fact that some men have an extra male or Y chromosome. This does not make them 'supermen', nor does it necessarily seem greatly to increase their sexual drive. On the other hand, many of the cases discovered have been among criminals and among the population of such institutions as Rampton, the special hospital in Nottinghamshire for very

disturbed or dangerous mentally handicapped people. The cases reported have been above usual height, but from the information at present available it would appear that there are considerable numbers of men with this abnormality in the general population who behave, as far as we know, in a perfectly normal way.

Some people have an extra female or X chromosome. This was one of the first reported human chromosome anomalies, and the discovery was made in 1959, the same year as that of Down's syndrome. It is, of course, possible to tell the difference between the cells of men and women by examining the chromosomes, but this involves a great deal of tedious and time-consuming laboratory work. Barr, a Canadian histologist, found a more obvious difference in the presence of a small mass of staining material outside the nucleus of the cell, now known as a Barr body. This can be seen in any suitable available cells without the use of cell culture. A cotton wool swab is simply used on the lining of the mouth and the smear transferred to a glass slide. The epithelial cells resulting from this 'buccal smear' can, after staining, be examined for the presence of Barr bodies. Male cells do not show them, and female cells do. The female cells are said to be 'sex chromatin positive'. Women who have extra X chromosomes —that is, three or more—show two or more Barr bodies. On the other hand, if a male is affected in this way he will have one Barr body (or occasionally more), like a female.

In fact such males are like females in many ways. They seldom marry, and often show little interest in women. Their sexual potency is limited and they do not have children because there is a poor development of the testis, which is small and underweight. The external genital organs are small, and the secondary sexual characteristics do not appear properly. There is little beard growth and the breasts tend to be abnormally big for a man, while his body fat has a female distribution, giving a feminine appearance. This condition is called the Klinefelter syndrome, and affected individuals tend to be of limited intelligence, though they are not usually very backward. However, a considerable number of them find their way into institutions, and the condition probably has an effect on behaviour as well as intelligence, more of them getting into trouble with the police. All of this suggests that the extra X chromosome has a bad effect on brain development, though it is not usually so severe as to cause death in infancy. Klinefelter's syndrome is commoner than Downs' syndrome among males, affecting about one in 400, though it is less common in all babies. Since affected children are not so delicate, there are probably more cases surviving in the community. But, again, affected persons are much less obviously abnormal than is the case with Down's syndrome, and many of them, being of near-normal intelligence, can manage to fend for themselves with a little help. Many have never been diagnosed as such. Some of them, the few who marry, may be recognized in clinics where they have sought advice because of sterility or inadequacy in sexual intercourse.

Incomplete females and superfemales
Some women do not develop normal sexual characteristics and have a condition which is the female equivalent of Klinefelter's syndrome. It is called after Turner, and is usually due to absence of one of the X chromosomes. In such girl children there is incomplete development of the breasts and pubic hair. They are dwarfed, and may show peculiarities of physical development, such as webbing of the neck. Some are retarded, some mentally ill, but many are of quite good intelligence. The ovaries are underdeveloped. They do not menstruate or have children, and seldom marry. In some at least there is also an effect on brain development, since they are occasionally epileptic or show other evidence of brain defect. One case under the care of the writer was profoundly retarded. She was exceptional in that she had two X chromosomes, as do ordinary women, but one of them was peculiar. Usually the X in an X chromosome is not symmetrical but there are long and short arms. In this little girl the faulty chromosome had two pairs of long arms. The effect was typical of Turner's syndrome, except that she was more retarded than most cases.

Other women have more than their share of X chromosomes. Biologists have used the term 'superfemales' in this connection, but it seems quite inappropriate for the condition in humans. Some of these women seem normal in every respect; they develop normal sexual function and appear intellectually normal. Others seem very abnormal and are grossly retarded, and may have cerebral palsy or epilepsy and evidently have abnormal brain development. One theory is that, in ordinary women, after a certain age of development only one of the X chromosomes functions and one is dormant. If the additional X chromosomes were dormant, then they might have no ill effect, which would account for the great variety in the effect of this abnormality. In any event, disappointingly enough, such women do not seem especially endowed with feminine charm.

There is a great variety of possible permutations of chromosome abnormality. For example, one child in the care of the writer had both the Klinefelter and Down's syndrome, so that he had a total of forty-eight chromosomes in each cell including one extra X and an extra

21. Some Klinefelter males have three or four Xs. The development of the brain is probably controlled by all the chromosomes, and it is unlikely that any major defect in them which can be seen under the microscope will be without effect on the growth of the brain, even though in some cases, such as certain triple X females, it seems to function quite normally.

Hydrocephalus
Many different forms of faulty development of the brain have only recently become known, but hydrocephalus, or 'water on the brain', was recognized by the ancients. It can be present at birth, but most cases start later, perhaps at three or six months. In many the defect was perhaps present at birth, but only showed itself later. Such infants have a normal head size and shape at birth, but at a later stage the head enlarges out of proportion to the body and becomes more rounded. In extreme cases, the head is enormously enlarged, so that the child may be quite unable to support it. For those who are not familiar with the abnormality, the sight of these children can be very distressing, but nurses and those who care for them—including, of course, their own parents—love them as much as ordinary children. Most of the content of the cranium or brainbox in such cases is, in fact, water, but curiously enough, even if the brain is thinned out to a thickness of half a centimetre around a vast mass of water, it still seems to function quite well in some cases. By no means all children with hydrocephalus are educationally retarded. Unfortunately, there are many other possible complications, including cerebral palsy, blindness and epilepsy. The sheer weight of the head may interfere with sitting up or walking and in severe cases there may be a danger of bed sores affecting the head.

Hydrocephalus is caused by a blockage in the flow of the fluid from inside the brain. This fluid is normally clear, like water, and is formed in the ventricles, or spaces inside the brain. From there it escapes through small channels to the surface of the brain, where it is absorbed back into the blood-stream. Sometimes these fine channels are blocked by brain malformation. In other cases, hydrocephalus is a result of meningitis, which causes a thickening of the meninges, the membranes covering the brain. This thickening and adhesion may prevent fluid escaping. A common form of meningitis which can produce this effect is meningococcal meningitis, or spotted fever. Fortunately, with modern treatment, the complication of hydrocephalus after meningitis can usually be avoided.

Hydrocephalus is often associated with another common malformation of the nervous system affecting about one in 300 babies' birth—spina bifida or open spine. In such babies the meninges in most cases bulge out in the form of a cyst in the midline of the lower back, though the affected area is sometimes higher. This permits infection to get into the cerebrospinal fluid very easily from the surface, and many children who suffer from spina bifida have the added complication of hydrocephalus following meningitis. Modern surgery spares the lives of many such children who would otherwise have died. Many remain well, but a considerable number require other help, including surgery for the hydrocephalus.

The treatment of hydrocephalus baffled surgeons for a long time, despite the use of much ingenuity. However, increasingly in recent years, surgical treatment has yielded better results following the invention of the Spitz-Holter valve and similar devices. This valve was devised by an engineer, who was the father of an affected child, jointly with a surgeon. If the valve is inserted in a catheter placed at one end in the ventricle of the brain, and at the other into a vein leading into the heart, the result may be a satisfactory flow of fluid without the risk of blood leaking back along the catheter. The outlook for children with hydrocephalus is now much better, though careful judgement is required since the surgeon must first be certain that he is really dealing with hydrocephalus while, on the other hand, he must not delay matters until damage has been done to the brain.

Before modern surgical methods were available, a number of cases of hydrocephalus 'arrested' spontaneously. That is, the head enlarged up to a certain point and then, somehow, the fluid found ways of draining and the process ceased. Such hydrocephalics survived, and a number of them may be seen in relatively skilled occupations. The writer remembers seeing one running a fruit stall without help in Sicily, and another working as a salesman in a busy store. Others have been successful in learned professions. As a group, however, like other children with damaged brains they are less intelligent than ordinary children in spite of the exceptions. A number are to be found in institutions for the mentally retarded, while others may go to schools for the physically handicapped. In cases which did not have the benefit of successful surgery, and which did not arrest spontaneously, the outcome was always fatal.

Tuberculous meningitis and encephalitis
Happily, tuberculosis is no longer the scourge in Britain that it once was. The younger generation knows of it as material for opera librettos and other romantic literature, or from accounts given by older

relatives. It was not only young adults and teenagers who were affected, but also children. Children's hospitals, such as the one where the writer is based, formerly provided for many children with chronic tuberculosis of bone, but there was also tuberculous meningitis, an acute and invariably fatal form of tuberculosis involving the brain. With the use of streptomycin, even this disease has become curable if it can be diagnosed early. Unfortunately, this is not easy, and there are still surviving a number of children whose brains were badly damaged before treatment took effect. As a result, they are seriously mentally retarded.

Tuberculosis is usually a disease of poverty, and as living conditions improve there should be fewer cases. Also, the general use of B.C.G. vaccine against tuberculosis should prevent open disease of the lung in adults, which should mean that children will seldom be exposed to infection, especially when this is taken together with more efficient treatment of pulmonary tuberculosis. Thus the tragedy of a normal baby suddenly becoming afflicted by severe mental retardation as a result of this disease may be avoided in the future.

Tuberculous meningitis, as it is usually called, is really a form of encephalitis or inflammation of the substance of the brain. Quite a few cases of mental retardation are due to encephalitis. It results in a loss of neurones and a scarring of the brain with an over-growth of glial cells. The degree of damage to the intellect varies enormously. In the early 1920s there were many cases of sleepy sickness, which was a form of inflammation of the brain. This disease affected the base of the brain causing symptoms like those in paralysis agitans, or Parkinson's disease. The face became expressionless, walking was difficult and the muscles became stiff. Apart from these effects, the personality of many of those affected people was changed, so that they became delinquent, having previously been of good behaviour A considerable number of children were so affected, and were housed in hospitals for the mentally handicapped. It is fortunate for this generation that the disease has now disappeared. It was due in all probability to a virus and there is, of course, no guarantee that it or similar diseases will not reappear.

Other viruses which cause inflammation of the brain and result, in severe cases, in all-round mental deterioration do not create a peculiar clinical picture like that in encephalitis lethargica, or sleepy sickness. Some of the common fevers, such as measles, can be complicated by encephalitis. In some instances there is acute and catastrophic damage to the brain. In others it seems in the light of recent work likely that measles can be responsible for a slow mental deterioration in children, causing a chronic encephalitis, sometimes lasting for several years and sometimes showing a characteristic electroencephalogram.

Other organisms than viruses may invade the brain. Syphilis was in the past well known as a cause of general paralysis of the insane, which is a form of syphilitic encephalitis. This sometimes affected the children of infected parents. Nowadays in Britain the condition is rare, and younger doctors working with the mentally handicapped may never have seen a case. The virtual disappearance of the condition results from a combination of better treatment and prevention, but it is always necessary to be on guard against infection during pregnancy, since there has of late regrettably been some increase in the incidence of syphilis.

It is not possible in one brief chapter to give an account of all the many factors which may so seriously affect the human brain as to cause mental retardation. No mention has been made of the effects of brain haemorrhage, which can occur at about the time of birth, of the effects of a shortage of oxygen at that time or of the effect of a serious loss of body fluid by the baby during dysentery or a similar disease; nor of those sad cases where a parent so batters a baby that his brain is irreparably damaged. Perhaps most of us at some time sustain some damage to the brain, and the wonder is that we do so well. There seems, however, to be a reasonable hope that with an improvement in living conditions there should be not only a decline in the child death rate, but also many fewer cases of serious damage to the brain from disease, injury or poison.

Chapter 3
The history of mental handicap

The human brain is relatively more developed than that of other animals, and it makes up a bigger proportion of the body weight. Some other animals also have a relatively highly developed brain—the anthropoid apes or dolphins for example—but they do not have man's adaptability. In general, they cannot make tools. They do not have a spoken or written language for communication or storage of information. They are not able to modify their living conditions to the extent that man can. They do not cultivate the ground or engage in stock breeding. Above all, there is nothing comparable to the elaborateness of human society, with its relative flexibility and adaptability, in the various societies created by other organisms, such as ants and bees. Consciousness in man is much more elaborate than in other animals, and gives him a greater potential awareness of time and space. Pigeons and other animals use the sun for navigation in a way impossible for man, but only man could invent the sun-dial or the compass. By co-operative effort and pooling of information, science has evolved, which has permitted man to split the atom and return from a voyage to the moon. The human brain has created science, giving civilized man the ability to control his environment for his own benefit, or to destroy himself.

Human society has evolved over many thousands of years though we have only a limited knowledge of events more than 4,000 years ago. The human brain has been evolving for a much longer period, though if we define man as 'social man', we can say that the *human* brain has had the same period of evolution as human society. Man depends on society, and, as an isolated individual, his capacity for survival is limited. Society makes use of a variety of human talent. There are some who, like Leonardo da Vinci, excel in many ways, but most bring a more modest contribution which usually includes specialization. A specialization, like that of the carpenter or surgeon, is developed as an acquired skill, but it must be based on natural ability. A person with cerebral palsy, minimal brain damage, or who is just very clumsy, would find it difficult or impossible to become a good carpenter or surgeon. By combining different individual talents, man, organized in society, is able to overcome many obstacles and to come to terms with an environment which might otherwise be impossibly hostile. At an early stage of human social evolution, when man was still a hunter, there was less scope for variety of ability. To this day, primitive societies such as those of the Eskimo and the Australian aborigines do not permit a high degree of specialization. They have only a limited use for the historian or philosopher and are chiefly concerned with the day-to-day business of keeping alive. Eskimos were, until recently, nomadic, and depended in part for their living on walrus hunts, which demanded an ability to travel in conditions of maximum danger. Such societies had little opportunity to maintain those who were senile, feeble-minded or short-sighted. Their potential for modifying their environment was very limited. With social development there has come an increase in material wealth, and, in particular, the growth of agriculture has allowed some of this to be set aside for the fostering of many individual specialties and talents. It is against this background of a more highly developed society that the diversity of the human brain's potential becomes obvious.

Few people are really good at everything. There is, however, a correlation between specific talents, so that those who are really good at one thing are more likely to be good at others. The 'natural fool' or 'village idiot' is the person who can do little or nothing, the few things he does do being done badly. His social contribution is, therefore, very small, or completely negative. Shakespeare's fools were not of this nature: they were more akin to court jesters and were permitted considerable licence. If they were abnormal, it was in the direction of insanity rather than mental retardation. Their lack of inhibition as well as royal indulgence permitted them to speak when others were silent. They held up a mirror to reality when courtiers would have been too discreet to do so. In this way they served a useful purpose.

An early English reference to mental retardation in our sense of the term occurred in the time of Edward II. The king's prerogative, affirmed in a statute of 1325, was to protect the land of idiots, take the profits from them to provide for their necessities, and to render the lands on their death to their rightful heirs. This statute, therefore, recognized that, in the case of idiots, there was little prospect of recovery. The same legislation provided for the safekeeping of the lands of lunatics, and mentioned that these might be returned to them on recovery. There was, thus, a clear distinction between the concept of mental retardation and mental illness, even though, at present, many people still confuse these. This difficulty, incidentally, comes in part from a fear of those who behave very differently from ourselves.

At present, as throughout history, contemporary jargon ma[y obscure] the issue. The writer knows that children in other wards in [a compre]hensive children's hospital refer to the patients in the war[d for dis]turbed children or to those wards for the retarded equal[ly as 'mental] cases'. This is just in the sense that both groups may show some imperfection of brain function.

Edward II's statute was concerned only with the upper class of the day who possessed lands of their own which might require protection. There was no particular provision for the poor. This distinction remained until 1959, for the Lunacy Act of 1870, which governed much of the legislation affecting the mentally retarded as well as the mentally ill, made separate provision for the well-to-do and for the 'pauper lunatic'. At that time, the village idiot remained the responsibility of his family and parish. Difficulties of definition which are still with us were present at an earlier date. The term 'idiot', in so far as this is in use in the international classification of diseases, means a profoundly retarded person or one with an I.Q. of below 20. In 1534, Fitzherbert defined an idiot as one who could not count twenty pence, or tell his age or name his parents. Swinburne, in 1591, mentioned measuring a yard of cloth and telling the days of the week. Both these tests foreshadow the much more elaborate test batteries devised by Wechsler and others, and contain a recognition of the different ways in which intelligence may be expressed, either in performance or verbally. A person who had palsy or who was clumsy might have difficulty with the measuring test, but could find the verbal task easier. On the other hand, a deaf person, or one with a speech defect, might be able to measure cloth but not be able to name the days of the week.

Historical frequency of mental handicap

As we have seen, mental handicap is relative to the attainments of others at the time in the same society. A white man left to himself in the Australian bush is likely to die and might be considered inadequate by the aborigine. The aboriginal sustains life and a kind of a society against overwhelming odds. This involves differences ranging from basic things like a better cultivation of the sense of smell to social attributes like the use of memory by the elders and the accumulation of tribal skill in such matters as the manufacture of weapons for hunting.

It is, therefore, difficult to say whether mental handicap is becoming rarer or more common. In fact, the question may not be very meaningful. There must have been many advantageous mutations in the course of the development of the human brain, and so it seems possible that many of the factors which led to the development and selection of the more favourable may be continuing. As we have seen, the more seriously mentally handicapped have few children, or none, so there is a continuing selection against unfavourable changes. On the other hand, it has been suggested by Tredgold Senior, and others concerned with the early days of the Eugenics Society in this country, that civilized conditions may provide protection for the 'unfit', and hence negate the positive effects of selection. Sir Godfrey Thomson in Scotland has been a vigorous exponent of this point of view, and it was his interest and energy which was in part responsible for the attempts to follow the trend of Scottish national intelligence by carrying out a second survey (1949), to make comparisons with a survey fifteen years earlier. Over that period there seemed to have been, if anything, a slight improvement in national intelligence. A more recent study, published by the Scottish Council for Research in Education (1967), showed that the average intelligence of Scottish children appeared to be two points higher than that of the American population used by Wechsler as a standard twenty years earlier. Thus there is as yet no solid evidence to support any suggestion that the development of social security will necessarily reverse long-term trends towards an improvement in intelligence.

Effect on historical changes of social factors
From the time of conception there is a continuous influence by the environment on the child. We know from the sizes of suits of armour and other evidence that there has been a growth in stature in historic times. This continues, and is manifest in countries like Japan, where great social changes have taken place in a short time.

Professor Butler has pointed out the great difficulty in distinguishing the many different factors which influence the development of human intelligence. One is the height of the mother. This is determined in part by the social class of the parents. If, however, it is taken separately it can be shown, with the assistance of a computer, that the factor of maternal height makes a positive difference in its own right to the outcome for the child. Professor Butler's report was based on an analysis of the births of some 17,000 children born during one week in March 1958. He and his colleagues were able to show the interaction of different factors on the school performance of seven-year-old children. Social class of the parents, the number of children born to the mother (birth rank), the age of the mother, prematurity or late delivery, smallness of the baby, maternal blood loss during the pregnancy, toxaemia of pregnancy, complications of labour and many other factors could all have a bad effect on the development of the child and his school performance. But one unfavourable factor on its own did not necessarily have any bad effect.

It might be supposed that it social conditions continue to improve, if maternal health becomes better and mothers become taller, if the poorer classes may expect in the future to enjoy some of the privileges of the rich, if better medical care is provided during pregnancy and delivery, then this will be reflected in a higher average intelligence and a corresponding reduction in the numbers of mentally retarded. It should not be forgotten, however, that not all social developments are positive. Whilst some aspects of sex equality seem positive, such as votes or equal wages for women, others are clearly negative. Among these may be listed the recent trend for the suicide rate in women to draw closer to that for men. Likewise, there has been a tendency for deaths from cancer of the lung to increase in women along with that of men. This appears to be due to the fact that cigarette smoking is commoner among women than it used to be, and might be looked upon as part of their 'emancipation'. However, cigarette smoking increases not only the risk of maternal ill health, bronchitis and cancer of the lung; it also means a greater risk of the baby dying or of being backward at school. It is usually considered that twenty cigarettes per day, or more, is 'heavy' smoking, but the study by Butler and his colleagues incriminates as few as ten cigarettes per day as having a bad effect on a baby during pregnancy.

It is obvious in the long term that if we contaminate our personal environment by smoking or drug taking, or the social environment by pollution by poisons, then we may undo some of evolution's positive trends. Attention has recently been drawn to the possible ill-effects resulting from an accumulation of mercury in tinned tuna fish and other marine products. Since this fish is caught in the open ocean, the warning indicated that the danger of poisoning had spread beyond limited areas. It is known that heavy metals can have a bad effect on the brain, and the expression 'as mad as a hatter' was coined because mercurial poisoning was an occupational disease with hatters, who used the metal in processing felt. It was recognized recently in Japan that mercury can affect the brain of an unborn baby—an experience resulting from the contamination of fish in a particular bay. But the recent findings have an even more serious implication for the future, unless effective steps can be taken to prevent the menace to future generations.

A similar consideration may apply to the widespread abuse of drugs. The effect of thalidomide during pregnancy is now well known, but other drugs can act like X-rays or radium and interfere with the genes. It is known that L.S.D. causes breakages in chromosomes when cells are grown in the laboratory in a tissue culture. It is also known that people who have received this drug show breakages in their chromosomes and other abnormalities which may last for years. This suggests that parents who have used this drug may be at greater risk for having abnormal children.

Early provision for the mentally retarded
At present we can but guess at long term trends in the absolute and relative incidence of mental retardation. In practice, the problem has steadily come to the fore with social development, and a recent study of the child population in the Isle of Wight has yielded valuable information from a well-defined area of the incidence of various disabilities among the sample chosen. A proportion of 2·53 per cent was regarded as intellectually retarded by the standard used. In mathematical terms, this was expressed as two standard deviations from the mean. This standard enabled children to be identified who did conspicuously badly by comparison with a control group of Isle of Wight children. However, the figure fell to 1·5 per cent if the Wechsler Intelligence Scale for Children norms were used.

It seems unlikely that the incidence of backwardness in children of this age was much less in the past than it is now, taking into account what we know of children in underdeveloped countries at present. However, it was not until Elizabethan times, that any special provisions and rules began to be made in Britain for the mentally retarded. This was a period of great expansion of trade, of the merchant class and of the cities. There was an increasing breakdown of the feudal structure, which had persisted to some extent in the villages. The establishment had, at that time, some doubtless justifiable concern over the possibility of 'beggars coming to town'. The existence of mobile bands of vagrants with no local attachment was a potential menace to established order. When times were bad, groups of tramps, tinkers, beggars, thieves, cripples and others could be swelled by landless peasants. A major purpose of the Elizabethan Poor Law of 1601 was to segregate the poor, the afflicted, the unemployed or the unemployable, and to restrict or keep a check on their movements. They were made a parish responsibility, and workhouses were created for them. This type of provision persisted almost up to the present day, and such workhouses were places where many of the mentally retarded were accommodated. The writer remembers that his interest in psychiatry was first kindled in a hospital, part of which was still officially designated as a workhouse and still ruled by a 'Master', so that the inhabitants, including some mentally retarded children, literally spent 'Christmas day in the Workhouse'. Dickens has preserved for posterity a record of life as it was in the last century in such institutions. In fact, at present, a number of such ex-workhouses are still in use for the accommodation of the mentally handicapped.

Revolutionary changes
With the gradual development of technique and increased social wealth, different forms of social organization became possible. The French Revolution sparked off fundamental changes in every aspect of living, including a fresh impetus to demands for individual liberty. Pinel, under the influence of the new humanism, wrote his *Treatise on Insanity* (1806), and a well-known picture shows Pinel striking the fetters off the lunatics in the Bicêtre hospital. He preached the value of work therapy and believed that, if the mentally ill were engaged in useful work, they could be brought nearer to health. He applied the same rule to prisons and hospitals, and made it clear that he considered that this applied also to the mentally retarded. The use of physical restraint gradually became less general and more humane methods were introduced.

The 'Retreat' at York, a hospital for the mentally ill founded by the Society of Friends, provided a fresh impetus in this direction. However, physical restraint is still used in Britain to the present day. Until 1959 an attempt was made to regulate its use by keeping registers in hospitals for the mentally retarded, as in those for the mentally ill. These registers were inspected by the Board of Control, who laid down methods of restraint of which they did not disapprove, provided that their use was authorized in writing by the medical officer in charge of the unit. The abandonment of this procedure and of the central inspectorate in 1959 may have been tacit recognition of the fact that in this and other respects the central body merely served as a 'rubber stamp', enabling those responsible for the conduct of institutions locally to shelve some of the responsibility. Pinel's principles are as relevant today as when he wrote. If sufficient staff are employed, and if the residential units for the retarded are small and homelike, and if every opportunity is taken to engage their inmates in suitable activity, there will be no need for physical restraint. 'Chemical restraint' is today a factor to be added, and the excessive use of drugs is, like the use of physical restraint, a path of least resistance and a confession of failure.

Legend and reality

The history of mental handicap is full of fairy stories and demonstrates the magical and irrational nature of much individual and collective thought. The magic in question is sometimes black, and sometimes white. The wolf boy of Aveyron follows the tradition of Romulus and Remus but unlike them he was not specially gifted. On the contrary, he was so devoid of talent that his devoted teacher, Itard, had to confess to failure in all efforts to educate him. Itard wrote in 1798 and again in 1801, and like Pinel was much influenced by revolutionary humanism. He, like his pupil, Seguin, who wrote in 1846, believed that it was essential to capture the interest of the subject in order to train him. Itard's wild boy was a young man who had been found wandering in the forest, and like Kipling's Mowgli he was thought to belong to the wolves. He was described as *Juvenis Averionensis* by the local professor of natural history in the belief that he represented a different species rather than the extreme range of human intellectual variation. Itard, however, gave a clear account of his observations, and in so doing may be said to have founded a school of the scientific observation of behaviour in the mentally handicapped. Seguin successfully developed Itard's work at a later date and added much to our understanding of the development of human behaviour and the manner in which it may be modified in the mentally handicapped. The early optimism of Itard and of Guggenbuhl, who founded a colony for 'cretins' near a mountain top by Interlaken, was disappointed, but they and others like them founded a positive approach to this most difficult of problems.

In a sense, it was necessary to rediscover the work of Pinel, Itard and Seguin at a later stage, bringing as they did, ordinary commonsense principles to bear on mental handicap. During the early years of this century, their teachings became overlaid by an atmosphere of pessimism and an outlook of passive helplessness. The approach of these earlier workers had been one of humanist and teacher. At a later period, there was a great interest in labelling and docketing various syndromes together with a realization that structural abnormalities of the brain in severe cases of mental handicap could not be cured. To the extent that the medical profession was concerned, the subject tended to be little thought about since there was no prospect of radical treatment or cure. Early enthusiasts in the field of heredity tended to believe that once a congenital defect had been established, it could not be modified. At a later date, Binet's work came to be interpreted in such a way as to lead to the belief that intelligence was a strictly measurable entity fixed at birth.

The Institution and the Victorians

It is sometimes suggested that, in simpler forms of society, the retarded are supported within the society, and all is well. While this may be so with the mildly retarded, the notion is, in general, as false and illusory as that of the 'noble savage'. If retarded children do not die naturally, they are in tribal groups often done to death, or else receive so little attention that the result is the same. In countries with ancient and more developed civilizations, the situation may be little better, and a retarded child may be kept locked in a dark room out of the neighbours' sight.

It is easy to criticize institutions for the mentally retarded, and many have done so. Recent dramatic exposures have emphasized the validity of such criticism. Nor can those who have worked in institutions for long periods be satisfied unless indeed they have themselves become institutionalized—which is a real danger. Russell Barton drew attention to what he called the 'institutional neurosis' existing within hospitals for the mentally ill. He suggested that many of the symptoms in long-term patients and much of their psychological dilapidation, were due, not so much to their initial illness, but rather to their long confinement, their isolation from society, their inactivity, and their being caught up in a rigid, impersonal institutional system. Bowlby, Robertson and many others have pointed out that similar truths apply to institutionalized children who are denied the normal stimulation which they would get from family life in the general community. There is much objective evidence to support this view in the case of children, particularly retarded children. Pauline Morris has recently delivered a very effective broadside at the institutions in her book *Put Away*.

It should be remembered, however, that those who founded the idiot asylums, like Guggenbuhl and Andrew Reed in Britain, were inspired by the most laudable motives. Their views were in many ways similar to those of Robert Owen, who, as a Utopian socialist, believed that a solution to problems resulting from the Industrial Revolution lay in self-contained colonies or communities. Owen's experiments failed because they were backward-looking and out of step with contemporary society. The asylums did not fail in the economic sense, since they were not conceived primarily for economic reasons. They did fail, however, to live up to the expectations of their founders in the human sense. One of the main reasons for this has, in fact, been economic in the sense that the institutions have always been run on a pittance. Another major reason has been a confusion of purposes, since, rather than being places of refuge, they have, over a long period, taken on something of the role of a prison or place of detention. Even the modest reform in the mental health legislation introduced prior to the Second World War, which allowed the mentally ill to be voluntary patients, was not extended to the mentally retarded, who continued to be committed to institutions by formal process. Restrictions on the discharge from the institutions of the mentally retarded were also stricter than on the mentally ill, illogical though this may seem.

The asylums should be seen in the light of possible alternatives existing in the mid-nineteenth century, when many of them were founded. There was no effective social security system, which has indeed only come into existence since the Second World War. The alternatives were the workhouse or a desperate struggle for existence in conditions where many children of normal intelligence succumbed to infection and poverty. The situation has changed since the introduction of the Mental Deficiency Act 1913, which became effective after the First World War. At this time, for reasons already mentioned, there was a great broadening in the concept of 'mental deficiency'. As a result of this as well as of a deliberate policy of segregation of the 'unfit' to prevent multiplication, large numbers of people were forced into institutions which became increasingly overcrowded and inadequate. If blame for the present state of affairs is to be apportioned, it does not lie with the original founders or primarily with their staffs, who have, for the most part, tried to carry out their tasks in conditions of great difficulty. The fault lies with society in general, and in particular with successive administrations at local and national level, which have only recently begun to take an active interest in the problem of mental handicap. The professions, including that of medicine in particular, do not have a good record in this respect, since they have usually chosen to turn their attention to something less distasteful, to areas which had a better status or which might be financially more rewarding. Langdon Down, who gave the first proper account of the syndrome which now bears his name a hundred years ago, was thought by his colleagues to be very odd indeed for having abandoned a fashionable practice to devote himself to this 'disreputable' subject.

Andrew Reed, the philanthropist, began his efforts to found an idiot asylum in 1840, and Park House, Highgate, was opened as a result in 1848. This was a 'charitable asylum', and was succeeded by an annexe at Colchester which was to become the Royal Eastern Counties Hospital, while a newly built 'model asylum' was opened at Earlswood by the Prince Consort in 1855. Royal patronage was extended in particular to 'the genius of Earlswood asylum' who would in modern terms have been described as a deaf-non-communicating patient with autistic features but who was in those days an object of particular interest to be exhibited to the royal patron, a particularly bright oasis in an intellectual desert; the models made by this patient are evidence of his considerable mental resources. It is interesting to note that the Earlswood Asylum was intended for the middle and working classes, but that paupers were ineligible. The Royal Albert and Star Cross, now the Royal Western Counties, are other well-known institutions built soon afterwards. Larbert is also well known because of the writings of Colonel Ireland, who based his books on his experience there.

The feeble-minded

Ireland designated his text as referring to idiots and imbeciles. He did not use the term 'feeble-minded', which became well established only at the turn of the century. Some homes for the feeble-minded were created around 1890, and the category of 'feeble-minded' was given official recognition in 1901, some 13,000 people being so designated. New machines and techniques were replacing child labour in the factories, legislation was being introduced prohibiting this in stages and attendance at school was being made compulsory. In this changing climate, the position of the feeble-minded became more difficult. They could not manage the ordinary school curriculum in the conditions of the time, and it was becoming harder for them to get suitable work.

Military standards

In Louis Napoleon's France, Morel became very worried about the poor standard of military conscripts, and so introduced the notion of national degeneracy. He produced three illustrated tomes which have influenced thinking on the subject of mental handicap to the present day. In Britain the Eugenics Society was founded in 1909, a number of its early supporters also being influenced by questions of military fitness. Among them, Tredgold considered that chief problem to be the prevention of propagation by the unfit. A year earlier, the Royal Commission on the Feeble-minded had reported and estimated that there were some 150,000 mental defectives in England and Wales. However, they had used this term comprehensively to include all the mentally disordered, making no distinction between the mentally ill the senile, the profoundly or the mildly retarded. This approach coincided with that of Morel, who thought that all forms of mental disability were related. Tredgold extended the notion of degeneracy even more widely, and believed that some kind of 'injury to the germ plasm' could produce a great variety of unfortunate results. It was, for example, thought at that time that such injury might result from an excessive consumption of alcohol on the wedding night, though no scientific evidence was ever advanced to support this view.

Yerkes in the United States during the First World War had been concerned at the number of recruits who seemed to be of low intelligence. The problem of mild mental retardation was again highlighted during the Second World War, and Eli Ginzberg analysed the American findings in his book *The Ineffective Soldier: Lessons for Management and the Nation* (1959).

As was pointed out by the Group for the Advancement of Psychiatry in America, a national emergency tends to sort out individuals with limited qualifications. The mildly retarded are conspicuous because of illiteracy, poor school records, and, in the United States, because of their geographical distribution. National minority groups are more severely affected, and nearly half those rejected during the Second World War on account of 'mental deficiency' were Negroes, whose rejection rate was six times that of whites. Actually, much of this rejection was due to illiteracy, and showed a close relationship, state by state, with the amount spent per head on education.

The Mental Deficiency Act 1913
Growing concern on the part of the pressure groups mentioned above led to the passing into law of the Mental Deficiency Act, 1913, which had the effect of encouraging an acceptance of life in an institution as the proper and natural thing for the mentally handicapped. The Act also had the effect of detaining all patients in such institutions by legal process. They were further segregated from the general population because the institutions as such had to be recognized under the Act. There was no way in which the institutions could take informal or other types of patients, nor in which ordinary hospitals could provide for the mentally handicapped. To many parents, the legal procedure seemed cumbersome, unnecessary and somewhat awesome, and many felt that they had no legal rights in the matter. Others felt that, in some way, they were being treated as if guilty of an offence in that they had to appear before a magistrate.

In fact, the Bill presented to parliament in 1912, and thrown out by the liberal interest, had been a much more stringent measure, and included a clause prohibiting 'mental defectives' from marrying. This was contrary to the usual sense of British law which holds that persons are capable of entering into contracts and legal obligations provided they properly understand what they are doing. This remains the actual situation at present with the mentally handicapped, as with the mentally ill. This situation, where each individual is judged on his own merits, is clearly much more satisfactory. Individuals placed in the same category vary enormously in their level of social competence. Also, there is a danger that if the law lays down that certain categories of people can or cannot do certain things, then the law may be 'bent' to include them in or exclude them from these same categories. If the matter is left open and, if the question is raised, it then becomes possible to give an honest opinion in a particular case, bearing in mind all individual circumstances. In most cases, of course, the matter will *not* be raised in any formal way, but will be decided by informal discussion among the parties concerned and their relatives.

Had the 1912 Bill become law, there would have been unending difficulties in deciding who was a 'mental defective' in so far as marriage was concerned, and some who could have made competent parents or spouses would have been debarred, while others far less able to fulfil these roles would have entered upon them without obstruction. The clause would also have prevented the legalization of children in some cases and disrupted families in others. The eugenic effect would have been negligible, since the more obviously retarded seldom have children and the great majority of the mentally handicapped, especially those whose defect is obvious, are born to normal parents. Clinical experience also shows that, where women of low intelligence do have an illegitimate child, despite much-publicized exceptions, this event is unlikely to be repeated. There is therefore no good reason for automatically confining such a young person to an institution for the remainder of her reproductive life. None the less, although there was no specific section dealing with this situation in the body of the 1913 Act, a ban on associating with the opposite sex was introduced into the terms of licence from hospital. Furthermore, the original Act itself laid down that a defective was liable to be 'dealt with' if she was in receipt of poor relief at the time of giving birth to an illegitimate child or when pregnant with such a child. Being 'dealt with' in this connection usually meant committal to an institution. It is interesting to see how the original Poor Law notion of protecting established society against the pauper came to be combined with that of retribution for wickedness and the then fashionable 'prevention of propagation', though it might justly have been remarked that this was indeed a case of locking the stable door after the event.

Civil Rights

The 1913 Act introduced checks on civil liberty which seemed at variance with other legislation in this country. The involvement of a magistrate in the detention of a person under the Act proved of limited value as a safeguard. The checks on the release of those detained were more stringent than in the case of the mentally ill. Detention of the mentally ill at Broadmoor usually followed cases brought to trial. Detention at Rampton and Moss Side, the comparable hospitals for the mentally handicapped, was seldom after trial, but was usually because the patient had been found difficult or judged dangerous when detained in an ordinary local hospital for the mentally handicapped. Patients who had managed to escape from hospital were frequently returned after a considerable absence, and on occasion the use of force in such cases led to violence and serious charges. In regard to female patients and marriage it was found necessary at one stage to circularize hospitals to the effect that marriage should not, in itself, be regarded as a reason for returning a patient to hospital! Despite the rigidity of the 1913 Act, its interpretation led to an even greater restriction of the rights of the individual than might have been intended. A person who was a defective was subject to be 'dealt with' if he was found neglected. This phrase came to be interpreted very widely, and the Board of Control found it necessary to review the detention of 5,700 such cases when the Lord Chief Justice ruled that a particular patient was not technically neglected when dealt with under the Act.

Role of voluntary organizations

An active part in promoting a revision of the legislation and bringing facilities for the mentally handicapped into the twentieth century was played by the National Association for Mental Health as well as by many professional and other organizations. Much impetus was, however, also provided by the parents of handicapped children, who formed an effective organization after the Second World War. Originally named the 'National Association for Parents of Backward Children', it is now well known as the National Society for Mentally Handicapped Children. From the beginning it has done a great deal to modify the law towards mental handicap and to press for adequate community provision for handicapped children and adults. The society has also continually kept before the public and the government the need to improve residential facilities.

In this connection it is worth mentioning the combined effect of the policy of institutionalization and the neglect of hospital premises during and after the Second World War. Little building took place during the twenty years after 1945. During the war, premises had often been used for other purposes and existing standards in relating to overcrowding had ceased to be meaningful. For a number of years a hospital admission waiting list of over 8,000 existed at a time when some 10,000 beds were out of use because of shortage of staff.

In 1955 the report of the King Edward Hospital Fund had this to say:

> In general it may be said that the average age of the mental hospitals is well over 50 years and that the majority date from the time when the mentally ill were looked upon primarily as potential dangers to the community. It was thought best to segregate them away from centres of population, in districts where land was cheap, so that extensive grounds might isolate them still further from the community. Notwithstanding the work of Pinel, Tuke and others at the end of the eighteenth century in advocating freedom from restraint, some of these nineteenth and early twentieth century buildings and airing grounds suggest that 'prison' would be a truer designation even than 'asylum'. Second to the protection of the community came the custodial care of the inmates. These were herded in enormous wards, of a size not found in any other type of hospital, with cells for the solitary confinement of the more disturbed patients. Sometimes dormitories were provided for the patients from two or three wards and contained perhaps 160 beds or more in close-packed rows. Patients were not expected to have any possessions and no lockers were provided. In some hospitals the patients' clothing is still rolled into bundles and tied to their beds at night, since no storage space is provided for them. Washing, bathing and toilet facilities were primitive and inadequate, even by the standards of the last century, and in some cases have remained so until the present day. Overcrowding occurs to a degree unknown in other hospitals.

This quotation applies to the mentally ill. It could have been written, with even greater force, of the mentally retarded, since the amount spent per head on such patients in hospital is appreciably less than that spent on the mentally ill, and a number of the hospitals are even older. Although some improvements have been made since this report was written, the basic problem of the institutional population has not been tackled, nor can it be without appropriate expenditure involving extensive investment in rehabilitation and alternative accommodation.

The Royal Commission

Much evidence on the state of the services for the mentally handicapped was heard by the Royal Commission on the Law Relating to Mental Illness and Mental Deficiency during 1954 and 1955. The commission, set up in response to the very considerable public pressure for a reform of the law, was able to set out certain principles as to the treatment of the mentally disturbed on the basis of the considerable measure of agreement between those who submitted evidence. It recognized that considerable changes had taken place in the social structure since earlier laws were enacted, and recommended an informal approach to many matters which had previously come within the scope of the Lunacy and Mental Deficiency Acts. This implied that use should be made of the existing service—the Health Service, for example—when this became necessary, in the same way as other people did who needed to avail themselves of the service. This meant that psychiatry would come closer to other branches of medicine. Similarly, the Commission recommended a normal use of welfare services by the mentally disturbed, which would again have the effect of the mentally ill or retarded using ordinary services instead of coming within the scope of special Acts as pauper lunatics or mental defectives in receipt of poor relief, as had previously been the case.

The Mental Health Act 1959

The 1959 Act provided a more up-to-date approach to mental disturbance, and did away with much unnecessary red tape and restriction of liberty, permitting a less formal, more humane and more commonsense approach to mental ill-health. To date, however, the Act has not been matched by any corresponding change in the available services. The reason is not difficult to understand, for it costs very little to change the law. But the cost of employing social workers in rehabilitation work, of building schools and training centres and of rehousing those who must have residential care in contemporary hostels would be formidable, even though this expenditure is inevitable and would in the long run prove to be sound economics.

The main effect of the Act was to permit the mentally disturbed to be admitted informally to any suitable place for treatment, care or observation. The same applies to the local authority services in that the old procedure of formal 'ascertainment' is now abolished and the authority attempts to make provision in its area for such people as appear to need a service. Up to the time of writing, this has included the provision of training centres by the local health authority, but in the future this function will be taken over by the local education authority. The Act does preserve powers of detention in particular cases, and these powers are, in the main, put into the hands of medical advisers—usually two, one of whom is required to have some special psychiatric experience. In a limited number of cases, authority for detention stems from the courts. In the ten years since the law was passed, the great majority of hospital patients have become informal and complaints of unjust detention seem to have been very few. A number of safeguards have been built into the Act, including the right of appeal to a Mental Health Tribunal, though this procedure still tends to be inadequate where patients have no family, friend or adviser.

The main guarantee of liberty for the mentally inadequate will be the provision of adequate education, training, rehabilitation, employment and of all the social or therapeutic services necessary for themselves or their families. Legislation alone cannot achieve this, unless it is followed by adequate financial investment in the field, adequate training of personnel and education of the public.

Chapter 4
The cultural, social and economic background of mental handicap

It has only been during the past hundred years that the problem of mental handicap has revealed itself in its present dimensions in the more technically developed countries. A visit by Hilliard to Ceylon on behalf of the World Health Organization a few years ago failed to disclose any significant problem of mental handicap. This is not to say that the population of underdeveloped countries is more intelligent than in Britain or the United States. Indeed, all the evidence suggests that, on tests standardized for developed countries, people in poorer countries tend to do less well. Earlier studies in Britain have shown that town populations have an advantage over rural ones, and Sir Cyril Burt's classic work carried out in London after the First World War showed the striking differences between London boroughs in regard to backwardness at school. He assessed backwardness at over 20 per cent in Lambeth, Hoxton and Poplar, and at barely 1 per cent in Hampstead, Lewisham and Dulwich. (It should be remembered that the geography of class distribution was a little different at that time.) Burt found that 30 of the backward and 7 per cent of the general school populations were below what he termed the 'poverty line'.

Susser and Stein, in a study of mental handicap, divided families into what they called 'aspirant' and 'demotic'. These families had different expectations of their children: an important factor in assessing the prevalence of mental handicap. The family, the school, the employer and society as a whole tend to make increasingly complicated demands on both child and school leaver. In many other countries, the level of child mortality is still high, and a few years ago it was much higher in Britain than it is now. The decline is sometimes attributed to antibiotics and advances in medical science, but this is only partially true. A main factor has been an improvement in living conditions. Figure 5 shows the dramatic decline in infant deaths in England and Wales. In Victorian times, families were large, but a working-class mother took the death of some of her children almost as a matter of course. In those times the main focus of attention of parents was the effort to prevent children from dying of hunger, malnutrition, overcrowding or poverty.

Parental expectations

At present it is taken for granted even in the poorest classes of Britain that children will attend school regularly: they cannot leave school before the age of sixteen. It is expected that when they do so they will be able to read and write, complete the many forms required at every stage of modern life, reckon change and do simple arithmetic. A majority of jobs will demand more than this, and there

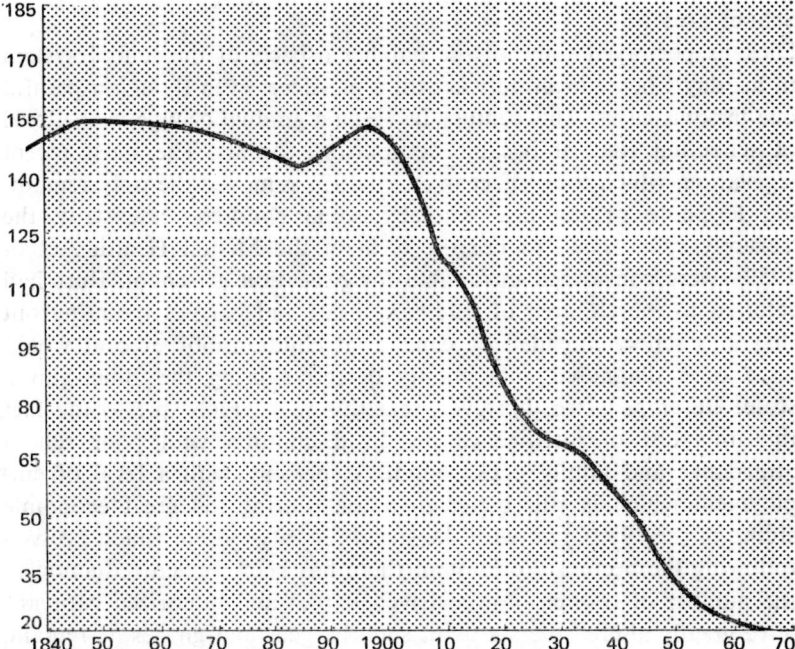

Fig. 5
Decline in infant mortality in England and Wales, 1840-1965. (Deaths below age of one year per 1000 live births)

are now not so many parents who do not appreciate this fact or who would begrudge their children education up to this level. On the contrary, most parents at every level of society appreciate that some effort at school is required to equip a child for work in modern society. The expectation is, of course, likely to vary greatly in different social classes, but the basic demand is the same. Illiteracy and an inability to do simple arithmetic or to tell the time are all things which make a child of school-leaving age conspicuous today, whereas even a couple of generations ago they would have been commonplace. Arnold Bennett in his novel *Clayhanger* gives an excellent account of the little lad whose task it was to get up in the small hours to light the fire in the pottery kiln. At that time, a child of tender years was already a potential source of income to a needy family, and the amount of skill demanded from child labour was limited. At present a large family is an additional economic burden, for the children's earning capacity cannot be expected to begin until at least the age of fifteen.

School provision
Dickens portrayed some of the harsher aspects of the school system in his day when education was still a privilege, even though a painful one in some cases. This century has seen a gradual change in the level of schooling since it became compulsory for all. The most recent legislation, which took effect in April 1971 removed the only remaining loophole in the law whereby some children—essentially the 'severely subnormal', to use the term of the Mental Health Act of 1959—were considered unsuitable for education at school. Burt had referred to the children of tramps, gipsies and bargees, pointing out that in a school attended by canal-boat children, 60 per cent would have been diagnosed as mentally defective using the Binet-Simon scale. He emphasized, however, that this was largely due to the fact that this test of intelligence penalized children with poor school attendance and family background. At present, with a level of employment which is still better than that during the great economic slump of the 1930s, and with the social security system which evolved following the Second World War, there has been a great reduction in the number of tramps. Power-driven barges and motorized caravans have greatly altered the status of such bargees and gipsies as remain. As a result, children in these groups, apart from being less numerous, have become more static and are likely to attend school more regularly.

At the same time, the status of the teacher has altered. There are now more teachers, and more with formal qualifications. The day of the pupil teacher and the 'uncertificated teacher' have gone. The size of school classes remains a major problem, but even here an improvement has taken place. The attitude of the teacher to education has also gradually altered. He is no longer primarily concerned with rote learning and the inculcation of the '3 Rs', by force if necessary. Despite all the present difficulties and stringencies, there is now some opportunity to assess an individual pupil's capabilities and to consider his education in the broader sense of social adaptation. At the same time the educational psychologist and other specialists have made their appearance on the educational scene. All of this has led to a gradual increase in the understanding of the problem of the child with special handicaps, whether these are intellectual, emotional or physical. While special classes or schools with teachers who may have special experience and knowledge of handicapped pupils provide part of the answer, there is also a better understanding of the variety of individual capacity and greater possibilities for integrating the unusual pupil into the group. Thus, although much remains to be done, we are entering a period when there is a gradually increasing awareness of the needs of the individual pupil, especially of those whose capacity for learning has been impaired.

Requirements of employment
The example of the teacher has been mentioned above in connection with improved professional qualifications. The need to establish these for teachers is self-evident, but a great variety of occupations which previously might have been looked upon as unskilled or semi-skilled now demand compliance with formal courses of instruction as well as evidence of a certain level of educational attainment. The burden of responsibility concerning any particular task, such as that of the steel erector, may have greatly increased while with automation, the number of employees assigned to particular tasks is gradually reduced, chiefly at the expense of the unskilled.

Levels of mental handicap
Against this changing background, the status of the mentally handicapped child is also changing. For practical purposes, it is possible to consider two levels of mental handicap. There are the more numerous children with mild degrees of backwardness. In their case, economic, social and cultural factors are very important. They may roughly be considered as that group who achieve an I.Q. of between 50 and 70 on standard tests, and a proportion of them will be singled out at school as 'educationally subnormal'. The less numerous group are those with an I.Q. below 50. A great majority of these will have forms of brain abnormality such as those described in Chapter 2. They are sometimes referred to as the 'pathological' group—the group which was under the terms of the Mental Deficiency Act, 1913, referred to as 'imbeciles' and 'idiots'.

At any stage of social development, these would be conspicuous by their limited ability. Many would doubtless die in a less developed society. By contrast, the mildly retarded are only obvious where there is educational opportunity and technical development, and are some-

is referred to as the 'sub-cultural' group of the retarded. In their social factors are very important. They are sometimes looked upon as being just part of the ordinary variation which is to be expected in humans in regard to intellect as for other qualities. They do not look conspicuously different, and would pass for normal in a crowd.

Interplay of pathology and culture
This way of looking at things has the attractiveness of simplicity. In fact it is an oversimplification. There is no such sharp distinction. Intelligence tests have limitations, and the same child may at one time be classed as mildly retarded and at another as moderately. That is, on one assessment he may have an I.Q. of 55 and a year later of 45. This does not necessarily mean that he has deteriorated in the interval, though if his parents have been told the two test results in the form of a precise figure they may be very worried. In fact it may be that a different test has been used or a different psychologist has examined the child; or he may have been assessed in a different locality. Perhaps he was not very well, or a little disturbed, or ill-at-ease when the second assessment was done.

Then, social factors are, after all, of some importance in deciding the level of attainment of the more seriously retarded children. The work carried out in the Brooklands unit by Tizard and his colleagues showed that it was possible to improve the vocabulary of children with an I.Q. between 20 and 50 by using a suitable régime. In this study, they were compared with other children remaining in the parent institution at Tooting with large ward units and a lower level of staffing. A film made at the same time demonstrated differences in social attainments, though these were more difficult to measure than language. It is also now generally appreciated that figures showing levels of intelligence are themselves subject to modification by upbringing and social or economic conditions. This is less true of the 'pathological' or more severely handicapped cases, but even at this level there is some impact.

There is no reason to suppose that pathology of the brain stops short at the more severely handicapped. In fact, there is ample evidence to the contrary. There are many people with epilepsy or cerebral palsy who are of quite good or high levels of intelligence. It is true that if a random sample of the cerebral palsied or of epileptics is chosen they will, as a group, be found to have a lower level of intelligence than a random sample of people. But among them there will be a fair representation of those in the ordinary range of intelligence and of the mildly handicapped. Although such people have these levels of intelligence they must have something wrong with their brain—some degree of pathology—otherwise they would not suffer from cerebral palsy or epilepsy. Intelligence in hydrocephalus has already been discussed, and it has been shown that this condition can be compatible with good intelligence. It seems a fair assumption that where people with a good intelligence have some brain pathology, they would have still better levels of brain function if they did not have the abnormality. On the other hand, there are abundant examples of people with obvious brain pathology who function well above average competence. The writer well remembers Wilfred Willett, who suffered from a paralysis of one side of the body due to extensive damage to the brain from a wartime head injury and who was yet an acknowledged authority on ornithology, had an encyclopedic knowledge of biology, and was an accomplished public speaker.

Most of the pathological conditions listed in Chapter 2 as well as very many others known to produce mental handicap can occur in a mild form. Thus, head injury and meningitis may reduce the level of intelligence without severely depressing it, so that an affected child who was previously of average intelligence may afterwards function at an educationally subnormal level. This applies to many inborn chemical errors, such as phenylketonuria, in which a few affected children who have not had treatment are retarded mildly rather than severely. It seems likely, in fact, that all the many things which may combine to interfere with the optimum development of the brain from the time of conception play some part in 'normal' variation.

Susser and Stein, mentioned above, studied patients who were found to be dull and who came from different types of family. Most of the children from 'demotic' homes, where there was no particular demand for scholarship, seemed clinically normal, while of those coming from 'aspirant' homes, a considerable number obviously had some abnormality of brain function. They considered the difference to be significant. While this is an interesting and useful contribution, it is clear that no such sharp division can be drawn. There will always be an interplay between the individual child and his environment. If, because of a fault in the structure or function of the brain, he is limited in his educational possibilities, a good home, skilled teaching and a stable social background will allow him to develop his potential to the full. If he is potentially of good intelligence, but has to face parental neglect and misfortune, inadequate schooling in an overcrowded class with inept teachers, and life in a background of poverty and unemployment, then his actual achievement may fall far short of his potential.

A further complication in the argument is the obvious fact that an unfavourable environment may cause many of the pathological conditions which interfere with brain function. Prematurity is one example of such a situation. Low birth-weight may be due to many different reasons: some babies are small because they are twins or triplets; others because they have a chromosome abnormality, or have been affected by German measles in the mother. But there is also a striking effect of social class and standard of living on birth-weight. Working class mothers in Britain tend to have babies with lower birth-weights than do mothers in the Registrar General's classes I and II, i.e. in professional and better off families. Poorer mothers also tend to have bigger families, and with repeated births there may be some exhaustion of their reproductive capacity. Studies in the United States have shown that Negro babies are more often small at birth than are white babies, and a number of workers found evidence to support the view that a good maternal diet will reduce the incidence of low birth-weight.

Family size

As mentioned above, family size may operate at a biological level. A mother may be exhausted by repeated pregnancies unless she has the advantages of a good diet and favourable material circumstances. The mother whose diet is not really adequate to maintain her own health may become anaemic after several pregnancies, though anaemia may only be one aspect of her poor state of health. She may also have a shortage of vitamin B.12 and of folic acid, both of which are essential for the normal development of a baby.

Family size can also act at a cultural level, by deciding how much adult time is available for the children, what facilities and playthings are provided for them, and opportunities for recreation and stimulation. The survey in Scotland (see p. 50) showed a fairly steady drop in intelligence in proportion to family size. Eleven-year-old children were studied, and the average intelligence of only children on the Terman-Merrill scale was 113, falling to 91 for those whose family sizes were eight and nine. While some have argued that these findings imply a possible decline in national intelligence, on the assumption that less gifted parents are more fertile, Penrose has pointed out that a different interpretation is possible. He suggests that if birth order is connected with intelligence, and if the first-born is, on average, a little more intelligent and the later-born progressively less so, then this would explain the drop in intelligence with family size. It seems reasonable to suppose that parents will be able to devote more attention to their first child, and that as the family size increases so standards of living and opportunities will be reduced. Such differences are, of course, not absolute and can be modified by such social measures as family allowances or better chances of housing for big families.

Relationship of mental handicap to delinquency, mental illness and other social problems

It is sometimes suggested that mental handicap and similar problems cause slum conditions. This view is not generally held at present, since it has been amply demonstrated that an improvement in living standards, better employment, building and social security programmes have done much to abolish the slums. Old ideas die hard, and the same arguments are being served up at present about immigrants in Britain. It is true of them that they tend to take poorer paid and unskilled jobs. They go to live in poor areas, and live in overcrowded conditions. Because of their low income, they live at a lower standard than people born here and so 'make' a slum in the eyes of the casual observer. Their families are often bigger, and they have less money to spend on their children, who may be somewhat neglected because both parents are out at work trying to make ends meet. The language or accent and vocabulary of the children may be different, as may their customs. The upshot is that such families have a higher proportion of children who are retarded at school. There is little good evidence to support suggestions as to any real difference in potential intelligence between people of different racial origin. It seems likely, therefore, that at present immigrant children in Britain are suffering from a temporary disadvantage which will be overcome to the extent that they can be integrated with the native population and are given equal opportunities in job selection.

There was at one time a prevalent notion that 'bad stock', could account for alcoholism, insanity, mental defect, tuberculosis, delinquency, prostitution and all manner of wickedness. The ghosts of this notion still linger, and are a source of embarrassment to parents with the misfortune of having had a handicapped child. They may still think of this as shameful, and uninformed or malign gossip can help to make them feel criticized and rejected. It is therefore important to make it clear that, whilst all manner of social problems can be found together in a slum area, there is no reason to suppose that this is necessarily because of some mysterious hereditary weakness in people living in that area. Many find themselves caught up in a vicious circle of events from which it is difficult to escape. This applies to such factors as living in a poor area and belonging to an unskilled class. Children raised in this situation are likely to have few advantages, and so may well repeat parental patterns. Those living in such poor areas are also more prone to delinquency, alcoholism, prostitution and mental illness. These problems will therefore be linked together by a common material and social environment. A number of examples have been much quoted in the past to support the theory of 'bad stock' or neuropathic diathesis, one of which was the Kallikak family in the United States. A large pedigree of this and similar families was collected, and it was shown that different members of the same family were delinquent, alcoholic, defective, insane and so forth.

On the whole, the more carefully study is devoted to consideration of possible connections between different disabilities, the less obvious do the connections become. Woodward, for example, carried out a careful analysis of the supposed connection between delinquency and mental handicap. She found no clearly established link, though there was a tendency for delinquents to be below average in school achievement.

This is of great practical importance for parents who may believe that, because a child is found to be mentally retarded or a poor scholar, he will become delinquent or anti-social when he grows up. The same consideration applies to fears that some parents may have about a child's sexual development. They may believe that backward adolescents are more likely to be promiscuous, to become prostitutes or have illegitimate babies. There is no statistical evidence to support such views, though occasional examples can be quoted of fertile mothers of low intelligence. This seems to be more than compensated for by the considerable number of individuals of limited intelligence who have no children. On the whole the more seriously retarded do not seem to have as strong a sexual drive as normal people, and they tend to be more biddable.

The separation of mental illness from mental retardation is a difficult problem. There is an administrative confusion, because some mentally retarded people are still housed in institutions for the mentally ill, while, to a lesser extent, the opposite is also true. Then there are retarded individuals who develop mental illness. The problem of childhood autism, which can be regarded as a form of mental illness, has already been discussed. Also, it seems likely that some conditions causing mental retardation in some individuals may cause mental illness or difficult and anti-social behaviour in others. This seems to be true of Klinefelter's syndrome, and also perhaps of Turner's syndrome. It may also apply to some chemical disorders affecting the brain, such as homocystinuria.

So far as the inheritance of the more classical forms of mental illness or of mental retardation is concerned, however, there is no good evidence to support any link. The two problems may be considered separately—this is important from the viewpoint of public understanding. The mentally ill can be unpredictable, and this gives reason to fear insanity. On the other hand, the mentally retarded tend to be more easily predictable than ordinary people, their thought processes being simpler and more transparent. There is no particular reason why the children of a parent who has suffered from schizophrenia or depression should be mentally retarded. Conversely, there is no very good evidence to suggest that the children of mildly retarded parents are more likely to develop such conditions as schizophrenia. Again, there is difficulty and room for difference of opinion in the diagnosis of mental illness, so that different investigations may yield different results.

Institutional surveys

Attempts are being made at present to base an understanding of the problem of mental handicap on surveys of the general population. This presents difficulties, for the reasons discussed in Chapter 1, and more detailed information is usually available for studies of patients in institutions. In Penrose's classical Colchester survey, it became evident that, of those patients in hospital, proportionately more of the severely retarded had been born to professional and executive parents, while the unskilled parents had a bigger share of the mildly retarded. As Penrose points out, this may be interpreted in a variety of ways. Better-off parents with mildly retarded children would have been better able to make arrangements for them outside hospital. He suggests that the severely retarded may be more evenly distributed among the social classes. Tables 2 and 3 show that, particularly in 1957, so far as all patients admitted to hospital were concerned, unskilled workers were greatly over-represented among parents of 'defectives', the figure of 36 per cent being nearly three times that of 13 per cent assigned to that class in the general population. When children under sixteen are considered, there is still an excess of parents in the unskilled group, or twice as many as in the ordinary population. The majority of children concerned would have been severely handicapped. In regard to the Fountain Hospital the difference was less marked.

There must, particularly at present, be an element of selection in

Table 2 Patients under sixteen admitted to mental-deficiency hospitals (related to social class of parents)

Social class	Percentage of parents of all defectives admitted		
	1950-1 England and Wales	1957 England and Wales	1961-2 Fountain Hospital
i Professional	12	16	25
ii Intermediate			
iii Skilled artisans	48	38	44
iv Partly skilled	15	10	14
v Unskilled	26	36	18

Table 3 Social class of parents of patients under sixteen admitted to mental-deficiency hospitals in England and Wales in 1950-1 compared with that of employed male adults in general population

Social class	Percentage of general population	Percentage of parents
i Professional	18	12
ii Intermediate		
iii Skilled artisans	53	48
iv Partly skilled	16	15
v Unskilled	13	26

regard to social circumstances of children for their admission to hospital. At one time there was a tendency to suggest automatically that admission to hospital was the correct procedure, and many medical advisers or others concerned would have spent time trying to persuade parents to part with their mentally handicapped children. Today, most of the effort is, for two main reasons, aimed in the opposite direction. Firstly, we believe that most retarded children, like ordinary children, do better if they are living at home; there is a good deal of research to support this view. Secondly, there is a great shortage of residential places for handicapped children. At the same time the growth of day facilities makes it much easier for mothers to look after their mentally handicapped children at home. In our own work we have found that we can offer short periods of care to help families in temporary difficulties, and that the few admissions for long-term care which are possible are entirely demanded by social consideration. As a result, the children admitted to our hospital group tend to have no effective family, or to have parents who are ill, or to come from very poor or very large families with severe material difficulties; or, by contrast, to come from families which are, perhaps, fairly well situated, but which are quite unable for psychological reasons to accept a retarded child.

The handicapped child in the home
Many parents manage very effectively to look after a quite seriously handicapped child at home. Cases admitted to hospital tend nowadays to be exceptional. In some instances, the conditions at home may be so unfortunate that they would appear to be unsatisfactory for the other children in the family, even though they may be of good intelligence. The handicap of the child with which we are concerned may therefore be incidental. The family may perhaps have only one room, perhaps taken up entirely by the parents' bed and by cots, leaving no place for the children to play. To have a backward, restless child at home in these conditions may be a trial for the child and for the parents. Children who are restless in these conditions may prove to be no great problem in hospital. Resolute attempts to modify home conditions in some cases meet a degree of success. It seems better on every count to try every measure, including application to the housing authority and advice to the parents on ways to obtain help, rather than immediately resorting to hospital admission, even if a place can be found.

The following example illustrates the difficulties facing such a family:

'Bobby was a retarded little boy aged 5 when we first got to know him. He came into hospital for a while and then went home; later attending the Hospital School daily. At school he could take off his coat and hang it on a peg; he could drink from a beaker; use a spoon; would help himself to a biscuit from the tin. He would open the door. He responded to regular potting with infrequent accidents. He would make noises if something was withheld from him but no speech was heard. He responded to facial expressions and showed the teacher what he wanted. He tended to be shut-in and to be on his own but he did respond to affection and freedom to express himself. He did not play with the other children. He was not aggressive. He responded to adult attention and went freely with an adult if his hand was taken. He did not join in group activity but looked on with interest. He could ride a tricycle; he liked to push a pram and pull a horse on wheels; to roll wheels or cars along. Any mobile toy attracted him. Robert liked water play, sand play, finger painting. He would build pyramid bricks sitting beside an adult, but lost interest if the adult moved away. When he was bored he just sat spinning a piece of spring.

Bobby was one of seven. The father was unemployed and mentally ill. The parents were said to be totally overwhelmed by the problem of looking after the children. They were unable to cope with Bobby and gave him very little stimulation. Bobby is said to have talked before he was separated from his mother when he was three years old, being then sent to a Residential Nursery where he stayed for two years. The family were evicted from their flat and all the family including Bobby have been living in appallingly bad accommodation; three overcrowded dilapidated rooms provided by the local authority. The children ran wild between the filthy back-yards and the main road, a few yards from the Thames.

In summary, although Bobby probably had limited potential to start with, his condition was made worse by the lack of a constant mother figure; by his mother's inability to cope and by lack of suitable provision for the family by the local authority.

It is worth mentioning at this point the sheer economic considerations involved in comparing hospital and home care. Even if it were still possible to care for a child in hospital for as little as £10 per week—which some institutions seem to manage to do—this is still more than the sum which would be needed in a minority of poor families to make the home conditions bearable. Although such families are not numerous, it would seem highly desirable to introduce a scheme whereby the parent could be paid to look after the child instead of using the elaborate and less satisfactory arrangement of admitting him to hospital. In fact, at the time of writing, a figure of £20 per week is a much more realistic figure for residential care for handicapped children if adequate facilities are to be provided, and it may well be suggested that, if less than this is spent, it can only be to the detriment of the residents.

From what has been said, it will be obvious that it is very difficult in some cases to separate the effects of having a retarded child from the cause of the backwardness. A mother may be depressed and the household disturbed. It seems possible that this may have helped to make the child more backward. On the other hand, a backward, difficult child may produce depression in the mother and so upset the rest of the family. The writer's impression is that if a family is well knit; if the ties between parents are sound; if the parents are mentally and physically well; if the physical circumstances are not too difficult; if the mother is able to distribute her affection between the handicapped child and the other members of her family wisely; if she neither overprotects nor rejects the handicapped child; if she is realistic and ready to accept the services provided (if these, indeed, exist); if the father and other children are ready to support the mother in her efforts and fully accept the handicapped member, then the presence of the affected child will not be resented and will not be a great burden. Unfortunately, not all these qualities are always present in many families and the handicapped member does impose a considerable material, economic and emotional burden, subjecting the family to a severe test. It should be added that, with wise parental management and example, positive qualities can be developed in the brothers and sisters of the intellectually limited child. Through him their own characters may be strengthened and endowed with the positive qualities necessary for civilized living and helping those in need. Equally, if the matter is mismanaged, then the other members of the family may feel resentful, jealous and cheated of attention or maternal affection, all of which may have a deleterious affect on their character and development.

Tizard and Grad carried out a survey (1961) on the mentally handicapped and their families, covering 150 London families 'with an idiot or an imbecile child at home' and a further hundred with such a child in an institution. There was no difference in the social class of the two groups. They assessed the families for income using the National Assistance Benefit scales and found that 25 per cent of the home sample and 13 per cent of the institutional were rated as poor. But if the institutional cases had returned home the difference between the groups would have disappeared. In other words, an additional 12 per cent of the families with a child at home were reduced to poverty by the child's presence. There are many ways in which a severely handicapped child can cause extra expense. In the first place, he has the same needs as any other child for food, clothes, etc. But he may also need special clothes and appliances. In some cases it is possible for parents to get help with chairs, etc., but they do not always know how to go about it. Some severely retarded children are disturbed and destructive. There may be much breakage of crockery and destruction of furniture. In some cases there may be special needs. The family may spend more on heating in the case of a child with Down's syndrome, who would be susceptible to cold weather. They may also have to buy special foods, as for a baby, where a backward child is unable to chew solids. A major factor would, of course, be loss of parental income. Many poorer mothers work and their earnings are an important contribution to the family budget. They can often manage to get someone to look after their normally intelligent children in the interval between school and their coming home or going to work, as the case may be, but it is more difficult to arrange this for a handicapped child, who may be restless or disturbed or subject to fits or incontinent or needing to be fed or other special care. Parents may not like to ask friends and neighbours, or these may be unwilling to undertake the extra responsibility.

The volume of work in the home may also be critically increased by the retarded child. If, for example, the mother has a normal nine-month-old baby and a five-year-old retarded child functioning at a nine-month level, she will have to change and wash both children, wash their clothes and feed them. The retarded child will need care, as for a baby, but being bigger the amount of work may also be greater. This situation can also make it difficult or impossible for the mother to seek part time employment.

The Tizard and Grad survey also demonstrated that, economic considerations apart, the families with a handicapped child at home were worse off socially. Their contacts with others were much reduced, 15 per cent of these families being classed as 'seriously' limited in their social contacts. The reasons may be varied. For one thing, as we have mentioned, affected parents have less money to spend. Then they have more work at home, so that there is less time for leisure activity. Then again, a seriously handicapped child is in many cases not easily portable. There may be a risk of incontinence; he may be physically handicapped and heavy; he might have a fit while away from home; or he might be noisy and difficult. Some parents may feel unable to take these risks, and embarrassed by them. They may feel that friends and even neighbours would be unable to tolerate their child, or that his presence would detract from the occasion. For similar reasons they may be shy about inviting friends home, and a teenage daughter may prefer to go out with her boy-friend rather than invite him home where he would see her retarded brother.

Parents with a retarded child below school age may be faced with a serious social problem. Children of school age can go to a junior training centre or special school, but for younger children there is little provision. Tizard and Grad reported that, in London, only a sixth of children of pre-school age attended an occupation centre, the rest being excluded 'not only from these centres but from the nurseries and nursery schools for normal children'. Conditions in this respect have improved since the time of their report but only marginally. The situation contrasts with that of the end of the Second World War, when access to day nurseries was relatively readily available.

Economic consequences of research, prevention, treatment and care
At one time education for the children of the poor was looked upon by opposing interests as wanton extravagance. At present, there are few voices raised against general compulsory education. On the contrary, it is recognized that, for purely economic reasons, adequate education is essential for national prosperity. Policy makers, however, do not seem to have the same rational approach to the question of mental retardation. Very little money is invested in research, prevention, treatment or education of the retarded. There has been some criticism of the cost of treating a child with phenylketonuria on a special diet, which is indeed very costly. The various special preparations are protein substitutes made by breaking down proteins into the amino-acids of which they are composed, and by recombining them in suitable proportions without the particular amino-acid (phenylalanine) which the body is unable to tolerate in any quantity in this condition. Others have reckoned the cost of screening for diagnosis and the cost of treatment, but this is still only a small fraction of the cost of keeping a severely retarded person throughout his life, much of it in an institution. A child retarded by this condition could reasonably be expected to reach the age of fifty or more, and is likely to be totally economically dependent. The cost of his care might well therefore total at least £50,000 in current prices. Of even more economic importance is the loss of his productive capacity; this could be reckoned minimally at an equal sum but is likely to be much more.

Similar arithmetic applies to almost every aspect of the problem, and is particularly applicable to the mildly retarded. There are no very precise statistics on the mental levels of patients in institutions for the mentally retarded. These certainly include a considerable number of people who are not retarded at all if intelligence is taken as the criterion. There are some who object to the use of intelligence as a guide to the degree of mental handicap, and it is clear that this can be very misleading if it is rigidly applied in the sense that many people who may be shown to be mildly retarded on assessment are economically independent. On the other hand, unless we use some such guide, then there is no precise way of defining just who is in need of help or treatment under the Mental Health Act as 'subnormal or severely subnormal'. In fact, the 1959 Act lays down, under the definitions of subnormality and severe subnormality, that these must include 'subnormality of intelligence', though there is no further definition of what this means. In reality, in hospitals for the mentally handicapped there are people with an average or above average intelligence on assessment. They are not numerous, but anyone who has experience of these hospitals will know of a few people like this. They are not usually detained, but they have not succeeded in adapting to life outside.

It has often been argued that a lack of social competence rather than a test of intelligence should be the criterion of mental handicap. This is, however, also difficult to define. Many school-leavers appear to adults, and particularly to their own parents, to be socially incompetent. In fact, they often are until they have had the opportunity to make mistakes and find out for themselves 'the hard way'. Parents, courts and other authorities are often too protective and too fearful of the capacity of a young person to make a successful adaptation. This is one reason why young people have, in the past, often been sent to hospitals for the mentally handicapped. If they then rebel against such detention, often unwisely, this only confirms the belief of the authorities that they are irresponsible, so starting a vicious circle.

If social incompetence, rather than intelligence, is taken as the guide especially for detained patients, problems of civil liberty may arise, as they have done in the past. This would leave the matter wide open for individual interpretation, and anyone whose behaviour seemed somewhat irresponsible might be so detained. The introduction of the phrase relating to intelligence may therefore be something of a safeguard besides such other provisions as the right of appeal to a tribunal. Similar considerations apply to young people committed by a court to hospital after being found 'beyond parental care and control'. It may well be that if the appropriate social agencies were able to deal with the problem more effectively, then there might be no need to take some of these cases to court. When young people appear before a court, charged with a minor offence, the line of least resistance, if they are of limited intelligence or have been to a special school, is to send them to a hospital for the mentally handicapped in the belief that expert help will be available there. In fact, overcrowding and limited staffing as well as a tradition of caution may preclude the hospital from providing the necessary rehabilitation. If the necessary social workers (in this case, probation officers) were available, normal probation procedure might meet the case. Tizard and Grad noted that, at the time when they did their survey, institutions could provide only five social workers to 5,000 patients and their families.

The Darenth Park study

In their earlier work (1956), describing conditions in the years after the Second World War, Tizard and O'Connor achieved considerable success in finding employment for the mildly mentally retarded. They introduced large numbers of patients into unskilled labouring jobs and into routine work in light industry. Since then there has been some change in the level of employment, the degree of automation and semi-automation has increased, technical requirements are higher and there is less shortage of labour. Be this as it may, the findings of these workers showed that at that time only a very limited effort was needed to achieve dramatic results in rehabilitation. The extent to which these results are relevant to the present situation is arguable, but the writer has himself found that successful placements in the community are still possible with relatively little effort. There are still, however, very few social workers being given this task as a priority, and few areas where there is a list kept of those employers who have suitable work for the retarded, or who are willing to help in their placement. The necessary explanatory work to convince employers that the effort is worthwhile is not done. Those who might be responsible are often overburdened and are often not convinced of the value of the effort or of its practicability.

At the time of Tizard and O'Connor's survey, the mean I.Q. of the feeble-minded young person detained in hospital was about 70. Many psychiatrists working in hospitals for the mentally handicapped believe that the nature of the resident population has changed in the direction of severe handicap. This may be true, but a recent survey carried out by the British Psychological Society did not provide any supporting evidence. Admittedly the survey was incomplete and further work needs to be done. The Society was able to collect information only from those hospitals where psychologists were employed. Incidentally, it is striking evidence of the inadequacy of our present services that there are still a number of such hospitals without the services of a psychologist. A further difficulty was that, in a number of hospitals, the function of the psychologist was limited. He could only see those cases specially referred to him, while presumably he would be unable to cope with the total case load involved in regular assessment of every inmate. On the sample available, the mean I.Q. of the 'subnormal' was again at about the 70 mark, in line with the Darenth Park finding. Even more surprisingly, the mean I.Q. of the 'severely subnormal' was 60. It seems possible that this latter curious finding relates to the interpretation of the Mental Health Act, since there are separate provisions in the Act for the subnormal and severely subnormal. This consideration would only apply to those patients who are legally detained, or about 5,000 out of a total hospital population of the mentally retarded of some 64,000. Efforts are being made to remedy the lack of precise information about this hospital population, but what is required in this connection can only be got by a detailed survey on the spot of a sample population. Attempts to collect information on level of intelligence by the Department of Health and Social Security centrally will not remedy the situation, since these will be dependent on the time of psychologists available in the hospitals and on the co-operation, ability and availability of time for those completing the return. In the meantime, the argument in favour of employing social workers with the specific task of placing this section of the hospital population in the general community is overwhelming, if only on economic grounds.

Work reported earlier by Hilliard and Brandon and continuing at present supports this argument. They demonstrated that patients who had spent varying periods of time in hospital could be got out into open employment and placed in the general community without too much trouble. In this connection a continuity of effort is needed. There are still those who believe that such people are correctly placed in hospital and view with apprehension their release into the general community. They lack confidence in their ability to survive. It is all too easy to prove the correctness of this viewpoint by sending people into jobs and recording the number of failures. It is necessary to find a suitable job, a helpful employer, to advise the patient on punctuality and behaviour and to be ready to help if he loses his job.

The reasons why young people are admitted to hospitals for the mentally retarded or are considered unemployable are manifold. Above a level of about I.Q. 50 it is often not intelligence which determines the issue, but other qualities such as willingness, working ability, persistence, sociability, ability to accept criticism constructively, good temper, friendliness. It is possible to help young people to develop these qualities, but it is none the less difficult to predict success in employment, and even if the young person loses his first job, he may gain useful experience, confidence, or even an awareness of his own limitations from the trial period which will stand him in good stead later.

If it is so relatively easy to get some patients out of hospital the question as to whether their presence there was really necessary becomes relevant. The conclusion must be drawn that if better social services for leavers from special schools and job-placement services for this group were available, then many such admissions could be prevented.

The last section of this chapter has been devoted largely to the mildly mentally retarded in hospital because they have been studied to some small extent. Much less is known about the large number of children with similar levels of ability who leave school, many of them finding jobs and others remaining 'unemployable'. Of all areas in the field of mental retardation this is one where the least effort has been expended and where the most immediate rewards could be won. It would be naïve to have expected immediate successes from the American 'Head Start' programmes designed to improve the educational and social level of the underprivileged children. There is, however, every indication that, by proper provision of educational, social and advisory services and by persistent effort, the contribution which this section of the community are able to make to their own and the common welfare would be greatly increased.

Chapter 5
Assessment

Traditionally, the mother's first question to the midwife is: 'Is it a boy or a girl?' Nowadays, with our increasing awareness of the risk of congenital abnormality, the question is more likely to be: 'Is it all right?' Many of the abnormal conditions which are recognizable at birth affect, or may affect, the brain and mental development.

Down's syndrome
Perhaps the best known and most obvious of these conditions is Down's syndrome, or 'mongolism'. The appearance is usually so characteristic that it is immediately recognized by the midwife or medical attendant. The grandmother or the mother herself may sometimes recognize the abnormality from the general rounded shape of the baby and from the characteristic features. At this stage, if there is any doubt, confirmatory tests can be done. These involve counting the number of chromosomes in the white cells in the baby's blood. Down's syndrome is, therefore, an example of a condition which is obvious at birth and which by its nature implies mental retardation.

Spina bifida
Spina bifida is another abnormality which is immediately obvious at birth. This condition does not necessarily imply mental handicap, and about half of the babies with spina bifida are likely to die before five years of age, despite the best efforts of modern surgery. Of those who survive, about 10 per cent are likely to be severely mentally handicapped. One third will have some degree of mental handicap.

Hydrocephalus
Hydrocephalus is less likely to be obvious at birth, and the great majority of cases appear during the first few months after birth. However, in a few cases the head is already enlarged at birth and may cause difficulty in delivery. Children affected thus early are less likely to survive. Bulging of the fontanelle, or soft spot, is an early warning of the development of hydrocephalus.

Microcephaly

Microcephaly, or, more generally, smallness of the head, may obvious at birth and may indicate limited possibilities for mental development. In mathematical terms a degree of smallness which makes the head circumference more than three standard deviations below the mean for the age and sex is usually associated with definite mental retardation. Tables are available showing the expected head size at any given age for girls and boys, and also showing how much variation can be expected within the normal range. At one month for example the average circumference of the head is 37·3 cm in boys and 36·5 in girls, whilst the standard deviations are 1·5 and 1·4 cm respectively, so that for boys at this age a circumference of 14·7 inches would be about right. In practice, it is difficult to measure fractions of a centimetre with an active child. The measurement is taken round the head just above the brows at the front and across the part of the back of the head which sticks out most. In some cases smallness of the head is noticeable at birth, but in others it results from failure of the head to grow after birth.

Deformities

Many other deformities, some of which are linked with mental retardation, are apparent at birth or become so soon afterwards. Some of these are rare, such as Apert's syndrome, in which the skull is an odd shape being abnormally high, while the eyes may bulge and the fingers not be properly separated. There may be a suspicion of possible retardation with other congenital deformities, for example if there is a cleft lip and palate, or perhaps a heart defect. There could be something wrong with the brain, too, since different defects tend to be associated with each other. Serious abnormalities of the eyes and ears may lead to a degree of backwardness from 'sensory deprivation', even if the brain is healthy.

Cerebral palsy

Cerebral palsy is likely to show up soon after birth if it is at all gross. This most commonly takes the form of spasticity, and the likeliest thing to be noticed by the parents is the lack of proper movements in the affected limbs, the child lying stiffly in its cot. The lack of 'give' in the spine may also be noticeable when the child is picked up. Severe cases of cerebral palsy are very likely to involve some degree of mental handicap.

Epilepsy

Convulsions may be the first symptom to draw attention to a backward child. Sometimes these occur soon after delivery, and may be evidence of brain damage which occurred during birth. Single convulsions are common during infancy, especially with measles or some other infectious illness or fever. They are not necessarily a cause for great concern, but every child who has a convulsion should be completely investigated, especially in regard to development. Convulsions in infants often take a different form from those in adults. Instead of the major attack of 'grand mal' the attacks may be brief and are described as a 'salaam spasm' or 'infantile spasm'. In such an attack the child goes stiff and bends forward; the face becomes expressionless and he looks 'absent'; the electrical recordings from the brain (E.E.G.) may be abnormal. The frequency of the waves may be reduced and the voltage may be too high. Very high voltage is called 'hypsarrythmia' and is sometimes a sign of the disease known as tuberous sclerosis. Other babies may have 'petit mal', momentary 'absences', which tend to be repeated very frequently. These produce a characteristic E.E.G. picture with cycles at three per second coming from the base of the brain. Still other types of attack can be seen in infants, sometimes with a tendency to continuous twitching of a whole or part of the body going on for hours or even days. The ordinary startle spasm of normal infants may be followed by a fit in such cases. Any of these findings indicates a need for very careful investigation and assessment of the baby. An electroencephalogram is essential in such cases, and appropriate drugs to control the epilepsy can be prescribed. A few years ago, phenobarbitone, or 'luminal', was most commonly used, but there is now a great variety of drugs available and the tendency is not to use phenobarbitone so often for fear of making the child 'dopey' as well as, in some cases, irritable. Another drug commonly used is phenytoin, or 'epanutin', which very occasionally has the disadvantage of causing swelling of the gums, and which may also cause giddiness and unsteadiness if the dose is too high. In some children it interferes with the body's balance of vitamin B, in particular with the fraction known as folic acid.

Screening
Any infant having fits, or at risk of mental retardation for any other reason is now usually subjected to screening. With young infants, this commonly implies brief admission to hospital, though much of the work may be done on an out-patient basis. It is customary to investigate specimens of the urine and blood. Amongst other things the amino-acids are of particular interest. They are abnormal in both blood and urine in phenylketonuria and also in a number of other

inborn chemical errors, such as histidinaemia, homocystinuria, maple syrup urine disease and many others, though most of these are rare. There are specific tests for some of them, but it is also possible to do general screening by paper chromatography, that is, by running the urine or serum through blotting paper. The different substances dissolved travel at different rates, and by appropriate staining after an interval it is possible to see a kind of pattern of spots. The intensity of staining and size of the spot indicates how much of the particular substance is present. There are characteristic patterns for each of the diseases mentioned above, as well as in many others. In other conditions, such as gargoylism, special tests are indicated, such as examination of a blood smear in which the lymphocytes may include abnormal collections of a stained compound. Various other chemical tests on the urine also give an indication as to whether this group of diseases is present or not. These mainly depend on the presence of a complicated chemical substance known as chrondroitin B, or perhaps heparitin. These are mucopolysaccharides—compounds of protein and animal starch which are common in the body but which accumulate abnormally in these conditions.

At present, routine screening of all infants is confined to the Guthrie test for phenylketonuria. This involves a heel prick for the infant before discharge from the maternity ward. The test is very ingenious and depends on the presence in the blood of an excess of the aminoacid known as phenylalanine. A micro-organism known as *Bacillus subtilis*, in common with man, finds phenylalanine essential to life and growth. A sheet of jelly or culture medium is prepared and the blood specimens to be tested are placed on it. The culture medium contains no phenylalanine, so that when it is inoculated with the bacillus the latter fails to grow except around those specimens of blood which contain excess phenylalanine. These specimens are thus clearly indicated, and the infants concerned can be further examined by taking another specimen of blood and testing it in more detail for amounts of phenylalanine.

It seems likely that, as technique improves, many further tests can be done on a single blood specimen as a routine for all babies. It should also become possible in the future to screen for many conditions such as the lipidoses, where the exact nature of the chemical error is still in need of clarification. Pre-natal screening of the amniotic fluid—if further developed—will permit diagnosis of a number of chromosomal and chemical errors early in pregnancy. At present, for example, the condition of hyperuricaemia can already be detected in the unborn baby at an early stage. This is a rare and curious disease in which, as in gout, there is too much uric acid in the blood. In the infant, this interferes with the function of the brain and causes mental retardation. It also causes the baby to pick at himself and bite his lips. It should not, however, be assumed that if baby does this he is necessarily suffering from hyperuricaemia.

Assessment of behaviour
In many infants, backwardness is not noted through any of the defects mentioned above. Most commonly, parents become concerned because of failure in normal development. They may get worried at any stage, and this will partly depend on their experience and expectation. Some are inclined to accept whatever their first baby does as right and are not worried if he is slow to sit up and take notice. Others, more sophisticated, may be continually checking him against standards or comparing him with neighbours' children. In the last analysis, progress in any baby can only be checked by noting his attainments and comparing them with available standards. Even if some particular condition has been diagnosed in the baby, it will not be known to what extent this has affected his mental development until he can be assessed in a standard manner.

There is very wide variation in the development of the ordinary child. Too much significance should not be attached to any one item, for example, walking. The facets of behaviour most closely related to measured intelligence are speech and social relationships. If these are coming on well, then the outlook for intelligence is probably good. Locomotion seems to have a less close relationship to intelligence. This applies to the age of sitting, standing supported, standing unsupported and walking, as well as crawling or shuffling along. Toilet training is also very variable, and is as much a reflection of the attitude of the mother as of the intelligence of the baby. In things like feeding too, much will depend on how the baby is handled. The parent or nurse, for example, may be asked if the child uses a spoon and fork or only a spoon. The mother may reply that he only uses a spoon, but may forget to add that she has never tried him with a fork!

Vision
Parents may become worried about the development of their baby at all stages (fortunately sometimes unnecessarily). The infant may be too quiet, too 'good'. He may not cry as much as the other children, may be too contented, too easily satisfied, less resentful if his feed is late. On the other hand, he may be petulant, miserable, continually

whining and never happy. Some parents are struck by the fact that their baby does not appear to see and behaves as though blind. In some cases there may really be something wrong with the eye; the retina at the back of the eye may be imperfect. There may be a disease of the optic nerve, an optic atrophy or in some cases the transparent substances through which the light passes, the optic media, may be cloudy. A number of premature babies who in the past were given too much oxygen developed scarring behind the lens, and this can still occasionally happen with the very small and delicate baby. The danger is, however, well recognized, and the pressure of oxygen in tents or incubators for premature babies is kept as low as possible, and also, where possible, oxygen is never given continuously.

More often in the case of backward babies who seem not to see, it is because they are so retarded that they have not learnt properly to react to light. At an early age a young baby 'conditions' to certain stimuli. Blinking takes place automatically if the cornea, between the lids of the eye, is touched. After a while, a normal baby reacts to the threat of touch as though it were an actual touch, and blinks when an object approaches his eye rapidly. This can be demonstrated by flicking the fingers of one hand at the baby. A very backward baby may fail to 'condition' and show no response to the threat, though on examination, his eyes may prove to be structurally normal. But his brain has been unable to build the necessary link between the actual touching of the cornea and the rapid approach of an object which might result in a dangerous touch. Already in this respect the very retarded child is showing his helplessness in the face of physical danger.

Feeding
Some retarded children experience no difficulty in taking their feeds at an early stage, though later they may be slow to progress through the different stages of taking solids, chewing, finger feeding, spoon feeding, learning to use a spoon and fork together and, most difficult, acquiring the art of cutting food with a knife. Others are difficult with feeding from the beginning, particularly spastic children, who may have difficulty in sucking and especially with swallowing. Swallowing is no problem for most of us. It is automatic, or at all events is learnt with a minimum of trouble. The mechanism is a very complicated one since the air passages are situated in front of the gullet. All the food must, therefore, pass across the airway and we live in continual danger of choking. Even in a normal baby the action is seldom perfect. Therefore, it is dangerous to give a small baby liquid paraffin, since some

of it may find its way into the lung and cause pneumonia. Such dangers are very real for the handicapped child, especially for the spastic, whose swallowing mechanism is imperfect and who can only take a very small quantity of food at any one time. Swallowing is slow, so that such a child takes a long time to feed. As they develop, these children will protect themselves by resisting efforts to feed them more rapidly and keeping food in their mouth until they are ready to swallow it.

Normally we protect our lungs by coughing when something goes the 'wrong way'. This efficient reflex saves us from a lot of trouble. It can be damped by alcohol or other anaesthetics, and a person who is drunk may drown in his own vomit. Choking with vomit will seldom happen with normal babies, but is a real danger with the retarded, especially if they are fed in the wrong position. The right position is, of course, sitting up. People sometimes feed retarded children lying down because it is quicker; the child must swallow it or it will choke. This practice is inexcusable.

Social responses

A very young baby conditions to being put into the feeding position. It begins to suck and make mouth movements when it is held to the breast, but before actual contact. It is responding to the messages fed in from the limb and trunk muscles, tendons and joints which give him information as to position. At a later stage, the baby conditions to the sight of the breast or bottle. These responses then become linked with the image of the mother, the sound of her voice or other features of her presence. With puppies it is easy to condition them to smell, so that if exposed to camphor when they are fed they can be made to crawl after the scent and neglect the mother's teats. At different stages the baby will react to anyone coming into the room, and then specifically to his mother.

Responses are, of course, positive and negative. When a child has learnt to distinguish people he may react positively to his mother by smiling. Having learned caution, he may show fear of a stranger, the corners of his mouth may drop and he may begin to cry. In other cases, he may show no apparent reaction to a stranger or become unusually still or inhibited. This is the very first evidence of shyness which is so important in building up a complex of social responses. The relationship can become quite delicate, even with a very young baby. The sight of his mother in a strange dress or any similar sudden transformation may quite upset the equilibrium and cause a panic reaction.

Another aspect of developing social relationships is the use of mother as a secure base from which to explore the world. The v minous skirts of Victorian days provided a convenient refuge for a numerous small progeny, who might be as cheeky to strangers as they wished so long as they were able, if they felt their security threatened, to bury their heads in the maternal draperies. This aspect of infantile behaviour has been well demonstrated in baby monkeys by Harlow, even using dummy or 'surrogate' mothers. It is this rapid change in the pattern of responses to differing social stimuli, the fear of strangers, followed by a rapid adaptation and a willingness to be entertained and to play, which characterizes normal social development. By contrast, the very backward infant is remarkable for the poverty of its responses to others. He may seem completely oblivious of strangers, where a normal child might be totally inhibited. These responses provide a rough clinical guide. They are difficult to measure, but attempts at standardization have been made and are included in a number of assessment procedures.

Toileting

There is perhaps greater variation in toilet training than in most aspects of human behaviour. With cats and other domestic animals which behave in a similar way there is a pattern of responses which seem to be inborn and which impel the animal to get rid of excreta —faeces and urine—by burying them. In humans there does not seem to be any inborn pattern of this kind and the whole procedure of socially acceptable responses has to be learned by a series of conditioning procedures. Bowel control is usually established in adults of ordinary intelligence, unless they have some physical abnormality such as paralysis of the lower part of the body. In severe cases of spina bifida control of the bowel may not always become fully established. Control of the bladder is much more variable, especially at night. Bed wetting in adults of normal intelligence is not very uncommon. During the Second World War, large numbers of children were evacuated from London and other densely populated areas, and experience at that time led to a revision of attitudes to urine incontinence, since this was found to be so common among children of all ages. More attention is paid to toilet training in homes where conditions are better, families smaller, more parental time is available, toilet facilities better, heating arrangements more efficient in winter and social conventions stricter. This produces a differential class incidence in incontinence.

A high proportion of profoundly retarded children may always be doubly incontinent, as will some children in the severely retarded range, but it should be possible to teach mildly and moderately retarded children clean toilet habits. Noting what they can do at any given age in regard to looking after themselves for the toilet is part of the process of assessment of the child's developmental status. At the same time, what is actually achieved may reflect the level of care and training as well as the child's potential. A vigorous programme in a children's hospital ward may result in quite a number becoming clean within a short space of time.

As in many other aspects of training, learning of approved toilet habits depends on a personal relationship with the mother. Most children are encouraged to sit on a pot at an early age, but, initially, few use it appropriately, and many regard it as a toy or a means of locomotion. The conditioning process largely results from the attitude of the mother to the child's performance or non-performance. Like all other forms of training, there are two aspects of learning. First, the child is rewarded with a smile or a word of encouragement when he has performed, and feels the absence of these rewards when he has not. Secondly, he is actively discouraged when he soils or wets himself. At a later stage, this will extend to many other situations and will in some countries, involve prohibitions on passing urine in public, the necessity of hiding the private parts, the use of public toilets where these are provided (learning in these circumstances to distinguish between male and female provision), learning an appropriate adjustment of dress, and achieving cleanliness in the use of the toilet. The acquisition of accepted taboos and responses is essential to social acceptance.

Speech and gesture
Speech and tool making are characteristic of man and are the basis of human society. Few animals can do much in either of these directions. Human evolution has depended on the development of those areas of the brain concerned with the use of the hand and the organs of speech, which are adjacent and form a functional unit. Gesture is an elementary form of communication; it develops before speech and accompanies adult speech to a variable extent in different cultures. The passenger in an Italian motor-car may justifiably feel some anxiety if the driver begins a conversation, since he finds it essential to remove both hands from the wheel for this purpose. Backward children may reach the stage of gesture but may achieve little in the way of words. This seems particularly true of Down's syndrome, since children with this condition have particular difficulty with speech.

Pavlov called speech the 'second signalling system', and looked upon words as secondary signals of reality. A child has an experience, such as eating an apple or an ice-cream, or, at an earlier stage, feeding at the breast. Later the sight of these things will excite him. A link has been established between the sight of the object and the taste, the experience of swallowing, the satisfaction of appetite. The baby begins to salivate and mouth at the sight of the breast; if denied, he may begin to cry. An older child will try to get the apple or ice-cream when he sees them. The sight of them now arouses a response and is a signal of reality. Signals provided by sight or feel of an object are primary signals of reality.

Words become secondary signals of reality when they are learned and used appropriately. If you say to a hungry man: 'Would you like a nice juicy beefsteak?' his mouth may water as though the dish had actually been set before him. Children are conditioned to use words by employing them in an 'operant' manner. Thus, if a child says 'apple' to his mother, even when no apple is visible, it is possible that one may be produced. If results of this kind are regularly achieved, then the child has acquired a means of controlling his environment, of making his wishes come true.

Speech may seem to develop quite suddenly at the age of two or thereabouts. It is only at this time that some parents become really anxious about a child who has seemed to progress normally up to that time. In fact, his delayed development might have been obvious at an earlier stage had they been able to see it. Speech is built up very gradually, beginning at a very early age. Most mothers begin to talk to their babies almost as soon as they are born. The young baby understands nothing of what is said to him, but this early stage of talking to the baby is extremely important. It familiarizes the child with the mother's voice, while all the attention he receives becomes connected with the sounds produced by his mother. He is soon able to distinguish her voice from others. Although the words initially have no meaning, the tone and volume become important. Some sounds and tones become connected with pleasant things, like feeding and caressing, others come to be linked with the mother's anger, perhaps with a slap, a shake or an absence of pleasant feelings. At the same time the different tones in a mother's voice become tied to variations in mother's expression, the smile, the loving look; or, on the other hand, the red of anger, the frown. In due course, in a normal child all this wealth of experience goes to form the basis of language. Words become linked to feelings and expressions and acquire an emotional content. All these many complicated linkages may fail to develop or do so only very slowly in the backward child. A minority of retarded children, those who are labelled as profoundly retarded, may never learn any speech. The moderately and severely retarded will be slow, but should develop a useful vocabulary given sufficient help and encouragement.

Maternal love is like other kinds of love in that it needs something to feed on. Mothers of ordinary children derive pleasure from seeing the development of their son or daughter from day to day. If the baby is breast-fed he responds to the giving of the nipple by vigorous sucking. At a later stage the mother's smile brings an answering smile. He responds to a caress, to the warmth of the mother, and he will eventually begin to respond to her voice, to produce recognizable words. Thus there is built up an emotional dialogue, a meaningful two way relationship between mother and child. If the baby is very retarded, he will be slow to respond and the mother may weary of her efforts. She may, in fact, wonder if she is doing the right thing by continuing to try to get her child to speak, to toilet train him, to get him to feed himself. The secret of success in the development of young retarded children is patience. Fortunately, most mothers are amply supplied with this quality and that is why most children do better at home than in institutions. If parents continue to persist gently in their attempts to train the child as though he were much younger than he actually is he will in fact respond.

Stages of development
All modern attempts to assess the developmental level of a child and his degree of backwardness are based on the assumption that there are regular stages. These succeed each other in a logical manner, and it is possible to work out when, on average, each stage should be expected. There are many ways of doing this. One is by use of the Vineland scale which gives a 'social quotient'. This is based on a series of questions concerning toileting and other skills, to the mother and from the answers it is possible to see how the child is doing socially by comparison with the expectation for his age. If he is doing half as well as the average child he will have a social quotient of 50. This figure is not in itself very informative and does not tie in well with later I.Q. estimates. An over-all figure may be misleading because it may hide the fact that the child is average in some ways but is failing in others. This could be because of unsatisfactory training.

Many different tests and scales have been put together with a view to helping to assess the level of development in a young child, and most of them cover similar ground.

A useful *ad hoc* way of collecting, recording and assessing available information has been devised by Miss Rosemary Shakespeare and Mrs Garfield, enabling development to be assessed in several different areas (Appendices 1 and 2). Like the Vineland scale, the result will depend mainly on information supplied, usually by the parent, though some may be gained by direct observation. Results obtained in this way are not to be used as a basis for calculating an I.Q., but simply as a basic guide to progress. Failure in locomotion is likely to be associated with a degree of cerebral palsy if it occurs in isolation. This would, however, be likely to have some effect on the other areas of accomplishment, which, it may be repeated, are also dependent on the necessary instruction and opportunity.

Piaget
The eminent Swiss psychologist Jean Piaget has devoted his professional life to the study of development in children, and has shown that they go through critical phases of development in a logical sequence. One example, which may be called the child's concept of the permanence of objects, illustrates his work. If we lose something, a pen, for example, and we want to write with it, we seek it. We move papers and other things which might have covered it until we find it. A very young baby does not do this. It may be possible to interest him in something, for example, a rattle. He will watch this with interest, perhaps grasp it and shake it. If it is taken away from him and hidden he may cry for a little, but he does not seek it. He behaves as though it did not exist. It only affects his behaviour so long as it is within sight or touch. He can be said to have no concept of permanence of objects. At a later stage, he will look for something which has been hidden, especially, of course, if he actually sees it being concealed. It may be said that the child has developed a memory and can maintain interest in objects when they are no longer immediately to hand.

It seems as though these phases in development happen suddenly and spontaneously, on their own, as a result of maturation, but this is not the whole explanation. Maturation of the brain is, of course, taking place during the first two years or so after birth. At the same time, the young child is very active, continually exploring himself and his environment. The very small baby indulges in hand regard. He holds up his hand and looks at it, moving the fingers. In this way he learns how he can control his hand and what it looks like at different distances. He can see his fingers moving and feel them moving at the same time. This is the basis of all skilled co-ordinated movements. Profoundly retarded children may be seen engaged in hand regard years after this stage would normally have ended, because they are, unfortunately, still at that stage of development.

Other examples of Piaget's methods deal with an earlier stage than understanding the permanence of objects. These concern the removal of a cloth from the face and gaining a toy by means of a piece of string attached to it. If a very young baby has his face covered with a cloth he may be distressed and cry, but he will not attempt to remove it. He has not yet, as a result of play and experience, been able to link this situation with the use of his hands. At a later stage he will promptly remove the cloth with his hands or sometimes he will move so as to displace it. Again, if a toy in which he is interested is placed just out of reach, but a string attached to it is left close to hand he will, if he has reached that stage, pull the toy to him by the string. This, however, demands the ability, on a basis of experience, to link the toy and the string with the possibility of achieving his goal. This is not just given but demands active play and learning. Spontaneous play cultivates these abilities in the child, but in most instances the child is actively aided and stimulated by adults and others.

Other examples derived from Piaget concern the constancy of number and mass. At an early stage of development children will judge quantity by a general impression conditional on circumstances. Thus, if a series of coins or counters is pressed close together, and the same series is shown spread farther apart a child who cannot yet count is likely to say that there are more in the second arrangement. Again (Figure 6), if he is shown fluid in a tall vessel he may say that there is more in a flat container, even if the fluid is poured from one to the other in front of him. At a later stage he comes to understand the principle of the conservation of matter, and will know that it must be the same amount as before, even though it is in a different vessel.

Piaget's work has been used by Dr Mary Woodward as a basis for studying the behaviour of young infants and assessing the levels of development achieved by them. Consequently it is also very valuable for assessing severely and profoundly retarded children, who may be at such an early level of development that, despite their real age they cannot be assessed on ordinary tests. For example, an average two-year-old will begin to score on the much-used Binet-Simon type of test and may be assessed on this if he is co-operative. A profoundly retarded ten-year-old may still be below the two-year level of development, but may be shown, by using Dr Woodward's method, to be say, at the IVth stage of the Piaget Sensori-motor scale, normally reached between the third and the ninth month of life. This information is valuable; it gives us some idea of the present position, it can be repeated to see if the first assessment was reliable, and it can be compared with other methods of assessment. If repeated after an interval, perhaps of a year, it will show whether progress has taken place, or, occasionally, deterioration. Once again, this is not a formal test, and it relies to a large extent on the spontaneous behaviour of the child being evoked by a skilled examiner. It does not demand formal cooperation, and it can be used on disturbed and withdrawn children.

Dr Ruth Griffiths has devised a scale for the assessment of infants and young children which is used fairly frequently in Britain and which enables a general quotient to be derived which she considers useful in predicting intelligence as formally measured at a later stage. The use of this method is valuable for screening, and any serious shortcomings on this method would suggest a long-standing limitation of intellectual

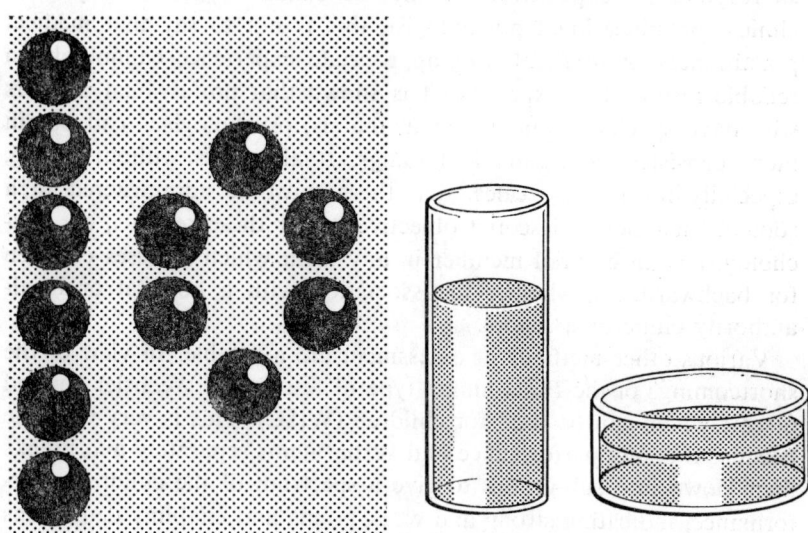

Fig. 6
Piaget's approach to phasic nature of mental development.

(a) Concept of number

(b) Conservation of matter

If child has learned number as rote series he may be able to count line of objects as on left correctly but he may count arrangement on right as 8 or more until he has concept of number as quantity

If child is shown fluid in tall glass on left and it is then poured into the low vessel on right he may still say there is more in the tall glass until he has a concept of permanence of matter

development. In this, as with all other methods, certain things must be assumed. The examiner must be thoroughly familiar with the method, and it is imperative that he or she should be familiar with young children; and, for our purposes, with very retarded children, including disturbed children who, if not out-manoeuvred may pull off his glasses, destroy his (expensive!) test material, wet the carpet or empty the contents of his ash tray over everything, seize precious records and crumple them into a ball. The experienced psychologist, familiar with these opening gambits, will have forestalled them by removing distracting objects or providing a line of retreat whereby he can retrieve his records or place them out of reach. He will turn the child's spontaneous activity to advantage in assessment, and will know how to outwit his 'testee' to mutual advantage. Even very disturbed children seem able to sense experience in the examiner, and so respond more positively. While the examiner will usually be a clinical or educational psychologist, this is not to say that medical practitioners or teachers with appropriate experience cannot obtain reliable results. But experience has shown that professional workers who have specialized in this area, that is, psychologists, can obtain more consistent and reliable findings. It also goes without saying, especially for formal scales, that these must be administered in a standard manner and scored objectively. For these reasons, the psychologist is an esential member in any team which assesses children for backwardness, whether in association with a hospital or local-authority clinic or a school.

Various other methods of assessment are available. In view of the shortcomings of the Binet-Simon type of test David Wechsler devised a scale which can be used for children (WISC). This is very valuable because it shows performance and verbal items separately and breaks them down into sub-groups to give a spectrum of the children's performance, indicating strong and weak points and enabling deductions to be drawn as to how far social background, educational opportunity or clinical state may have interfered with development. However, this scale only begins at a six-year level, and is therefore unsuitable for severely retarded or very backward children. For similar reasons, Raven adapted his 'matrices' for use by children, colouring them to add intrinsic interest. These matrices form a graduated scale of visual problems, a pattern being shown with a piece missing. The missing piece is shown below, together with several other wrong choices. The child has to indicate the correct piece which would complete the pattern. This method was originally produced by Raven as 'culture free', that is, it should be less influenced by schooling and background than the Binet.

The Binet-Simon scale was originally produced in France. It was then used in the United States in various revisions, and came back across the Atlantic as the Stanford revision of the Terman-Merrill. Thus it is standardized on an American population. Basically it still consists of a hotch-potch of items, many of which are as much tests of school knowledge or general knowledge as of commonsense. The first item in the 1937 Terman-Merrill revision is, for example, a performance item, and consists of a board from which a circle, a square and a triangle have been cut out. These are then placed under the appropriate holes, and the task is to fit them back correctly. This is a test of visual analysis, of manual dexterity, eye-hand co-ordination and a willingness to co-operate as well as an ability to persist with a task until it is finished. It is designed for the average two-year-old. On the other hand, many items, especially for the later years, are estimates of verbal facility and as such are much influenced by background and schooling. Thus, at age VIII: 'In what way are wood and coal alike?' The answer is likely to be made easier by practice in verbal definition such as the child is likely to get at school. On the other hand, this question illustrates the dependence of this type of test on particular social surroundings, since a child acquainted only with central heating may not see the point of it. This is particularly true of institutions, where coal and wood for kindling are now usually things of the past. The later items in the scale are of limited application to the mentally retarded, but it is success with this type of item which is used on this scale to distinguish backward children from the general population. It should, therefore, be pointed out that these are very much tests of school-type learning; for example, 'Which direction would you have to face so that your left hand would be towards the East?'

Despite its shortcomings there has been a much bigger accumulation of experience with the Binet type of test in relation to schoolchildren than with any other. Teachers are familiar with it and know how to use it. The latest Terman-Merrill revision reduces some of the more obvious statistical difficulties with the earlier type of scale. The results seem to predict success at school fairly accurately, but they heavily penalize children with a poor background and those who have missed a lot of schooling. So we may be arguing in a circle, since these are children who will most likely do badly at school, even if their 'native' intelligence really is better than a Terman-Merrill test would suggest. The difficulty in interpretation is greater because the

Terman-Merrill test gives a much poorer indication than the Wechsler of where the shortcoming might be. It is unfortunately common practice to give a child on one occasion an I.Q. in this way and for it to be allowed to follow him through school and later life, influencing all decisions taken on his behalf. Often we do not know the scale used, the date of the test or who carried it out. The writer has frequently seen a patient of about twenty-five who may have had the odd job or two and then stayed at home for a while, and he has been told her I.Q. was, say, 49. But a Wechsler may show a performance quotient of 80 and a verbal of 65, which would suggest, other things being favourable, that she is a very suitable candidate for open employment. On investigation it may be discovered that she was last assessed at the age of twelve, presumably on a Binet-type test.

In assessing a child we are not concerned with some kind of abstraction. The assessment is directed to advising parents and child about education, employment and social adaptation. It is important to distinguish between handicaps connected mainly with intelligence and those which are due to some other factor. At the same time, we must think of the child as a whole. A child of twelve with a Wechsler I.Q. of 55 may be willing, steady, persistent, kindly and helpful. He may eventually succeed in finding a job in open employment, despite his low intelligence. Another may have an I.Q. of 70, but be difficult, unstable, unable to concentrate for long and finding work discipline difficult to acquire. Here the problem is perhaps emotional rather than intellectual. An analysis of the situation within the family of the attitudes and relationships, may suggest ways in which the child can be helped to stabilize. It may be that he is over-protected by his mother, that he uses various devices to gain her attention, or that he plays off one parent against the other. In some such families the child still sleeps in the same bedroom as the parents, even though there is a separate room available. Persuading the mother to move him into his own room may be a definite move towards emotional maturity.

No assessment is complete without consideration of all the different problems which a handicapped child may have to encounter. These include difficulties of vision, hearing, movement (cerebral palsy), epilepsy, temperamental difficulties, social problems and many others. Such an assessment can best be carried out by a team of workers, including a psychologist, a social worker, a psychiatrist and/or paediatrician, a speech therapist and, on occasion, others.

Chapter 6
Causation

Some of the causes of mental handicap have already been reviewed in the previous chapters. Quite frankly, in a majority of cases, we do not know the cause. Some general principles are, however, obvious. Public health spells mental as well as physical health. Healthy mothers make healthy babies. The better our surroundings, social services and schools, the fewer mentally retarded children there will be. People who live in slums are more at risk of having backward children, and the worse we make our cities and the world we live in, the greater is the likelihood that damage will be done to the brains of future generations.

It may be useful here to divide the causative factors into genetic and environmental, into 'nature and nurture'. This division is quite artificial, because a disease or a disability is seldom caused solely either by genetics or by the way we live, but it helps us to understand what happens. Both elements make a contribution. To take an example from general medicine, gout is usually considered to be hereditary. If the person liable to gout because of his ancestry eats a diet made up of things like kidney and sweetbreads, he is very liable to an attack. If, however, he takes a largely vegetarian diet or eats only muscle meat, he may remain free of the disease.

This kind of thinking also applies to mental handicap. For example, there is a rare hereditary milk sugar disease known as galactosaemia which can damage the brain, and represents an inborn error of the metabolism. Garrod described a number of such inborn chemical errors when he became interested in the subject at about the turn of the century, and he foresaw that more would be discovered. The diseases he described did not seem to have much effect on the brain, but those described later do so in many cases, the best-known example being phenylketonuria. In galactosaemia the baby is unable to use milk sugar which is lactose. For ordinary babies, mother's milk is nourishing and natural. For babies with galactosaemia every feed of milk contains a dose of poison. The galactose derived from the milk sugar builds up to a very high level in the blood and interferes with the normal chemical processes. As a result, the liver, the lens of the eye and the brain are badly damaged. The infant becomes yellow, the lens is clouded with cataract, and the brain functions abnormally. If nothing is done the baby may die soon after birth. If he survives the illness the brain is likely to be permanently damaged and the child mentally retarded.

Galactosaemia is one of the conditions which conform to Mendel's laws of inheritance. It is carried by both parents, who are both unaffected. However, the fact that they are carriers can be demonstrated by giving them a loading dose of galactose. They do not get rid of this from the blood as quickly as do people who are not carriers. A curve can be plotted showing how quickly the galactose is removed from the blood, and carriers can be detected with a fair degree of confidence. Other members of the family such as uncles, aunts, or cousins, may be affected, and the disease is more likely if the parents are related by blood. Recent work has enabled the diagnosis of galactosaemia to be made on a few drops of blood. As in many other such hereditary disorders, there is a missing enzyme. An enzyme is a substance which permits a chemical action to occur, and the body contains a very large number. Some are in the gut, and carry out digestion. Some are in the blood, and carry out chemical work there. The liver is very rich in enzymes and makes many, while the delicate functions of the brain and other parts of the nervous system are entirely dependent on a proper balance of enzymes. The amount of any one enzyme in the body is extremely small, but they are very potent in proportion to their quantity. The recently developed nerve gases, which pose such a threat to mankind, owe their effect to interference with the action of the enzymes of the nervous system such as cholinesterase. It is sufficient for one droplet of such a gas to fall on a man's body to kill him. The pattern of enzymes is laid down by the genes, which make up the chromosomes of the cell nucleus. A fault in a gene determines an abnormal enzyme, which is then unable to carry out the work normally done by it. In galactosaemia, an enzyme involved in changing the sugar galactose from the milk to glucose (the sugar most used by the body) is missing or faulty. In the case of recessive conditions, such as galactosaemia, two faulty genes are necessary, one from each parent, for the disease to show itself in the baby. The risk of another child being affected is then one in four. On average, half the children of two carriers are also likely to be carriers.

In phenylketonuria, another recessively transmitted condition, a fauly gene is responsible for the failure of the enzyme which normally transforms the aminoacid phenlyalanine into tyrosine. Phenylalanine, like galactose, derives from the mother's milk, and here also normal milk is poisonous to the baby. If however, the environment of either of these babies is altered they may develop normally. Both the galactosuric and the phenylketonuric baby can be raised on a milk substitute which permits normal development. So, in a manner of speaking, it is not the disease itself which is inherent, but rather the predisposition to it. If an environment suitable for these unusual children is provided, then they can survive and develop normal mentality. In these conditions it is the genetic factors which play the main role so that it is excusable to use a kind of shorthand and to say that the diseases concerned are inherited. In other conditions, such as spina bifida or anencephaly (absence of the brain), there are, so far as we understand, genetic factors, but these may be less important than environmental causes.

Mutations

Evolution has taken place because of mutations, and it continues to do so. Mutations are changes in the pattern of genes, the hereditary material. Each species changes gradually as a result of favourable mutations and so becomes better adapted and more able to survive. These changes seem to happen in a random manner, and most of them are unfavourable, so that affected individuals die, or are less likely to survive. So far as we know, all the genetic causes or genetic contributory factors in mental retardation are the result of such unfavourable mutations. Mutations are, therefore, a mixed blessing. On the one hand, they are in the long term essential to survival of the species and allow for adaptation to meet changes in the environment. There have, for example, been drastic changes in the climate in the past, and these are likely to occur again in the future. Man is able to meet them to some extent by artificial control of the environment, but biological as well as social adaptability is likely to remain important. Social adaptation itself depends on the human brain and its ability to provide a stable society.

On the other hand, the many unfavourable mutations which occur cause thousands of individual tragedies for families all over the world, and many of these are connected with imperfect development or functioning of the brain. We have only limited information about the causes of mutations and the manner in which they take place. We have, in some respects, more information about other species, such as the fruit fly, *Drosophila*, than about man himself. The rapid breeding of such organisms and the short time interval between generations means they can be experimented with and subjected to all manner of trying conditions. In man, however, mutations which are 'dominant' are immediately expressed in the affected individual. This applies to conditions such as tuberous sclerosis and Apert's syndrome, both of which affect the brain. Another condition which appears to be passed on in a dominant manner is known as Marfan's sydrome. In this state the fingers are long and thin (arachnodactyly) and there may be a dislocation of the lens of the eye. Marfan's disease may sometimes have been confused with another disease which also produces mental retardation and eye symptoms, and which is called homocystinuria. However, a number of pedigrees of Marfan's disease show direct or dominant transmission, whilst homocystinuria is most likely recessively transmitted. Each of these three dominant conditions is very variable in its effect. Some individuals are very seriously affected, whilst others are nearly normal in their mentality. It is this variability of expression which makes it possible to establish that the condition can be passed on. Naturally, severely affected cases do not reproduce, and it is only mildly affected patients who marry or have children. Another dominant condition, which is well known because of its frequency, but which does not usually cause mental retardation, is the form of dwarfism known as achondroplasia. It has been suggested in Apert's syndrome, in Marfan's syndrome and in achondroplasia that the age of the father is important in those cases which arise as a result of a fresh mutation, more affected children being born to older fathers.

We do not know whether these dominant conditions are becoming more or less frequent, but if no change is taking place then there must be a state of balance. Many of the faulty genes are lost, because those possessing them do not have children. The balance is made up of new mutations. These affect children whose parents are normal, and in tuberous sclerosis they account for the great majority of cases. It is usually thought that the sperms are less likely to deteriorate with age than are egg cells, which are most commonly at fault in conditions due to chromosome abnormality. It does seem, however, that in the dominant conditions just mentioned some fault in the sperms may have occurred in connection with the age of the father. Fresh sperm cells are continually being formed. On the other hand, the egg cells are already formed at a girl's birth. It is this difference which is thought to be responsible for the fact that, in the majority of conditions where parental age is important, the effect seems to originate with the mother rather than the father. Professor Penrose has suggested that the frequency of tuberous sclerosis in England may be of the order of one in 30,000. Using this figure, and reckoning half the cases as due to new mutation, he estimates that the frequency of mutation in man for each gene at risk might be of the order of one in 120,000 or eight per million. However, recent work in both Britain and Poland suggests that a bigger proportion than half the cases is due to mutation, and if so, then man is perhaps more mutable than this.

Radiation

It is well known that X-rays and similar irradiation is harmful to human tissues and can cause damage to the brain. The dose used in taking a routine picture of a bone to check for damage is very small and creates little risk for the patient, but there is a slight risk for those who work in an X-ray department, which becomes serious if they do not take every precaution. It is known that harmful irradiation can be associated with mental retardation. American and Japanese workers who have studied the effects of the atom bombs at Hiroshima and Nagasaki have found that women who were pregnant at the time, who survived the explosion but who were within a certain radius, had microcephalic children.

Work published in 1927 by Murphy in the United States reported a large number of cases in which the mother had been exposed to X-rays during pregnancy and was subsequently delivered of a microcephalic child. The doses had also been very considerable, the irradiation having been used to treat some condition in the mother and not for diagnosis. Since that time the danger to babies of the use of X-rays for treatment during pregnancy has been realized, and this would not now happen. If it became essential, as in treatment for cancer, the pregnancy would be terminated. However, the writer has had a case of a microcephalic child born after treatment had been given in ignorance of the fact that the mother was pregnant. The developing brain is particularly sensitive to harmful influences such as X-rays because the cells are dividing rapidly. It is now considered desirable to avoid the use of drugs and even of diagnostic X-rays during pregnancy unless these are absolutely essential.

Certain forms of radiation such as X-rays and rays emanating from radium,) cosmic rays and, in general 'ionizing radiation' damage living tissue. Damage is more severe in tissues which are growing actively, and seems to be mainly to the nucleus of the cell. Tissues grow as a result of cell division, and this is also necessary to replace lost cells such as those shed from the skin or gut. In the adult brain very little cell division is taking place, so it is not so easily damaged by radiation as other tissues. It can, however, be seriously affected by large doses. The brain of the unborn or young infant is quite a different matter, since active growth and cell division are taking place. After exposure of tissue to a heavy dose of X-rays some cells die, but in others it can be seen that there are breaks in the chromosomes. The chromosomes are responsible for the process of cell division and copying, whereby a new cell is just like the old one which it replaces. In tissue so damaged the chromosomes are fragmented, and afterwards they may join up again the wrong way round. Normally at cell division, the twenty-three pairs of chromosomes line up opposite each other and the two members of each pair look identical except for the sex cells in the male. In some ways, the members of each pair seem to 'recognize' each other so as to take their proper place. After damage this mechanism may fail, since the members of the pair are now no longer necessarily identical. The whole process may be thrown into confusion, and cell death may occur. Sometimes there can be a cancerous change due to the formation of a new type of cell. In the unborn child the effect on the brain is due to loss of cells and interference with the critical stages of development.

In addition to their effect on the unborn baby, X-rays are mutagenic. That is, they speed up the rate of formation of new mutations. There is plenty of evidence to show this from experiments with plants and animals. New varieties can be produced artificially by exposure to X-rays, and the mechanism is similar to that just described. In men or women who have been exposed to X-rays to the testes or ovaries, the sex cells may be damaged and the genes which make up the chromosomes altered.

We do not know what causes random mutations. There is a certain amount of 'background' radiation to which we are all exposed. In some areas there is more of this because the rocks are more radioactive. In very high areas there are rather more cosmic rays, and some deep mines may contain more radioactivity. In addition there is a certain amount of artificial radioactivity. Attempts have, however, been made to cut this down to a minimum, and there are now careful safeguards in most places where it is used. It is also known that some chemicals, such as colchicine from meadow saffron, and also infectious agents can damage the chromosomes and cause mutations. The various chemical substances used against cancer will cause mutations. The drug L.S.D. causes breaks in the chromosomes and can be regarded as dangerous from this point of view. It therefore damages not only the brain of the adult who takes it but may also place future generations at risk. Chromosome breaks have also been observed after an attack of infectious hepatitis (jaundice) and if human cells are grown with the hepatitis virus they will develop similar abnormalities in the chromosomes.

Chromosome abnormalities which are visible
Usually, when we speak of mutations, we think of conditions in which just one gene or pair of genes is abnormal. However, the cause of abnormalities in chromosome size, shape, arrangement and number may sometimes be the same. It has been suggested that infectious jaundice may be one of the causes of Down's syndrome, and possibly of other chromosome abnormalities. Work in Australia by Collmann and Stoller showed that there were more cases of Down's syndrome in years when there had been outbreaks of hepatitis. At present an investigation is being undertaken on mothers of babies with Down's syndrome to see if they have had any greater exposure to X-rays. In the formation of the sex cells, the twenty-three pairs of chromosomes normally separate in the 'reduction division', one member of each pair going to either pole to form two new cells, sperms or ova each of which contain only twenty-three chromosomes. If a pair fails to separate, this is known as 'nondisjunction', and was first described by Professor Ruggles Gates in 1908 in the evening primrose. The plants he studied were hybrids, and the chromosomes were unable to pair properly because they came from different species. This kind of situation does not apply to man since all men are members of one species. We are not concerned here with the special case of the very few children with Down's syndrome who grow up and have children of their own. In them there is, of course, a different chromosome number and there is a certain resemblance to the situation in the plant hybrids mentioned above, but there are only a handful of such cases reported.

Some families seem to have a tendency to more than one case of chromosome abnormality, and such a family was reported in which there were two girls with Down's syndrome, a boy with leukaemia and a boy with Klinefelter's syndrome. This is rare, and may be due to some damage having been inflicted on the sex cells of one of the parents by a mutagen, so making a variety of abnormalities possible. Fortunately we usually regard mutations as single events and can reassure parents by saying that they are very unlikely to affect more than one child in the family.

It should be mentioned at this point that there is absolutely no biological or scientific support for the view formerly held that 'miscegenation', that is, racial mixture, has a bad effect and might be harmful both to the physique and mentality of offspring. When different human 'races' are scrutinized very closely, they are seen not to be genuinely distinct. There are very wide individual differences within them, and these are often greater than the differences between different national groups. The impression that such mixtures have a bad effect has probably arose because, in some cases in history, groups of people of mixed origin have been rejected and underprivileged and so had little opportunity for education or advancement.

In considering the causes of mental handicap, it is of interest to note a certain overlap with the study of some forms of cancer. This applies to mutations, and more particularly to chromosome abnormalities. It has long been recognized that children with Down's syndrome are more liable to leukaemia. This probably applies to other visible chromosome abnormalities, and also to other types of cancer besides leukaemia. It is now established that in one form of leukaemia there is an extra chromosome, the so-called Philadelphia chromosome. This is now thought to be chromosome number 22. This is a very similar chromosome in size and shape to that which is responsible for Down's syndrome, and there has been much difficulty in distinguishing between the two. It seems possible that further research into leukaemia and cancer in general may throw light on some causes of mental handicap, and vice versa.

Inheritance of chromosome disorders
Chromosome errors big enough to be seen under the microscope are not inherited according to Mendel's laws. The simple rules which he discovered in plants in a monastery garden over 100 years ago apply with surprising accuracy to point mutations, that is, to errors affecting single genes. They do not apply to such conditions as Down's or Turner's syndromes. In fact, most of these errors are sporadic, and are unlikely to be repeated in another baby born to the mother of the affected child. It is, therefore, usually possible to reassure the mother of such a child, and to explain to her that in the ordinary way these conditions are not hereditary. As we have seen, the error of 'non-disjunction' is the common explanation for a number of chromosome abnormalities, and this is more likely to happen with older mothers. It is possible to work out a table showing the risk according to maternal age. The average risk of any baby having Down's syndrome is about one in 600 live-births.

Dr Court Brown, who contributed much to our knowledge of the subject reported, that about 1 per cent of live-born babies have some detectable chromosome abnormality. He also suggested that about 0·5 per cent of the ordinary population carry some structural rearrangement of the chromosomes which can be detected in the dividing cell. However, he thought that it was possible that such rearrangements might be present in 5 to 10 per cent of the population, although present techniques often fail to reveal them. If spontaneous abortions are studied it is found that of babies who abort, about 20 per cent have some chromosome abnormality, rising to 30 per cent if abortions in the first three months of pregnancy only are considered. It is obvious from this that many of the babies who are seriously malformed or abnormal fail to survive at this early stage of development and are accordingly expelled from the womb. These facts are worth bearing in mind for those concerned with the ethics of therapeutic and preventive abortion.

The risk in Down's syndrome, while much less than one in 600 for younger mothers, rises to something less than one in forty at the end of the reproductive phase of life, that is, for mothers in the forty-five to fifty age group. Work carried out by Professor Berg and the present writer showed, however, that there is a slight but appreciable risk of recurrence in the same family, and that this is greater with younger mothers. We found seven second cases among 367 live-births to mothers who had already had one affected baby. This was several times greater than we would have expected if we took the age of the mothers into account. Another report by Carter and Evans at the same time showed that it was the younger mothers who, if they already had one affected child, were likely to have another. In other words, there is a low initial risk that a young mother will have a baby with this form of handicap. If she does so, however, she is more at risk of having another one.

The explanation for these findings is now clear. Older women have such babies more often because of their age, although we do not know how this works. In younger mothers we have to seek some other explanation. This can be found by study of the chromosomes in children of such young mothers, which shows in some cases that there is what is called a 'translocation'. A chromosome count shows the correct human number of forty-six per cell. However, on closer inspection there is found to be something wrong with one of these chromosomes. It is bigger than it should be, and has an extra bit of genetic material stuck to it. This is, in fact, the greater part of one of the little chromosomes which is usually called number 21, and which is responsible for Down's syndrome. Babies who have this 'translocation' are just like all other babies with Down's syndrome to look at, and so far as we can tell they do no better and no worse than the ordinary cases who have a free extra chromosome. So far as the child is concerned, this finding is of no importance. It can, however, be quite important from the point of view of advising the mother. Examination of the chromosomes of the parents in such cases may show that one of them, usually the mother, also has such a translocation. However, the affected parent will be for all other purposes a perfectly normal person. The reason for this is that when the chromosomes in the affected parent are counted there are only forty-five. One of the little chromosomes is missing, and this again is chromosome 21, which is hidden by attachment to another chromosome. In effect, then, the mother, if it is she who is affected, has a normal set of chromosomes from the point of view of her own development. But there is real risk that the translocated chromosome might be handed on to a child. Theoretically, it might seem that this risk is one in three, but in practice it works out nearer to one in ten. This could be for the reason already mentioned, that some affected egg cells may be fertilized but fail to survive.

If the father has such an unusual chromosome arrangement and is theoretically a carrier of Down's syndrome the risk of his having a child with the condition seems much less. We do not know exactly why this is, but one interesting possibility is that sperms carrying an extra translocated chromosome might be less efficient, less speedy, and so fail in the race to fertilize the egg cell. In practice, very few abnormal children are born to fathers with such a translocation.

There are some special cases in which Down's syndrome may be passed on by a 'carrier'. Sometimes two of the smaller chromosomes are stuck together in the parent, perhaps numbers 21 and 22, and this will carry the same risk as if the translocation were on to one of the larger chromosomes. If, however, the translocation is 21/21, then the expectation is that all children of that parent will be affected. This is, fortunately, a very rare situation. All these special risk families are now open to checking of each pregnancy, after the first instance has revealed the abnormality in the mother, by the technique of amniotic puncture. This should theoretically make it possible to say whether the baby is affected at a stage early enough to terminate the pregnancy without an open operation.

The special case of the 'mosaic' mother may be mentioned here. For reasons which we do not fully understand, some people are rather special in that they are really, as it were, two or more people mixed up together. Their blood can show that the blood cells are of different kinds with different groups. Now that so much more is known about chromosomes this is a very good way in some cases of showing the difference between the cells. In the case of mosaics of Down's syndrome, some cells may have the correct number of forty-six and others of forty-seven. In theory, it is possible to have a whole range of people varying from those with only 1 per cent of abnormal cells in their body to 99 per cent, and all these would be mosaics for Down's syndrome. In practice, we usually come across two kinds. Sometimes, when a child is born with Down's syndrome and his chromosomes are examined it is found that a minority of his cells have the normal number. At the other end of the scale, when cells from a mother of a child with Down's syndrome are examined it may be found that she herself is a mosaic, and that a minority of her cells are abnormal. In such cases we assume that the ovaries are mosaics, some of the egg cells being normal and others abnormal. Such 'mosaic' mothers often look just like anyone else. In some cases they may have some mini-symptoms of Down's syndrome themselves, perhaps the epicanthic fold, a little fold to the inner angle of the eye, perhaps a curved little finger, perhaps a so-called 'simian' crease, that is, a crease right across the palm instead of the usual two incomplete transverse lines. It is impossible to say precisely what the risk might be in such cases of another child being affected. It would certainly be higher than in ordinary cases. Perhaps the percentage of abnormal cells in a culture from the mother's skin might give us some idea, since this seems a slightly more reliable guide than a culture from the blood. Until more mosaic mothers have been studied, we might guess that if there are 10 per cent of abnormal cells in such a culture the odds might be 20:1 in favour of a normal child in the next pregnancy.

The question of direct inheritance of Down's syndrome has already been mentioned. About half the children with this condition die before the age of five or so. A majority of the remainder will grow up and reach sexual maturity. The girls usually menstruate in a normal manner and the boys are potentially fertile. The latter are, however, not likely to be very acceptable mates, and would in most cases lack the initiative and sophistication to make successful overtures. Women with the condition are likely to be looked after by their parents or other members of the family, or to be in the care of some residential unit, so that pregnancy will be a rare event. About half the cases reported of a woman with Down's disease mothering a child have resulted in a child with the same condition. This might be a theoretical expectation, since when the mother's cells divide to form the ova, if there are forty-seven chromosomes in the parent, then two ova, one containing twenty-three and one twenty-four chromosomes might result. Such cases are likely to become rarer. Apart from improving standards of care the climate of opinion is moving in the direction of not permitting such a high risk pregnancy to continue. This possibility does not arise with Turner's or Klinefelter's syndromes, since persons with these conditions are infertile. Females with an extra X chromosome and males with an extra Y are fertile, and theoretically it seems that half their children might have the same chromosome constitution as themselves though, also theoretically, some might have Klinefelter's syndrome. However, as mentioned, many people with these peculiarities are outwardly quite ordinary.

Causes operating during pregnancy
The first part of this chapter has given a very short account of some of the ways in which heredity can cause mental retardation. The story is, of course, very incomplete. Already vastly more than this is known and before many years have passed we shall have much more information at our disposal and many new techniques for investigation.

We now come to the stage when conception has happened. The fertilized ovum has to find a suitable nesting place in the womb and is dependent on the mother for all its nutrition. At the beginning the rate of growth is very high, but with time this gradually slows down. In the early stage, when the new baby's brain, heart and other organs are being shaped, it is very easily damaged. But things can go wrong at any time during pregnancy, and, of course, during and after delivery. This is one good reason why it is important to have proper ante-natal care during pregnancy as soon as possible, and also why delivery in hospital is safer for both mother and baby.

At one time there were all manner of superstitions about pregnancy. One widespread belief was in 'impressions', and it was thought that if the pregnant woman saw horrible things it would have an effect on the baby. The effect of emotional stress during pregnancy is not known. Some workers, such as Stott, have thought that they have been able to show a bad effect on the baby, but there is no acceptable proof of this. When the extra chromosome in Down's syndrome was demonstrated, Stott suggested that the effect of emotional stress on the mother was to interfere with the mechanism whereby the uterus rejects some embryos with this condition. The theory is ingenious, but improbable.

We do know, however, that certain infections, maternal ill health, loss of blood by the vagina during pregnancy, X-rays or radium, certain drugs and smoking are all bad for the baby. Dr Alison McDonald found that if mothers were doing heavy work during pregnancy there was a greater risk of brain abnormality in the child. This does not necessarily mean that the heavy work was in itself harmful. These women might have been poorer, less well nourished or worse off in some other way. Perhaps they smoked more.

Infections
At one time it was well recognized that syphilis could cause mental retardation, but the part played by this infection has been wildly exaggerated. Laboratory results obtained some forty-odd years ago when the writer was a student were often unreliable, and the elementary precaution of sending a second specimen for examination was not always taken. Today there are a number of new techniques, and diagnosis can be made with confidence. Syphilis, a disease caused by the micro-organism known as the spirochaete, was in the past commoner than at present, though, regrettably, there has been some increase in the number of new cases reported in recent years. This emphasizes the desirability of continuing routine examinations of the blood of expectant mothers to make sure that they do not have the infection. Since the introduction of penicillin and other improved treatments, infected adults are more likely to be treated effectively and less likely to pass the infection on to their children.

The fertilized ovum buries itself in the wall of the uterus. As it grows, it develops membranes around it through which the food supply is organized. From these eventually develop the afterbirth or placenta, in which there is a constant interchange of substances between the mother's and the baby's circulation, though these are separate. The placenta gives some protection to the baby as well as nourishing it. But it is not difficult for harmful influences to overcome this barrier. Drugs can get through, and so can infections such as syphilis. For the baby to become infected with syphilis the mother must have the disease, though she may have contracted it from the father. The spirochaetes may be demonstrated in the brain of an infected baby. Some infected babies are stillborn and others die early, but others may seem outwardly normal and only later show signs of syphilitic encephalitis, or 'general paralysis of the insane'. The writer had one such case in his care a few years ago but now has none and the condition is a medical curiosity. This fortunate situation is doubtless due to better treatment and routine testing during pregnancy, but if vigilance were to be relaxed the danger could return. Even if the brain has become affected, effective treatment is possible if begun before symptoms have appeared. But prevention is much better than cure!

Rubella
Rubella or German measles, is far commoner as a cause of mental handicap than syphilis, and during the epidemic in the United States

that began in 1964, it was estimated that some 10,000 to 20,000 babies were affected. These figures are probably a conservative estimate since it is now realized that the way in which the disease shows itself in a baby can vary greatly. Ears, eyes, heart, brain and other organs can all be affected. A seriously affected baby may end in abortion or stillbirth, but those that survive with the fully developed syndrome may be blind or deaf, or have a hole in the heart and a small head with a faulty brain. Very mild cases may be nearly normal babies, but at one or two years old they may be discovered to have faulty hearing for the higher tones.

In the great majority of cases German measles is a very mild disease when it affects children or adults, though it may occasionally cause encephalitis, and so mental handicap but this is exceptionally rare. On the other hand, for the unborn child it is a great menace. This danger was not appreciated until Gregg, during an epidemic in Australia, made the brilliant deduction which led to the exposure of the role of the disease. He noted that a considerable number of children suffering from cataract and other congenital deformities had all been born at about the same time, and that their mothers had all suffered from rubella during the early stages of pregnancy. It appears that the closer to conception the infection occurs, the greater is the risk to the child. It has usually been considered that the risk is confined to the first three months of pregnancy. This is broadly but not strictly true. Some babies are damaged later, and in others the infection seems to smoulder on.

There have been many recent developments in this field. The diagnosis of rubella is not always easy, as a number of different infections associated with a rash can look very similar to rubella. There are, however, serological tests which can now be done and which are very accurate, indicating definitely whether or not the infection in the expectant mother, or to which she has been exposed, is rubella. The same test would also indicate in cases where the expectant mother has only been exposed to the disease but had shown no symptoms whether she had had it in a mild form, and whether the unborn baby was at risk. If the answer is positive, the question of terminating the pregnacy might arise if the parents wish this. The same tests indicate how much immunity a woman has to the disease. At one time efforts were made to protect the unborn baby by giving gamma globulin to a mother who developed or was exposed to rubella. Unfortunately this cannot be shown to be of any value. A measure likely to be much more effective is the general release of the vaccine now recommended by the Department of Health and Social Security for the inoculation of teenage girls to prevent rubella during pregnancy.

A whole series of other infections may well be capable of damaging the baby during pregnancy. McDonald found that, where the mother had pulmonary tuberculosis, the outcome for the baby seemed less favourable. Fortunately this disease is now much rarer in Britain, and any bad effect was probably because the mother was in a poor state of general health; it would not be due to an actual tuberculosis infection of the baby during pregnancy.

Following an outbreak of Asian influenza in Dublin Coffey and Jessop considered in 1959 that mothers who had had the illness gave birth to more malformed children. Others' works have failed to confirm this and as yet there is no clear proof of any ill effects of influenza on the baby during pregnancy. Another disease which is little known but which definitely causes mental handicap in some babies, is toxoplasmosis. This may affect the mother during pregnancy and spread to the baby, damaging the brain. Affected children may have hydrocephalus and be blind, or have an eye defect which takes the form of scarring of the retina. There may be chalky deposits on the brain. Fortunately, such cases are very rare although the disease, on the contrary, is very common. It is possibly more frequent among agricultural workers, but it is not uncommon in towns. The infection is caused by protozoa. These are not bacteria but are single-celled organisms which can be classed as animal rather than vegetable. The disease affects many animals including birds and domestic pets as well as farm animals. Many of us have the disease but it is seldom diagnosed and probably does not do much harm to most of us.

From work carried out in London by Professor Elek and Dr Stern, at St George's Hospital it would seem that a disease caused by the cytomegalic virus is more important in this area than toxoplasmosis. The disease is so called because the virus causes affected cells to increase in size and become giant cells. The virus lurks in the cells of the salivary glands, but can affect the brain of the unborn baby and may cause microcephaly. It is perhaps not an uncommon cause of this condition. Tests on the serum of mother and baby soon after birth will reveal infection which is common and which probably causes little damage in the ordinary way. Not enough is known about it to decide whether it would be useful or possible to prepare a vaccine which might be used in the same way as rubella vaccine. Further studies are urgently needed.

Damage at the time of birth

Man depends on the use of his brain for survival, and in the course of his evolution it has grown until it is now bigger in proportion to the body than in any other species. Because of this growth in head size, the female pelvis has also had to adapt to permit the passage of an infant's enlarged brain box. Although considerable growth of the baby's brain takes place after birth the human infant is, though very helpless, much more mature in terms of weight than the young of many animals. A nine-month pregnancy is a very long time for an animal of human size. It is not surprising that adaptation sometimes fails and that damage to the infant (and to the mother) is done at the time of birth.

Physical growth is in part dependent on genetic factors, on heredity. In part it is decided by nutrition and state of health. Height of children is influenced by their social class and by the country in which they live. A Glaswegian baby who, at the turn of the century, emigrated to Australia from the Gorbals would have been likely to be taller than her cousin who remained in the slum environment. The height of the mother, and her general physical development, is also important in successful childbirth. At one time when the Germans called rickets 'Die Englische Krankheit' ('The English Disease') it seems likely that deformed rickety pelves may have caused much infant and maternal death or damage. In the condition known as osteomalacia, the bones are quite soft and the pelvis may be very deformed indeed. This state develops today in women in Asia and other areas where there is an extreme deprivation of vitamin D in the diet.

The size of the baby can also depend on class. Very small babies are commoner among poorer mothers, and some of these may be 'small for dates'. Thus, for example, one baby seen by the writer recently was very retarded. His birth weight was 3 lb 4 oz., or less than half the usual weight, but the pregnancy had run for its full nine months. Either, therefore, there was something wrong with the baby, or else the mother was for some reason unable to nourish him properly in the womb. Other babies are born prematurely by date, for example at seven months instead of nine. In either case small babies are more delicate and more at risk for brain damage. This may sound illogical, since it has just been pointed out that head size is one of the problems in the process of being born. However, babies premature by date are incompletely developed and not properly equipped to face an independent life. One of the many things that can go wrong with them is that they become jaundiced. If adults are jaundiced the brain is protected from any harmful effect from the bile in the blood because there is an enzyme in the liver which makes it harmless. This enzyme is not, however, developed in babies born at seven months of pregnancy, so, if they become jaundiced, the brain can be seriously damaged. Such babies often become athetotic. Athetosis is a form of cerebral palsy in which attempts to perform any act like picking up an object become very difficult because there are constant writhing movements which cannot be brought under any smooth control. These prevent the sufferer from keeping his hand steady for any voluntary action. Fortunately, exchange transfusion now makes it possible to prevent the effects of severe jaundice in the newborn. With much care, most small babies do very well, but unhappily a considerable number of the smallest still do badly. Perhaps it will be possible to stop so many babies being small. For some countries and some classes this has been partially achieved but, even in Britain we are still very far, as Professor Butler has pointed out, from being a classless society in this respect.

If a baby is genetically fortunate in the choice of his parents, if he has a healthy mother who can nourish him well in her womb for nine months and no longer, if he has a good obstetrician to care for him before he is born and whilst he is being born, if he has loving parents who care for him well, he must still face the hazards of infancy. A century ago, one third of all babies died in infancy, as still happens in some countries. It is perhaps difficult for young parents to realize how quickly things have changed. The biggest change has been in the standard of living and in hygiene but an important contribution has been made by developments in medical science as well as the National Health Service. The large hospital where the writer is based was, half a century ago, full of children chronically ill with physical conditions. Many of the conditions which then caused chronic illness, and which often affected mentality, are now curable. The example of meningitis has been mentioned but there is as yet no treatment for some diseases causing mental retardation in young children, such as viral encephalitis. There is still much to be done. Above all, even if we confine our attention to severe retardation, we have as yet no clue as to why so many tragic cases occur. The small areas of knowledge that we have gained are oases in a vast desert of ignorance.

Chapter 7
The services

The writer has spent many years in pressing for more adequate services for the mentally handicapped. Paradoxically, in order to get adequate services for the mentally handicapped it is necessary to abolish them. Perhaps a few examples will explain this seeming contradiction.

Shortly after the Second World War, we asked for free milk for our children in the institution where I was then working. We were told that we could not have it as our children did not attend school! They were excluded from the education service under section 57 of the Education Act, 1944. In this respect, by being regarded quite separately, they were at a disadvantage. It seems clear that, as with epileptics and other handicapped groups, separate provision may defeat its own ends. Quite often a problem which arises with a retarded child is not essentially a product of the retardation but concerns the child as a child. If the general services and social conditions were adequate then much of the problem might disappear. We often advocate entry of mildly retarded children into special classes or schools. A major advantage of such classes is that they usually contain less than twenty pupils, whereas the ordinary class may contain as many as forty. It is generally considered that a class of forty is too big by any standard, and that it would be an advantage to all children if classes were smaller and if teachers had an opportunity to get to know individual children better. Children differ, not only by measured intelligence but by temperament and attitude, by upbringing and character. Each child is worthy of a special and individual approach. Many teachers in special classes are specially qualified for this work. They have acquired experience or have taken special courses to help them to understand handicapped or disturbed children. If such experience and instruction is helpful in understanding children with special problems, it can hardly fail to be helpful simply in understanding children. It could reasonably be suggested that all teachers should be so equipped.

The time has come to press for general reduction in class sizes and also to do research on desirable numbers. In this connection research is urgently needed on techniques of teaching with reference to class structure, the use of teaching aids and the effect of these considerations on the desirable numbers in class.

Big advances have come about in providing for the mentally handicapped simply by undoing previous special measures. The removal by the 1959 Act of the necessity for formal certification and detention in a hospital or institution has swept away a great deal of red tape and has enabled attention to be focused on more positive work for the handicapped. It has also reduced the likelihood of unnecessary detention. At the same time the compulsory 'ascertainment' procedure was abolished. This procedure previously created two separate groups of children—normal and mentally handicapped. If an approach was made to the local authority for help for a retarded child to, for example, the children's officer, this was usually met by reference to the mental health section of the health department. Much of the little time that was available for such children was devoted to formalities. Indeed there was a tendency for the children to be seen for ascertainment and not primarily to find out in what way they could be helped.

A further development which is now pending is of the same order. This is the modification of the 1944 Education Act to permit the inclusion of all children within the educational system. There will no longer be educable and ineducable children, but just children. It is to be hoped that suitable arrangements will be made for those who were previously regarded as 'ineducable'. They will in future attend school rather than 'training centre' and they will be taught by teachers rather than by supervisors.

From this and what has been said earlier, it may be seen that it has been necessary to convince the public and the authorities that the needs of mentally handicapped children are primarily those of children, and do not differ very markedly from those of others. The use of probation for retarded offenders charged with petty crimes has already been mentioned. Similar considerations apply to illegitimate or neglected or deprived children who are also retarded. If they are treated in the same way as ordinary children would be in the same circumstances, the total size of the specific problem of mental handicap will be reduced.

Prevention

Services for the mentally handicapped should be viewed broadly to include the whole range from prevention to amelioration and long-term care for the aged as well as for those who are very severely handicapped or disturbed. With regard to prevention, the first need is for adequate research, on which at present very little money or time is spent. A second need is for education of the public, the professions and the authorities in this matter. There is a gradually increasing public awareness of some of the problems concerned, and this also applies to the professions.

In the years just before the First World War the ABO blood groups were something of a novelty to medical science. Today very many people will know their ABO blood group through having given or received blood, or through military service, or through being grouped prior to an operation. This is one example of the increase in knowledge of ourselves. It has little direct reference to mental retardation except to the rare case of ABO blood-group incompatibility, which very occasionally produces jaundice in the newborn with attendant brain damage. Just before the Second World War, a fundamental discovery was made about blood compatibilities, and it was realized that many of the difficulties with transfusion that had been experienced were due to what are now known as the Rhesus blood groups, so called after the monkey of that name. It is now routine in ante-natal care to investigate the blood group of an expectant mother. If she is among the minority of Rhesus negative women, this is specially noted, and during pregnancy the antibodies to the Rhesus antigen D will be measured. If these are high, action may be necessary and the baby may require exchange transfusion soon after birth. If it is the mother's first child, antibodies are unlikely to develop during the pregnancy but may occur after the delivery, and will be a threat to the second child. This can now be prevented by giving the mother antibodies after the delivery which will react with any Rhesus positive cells that may have leaked from the baby into the mother's circulation, and so will prevent her from being immunized to subsequent babies.

Many women will now know their Rhesus blood group. If women are Rhesus negative it is possible that some of their daughters may also be so. Understanding and interest in the Rhesus blood group may be transmitted from one generation to another and as the daughters grow up they will be motivated to know their Rhesus blood group. In the same way knowledge of rubella is extending. A pregnant woman who discovers that her friend or neighbour has rubella may know that she should avoid her friend's company until the infection is over. If she has been exposed to infection, she may herself consult her doctor about the danger. Knowing the danger of rubella, mothers who are so informed will support the new measures of rubella vaccination for their daughters.

Apart from such particular examples of prevention, there is a growing readiness to seek and accept care in and before pregnancy. At present, few of us know much about our genetic constitution. Families are small and in large centres of population, such as London, parents only know their immediate family. They can give no information about remote relatives. With the development of modern techniques and the National Health Service having led to improved medical records, information about genetic potential is accumulating. Screening at birth should permit a recognition of most cases of phenylketonuria in the population, including all the mild forms. Thus affected families and their relatives will become aware of the problem. Enquiries are often made about the risk of brothers or sisters of patients passing on the condition to their children. Some relatives may be sufficiently interested to find out if they are carriers, now a quite feasible process which has a considerable degree of reliability. A similar situation applies to families of actual patients with other conditions of genetic origin, such as homocystinuria or histidinaemia. Before very long, fresh technical developments will occur so that it will be possible to examine blood and urine from every new-born baby and find out whether he is suffering from a whole range of chemical disorders. It should also be possible to check on the carrier state for many diseases, that is, whether an individual carries a faulty gene, like that for phenylketonuria, without himself suffering from the disease.

Genetic counselling

Few people embarking on marriage are worried about genetic risks, but with the gradual increase in our knowledge there is likely to be more concern. The particular families mentioned above are those who are certain to be among the first interested. A member of such an affected family may himself wish for reassurance that he will not have children with a familial disease. His proposed partner, when she learns of the abnormality in the family, may wish for the same information. Increased public and professional understanding of these problems is sure to create a greater demand for expert advice.

At present the most active demand for genetic counselling comes from parents who have already had one affected child and who would like information about the risk of having another. Some parents who carry the burden of a severely retarded child do not feel that, in any circumstances, they would be prepared to undertake another pregnancy. Perhaps they feel they already have as much as they can cope with in the care of the one abnormal child. Others may be deterred because they would not take the risk of another affected child, despite any amount of reassurance that the risk is very small. On the other hand, some parents, for religious or other reasons, accept what fate brings them. There are a few who, *because* they have an abnormal child, are all the more determined to try to have a normal one. An increasingly large number of parents is, however, prepared to ask for and accept advice in regard to the risk which they carry.

A number of agencies are now able to offer genetic counselling at different levels of authority. To an increasing extent, general practitioners are informed about these problems and are able to get further advice. The first step in seeking genetic counselling should, therefore, be through the family doctor. Physicians, biochemists and other scientists are involved to varying degrees. The obstetrician is obviously very much interested in questions where there is a possible unfavourable outcome to the pregnancy. On the other hand, many obstetricians do not know from their records what has been the outcome in the case of many babies whom they have delivered. A child will perhaps have been discharged from the maternity unit apparently well, and only much later has retardation become apparent. In such cases the paediatrician or children's specialist is more likely to be involved. It is no secret that the care and counselling of the mentally retarded and their families has not hitherto enjoyed great professional popularity. The physician has often felt that, since he could do little in the way of curative effort there was nothing to be done. There is, however, increasing interest among paediatricians at present. This is doubtless due in part to an improvement in child health, so that the time of the children's specialist is less taken up by more pressing matters. A number of paediatricians have taken a special interest in mental handicap, and some of them are interested in genetic aspects and are in a special position to advise on genetic hazards. Most psychiatrists who have the care of the mentally handicapped no longer content themselves with a custodial role, but now conduct active out-patient work based either on the hospital service or jointly with the local authorities. A number of these psychiatrists have special knowledge and experience of the manifestations of disease in association with mental handicap, experience of work with affected families, and knowledge of the genetic principles involved. As psychiatrists, they should also be equipped to understand the special attitudes of parents already often harassed and aggrieved, and anxious about the future. Too often parents feel that the problem of a handicapped child is one which is not interesting to their professional advisors or is, indeed, downright distasteful to them. If genetic counselling is to be of value the counsellor must be equipped not only with a knowledge of genetic principles but also with an understanding of the mechanisms which lead to resentment or a readiness to accept advice.

In view of the increased need for general practitioners to be aware of genetic problems upon which advice might be sought or in which they might feel it proper to give advice the Ministry of Health issued a brief guide to some common hereditary problems. Mental retardation receives a brief mention, but no guidance is given for counselling that majority of families with a seriously retarded child where no explanation for the condition is available. It also states that the greater part of the mentally subnormal, especially those of mild degree, are anatomically and physiologically normal; their dullness of intelligence represents only the tail-end of the normal range of variation. This is a curious but often repeated statement. Of course, there is variation in all characters. To say that a character has a 'normal range' is a technical and mathematical expression. It does not tell us why some people are shorter or less intelligent. There is every reason for believing that the mildly retarded are not physiologically and anatomically normal, as nearly all the conditions which produce severe retardation can also produce mild forms. The Isle of Wight survey provides further evidence that the mildly retarded often have additional handicaps. It seems just as important to screen the mildly retarded for genetic errors as the severely retarded.

The booklet lists a number of genetic advisory centres, which are for the most part attached to teaching hospitals, research units or children's departments. Few of these units have taken any broad interest in the problem of mental handicap though they continually deal with particular diseases. The psychiatric unit listed has concentrated in the main on problems of the mentally ill rather than the mentally handicapped. There would appear to be room for shifting the emphasis in genetic counselling in mental handicap to a closer link with units with a specific interest in the mentally handicapped. It might be helpful if, in a future edition of such a booklet, some indication could be given on where advice should be sought for the counselling of families of the mentally handicapped. It is true, as mentioned above, that services for the mentally retarded should be widely based and not isolated. In this particular area, which has in the past suffered both from neglect and misinformation, there is probably room for some specialized units with a research bias to provide reliable information for the service generally.

Early enthusiasts for eugenics have sometimes given the impression that they were speaking from positions of superior wisdom and have, as it were, 'talked down' to those afflicted with the burden of a handicapped child. There is certainly no room at present for this type of attitude nor is there any basis for it, since members of the professional classes are, like others, often afflicted in this way. What is needed is informed discussion on the basis of such knowledge as is available. If the patient is referred to the expert in the field it seems best that he should discuss the problem with the members of the family concerned and report back to the general practitioner and school medical officer where the latter is involved, as he probably will be. Most families will then feel the need for further discussion with their local adviser to check and clarify the advice which they have been given.

Advisory Clinics
There is a great need for general advice for families with a retarded child. Parents of a seriously handicapped child need to be able to discuss their problems with a sympathetic listener. They can go to their general practitioner who may, or may not, have a particular interest in or knowledge of the problem. He may then refer the parents elsewhere but at present there are only a limited number of clinics able to offer advice on all aspects of the problem.

Parents will wish to know if indeed their child is retarded. They will want to know authoritatively how much he is retarded. They will want to know the likely outcome, his outlook for life, for education, for employment. They may wish to know the reason for the child's backwardness. They will certainly ask for advice about treatment and the prospects of improvement. These are some of the immediate questions which arise about a baby. At later ages different matters come into question. There may be the problem of finding a suitable play-group, day nursery, school; or, perhaps, short-term residential care, or, as a last resort, long-term care. For parents materially or psychologically unable to provide for a seriously handicapped child the matter of residential care emerges at an early stage. In other cases the child may be illegitimate and the mother may doubt her ability to care for him. Incidental diseases and their treatment may also make difficulties. Parents may feel that, because their child is retarded, there may be less willingness to provide treatment and facilities. In the case of Down's syndrome there may be a 'hole in the heart' which in another child could be successfully operated. Some children with Down's syndrome have successfully undergone such operations. Most of us would agree that the wisest and simplest course in all such matters is to treat the retarded child in the same way as any other child always provided in, say, the case of major surgery, the patient is able to stand up to the proposed operation. But these matters will need much discussion, and parents will be glad of advice from those who have a sympathetic understanding of their problems.

It has been pointed out above that, so far as possible, ordinary services should provide for the mentally handicapped child. To some extent this is increasingly being done. On the one hand the children's specialists in many areas have taken an increasingly active interest, especially in the problems of young children. In some cases, however, it would seem that it is easier to get advice on the nature of the physical abnormality and its possible cause rather than on other aspects, particularly disturbances of behaviour which may present a problem with older children. These latter aspects may be provided for by clinics conducted by the health departments of the local authorities, by school medical officers and educational psychologists. However, there is great variation in the extent of provision made by local authorities. Some of them, for example, do not employ educational psychologists for this type of work. Many clinics are now conducted by the staff of hospitals for the mentally handicapped, either on the premises or by arrangement with local authorities and general hospitals in the area.

The needs of parents for appropriate clinics were set out by a working party organized by the National Society for Mentally Handicapped Children in a report published in 1967. This called for a multi-disciplinary team which could tackle all the different aspects of the problem. By this they did not mean a number of doctors in different specialties working together. It is taken for granted that all the appropriate specialists will be available for consultation, including eye and ear specialists, the orthopaedic surgeon or the neurologist, if necessary, and such others as may be required. The core of the team should be made up of members of the different professions involved, usually a physician with a special interest, a psychologist and a social worker. Others involved may be a teacher and the speech therapist. Logically, such clinics should be set up jointly by the hospital service and local authority. The physician who usually takes a leading role may be a children's specialist, a local authority medical officer or a psychiatrist. All these may work together. In practice some areas have a clinic which may deal primarily with some aspect of the problem. In other areas facilities are not adequate and there is a great need for better provision. Screening and assessment are excellent things in themselves, but they are not enough. There must be provision for continuity in advice, for appraisal of family circumstances and attitudes, for help in overcoming specific behavioural difficulties. These may include temper tantrums, difficulty in feeding, disturbed behaviour, destructiveness, self-destruction, noisiness, aggression towards other children, wandering, and, at a later age, pilfering, truanting, importuning, loss of employment. Much psychiatric and social worker help may be necessary with the family as well as material assistance to enable it to hold together under the stress imposed by the handicapped child. Sometimes the stress is physical—loss of income, reduced standards of living, greater expenditure—sometimes it is social and psychological—reduced contact with friends, loss of the innocent pleasure in which most parents indulge of boasting of the accomplishments of their children and of projecting their own personality into them.

There have been considerable improvements since Tizard and Grad's London survey of the problems which families of handicapped children face. (But much more progress has been made in providing day units than the other facilities they recommended.) Writing in 1963 Tizard reminds us that in that survey 14 per cent of cases seemed to have been badly handled at the time of disclosure of the child's backwardness to the parents, and that in a further 14 per cent there were unsatisfactory features. He suggests that 29 per cent of mothers with children in long-stay hospitals for the mentally retarded felt that they could have coped if adequate domiciliary services had been available. He comments that the problem of long-term management of the mentally handicapped are today often neglected because no-one is really responsible for them. (At this point he is commenting on Mary Sheridan's advocacy of a screening procedure of 'at risk' babies to be conducted by local authorities.) A difficulty about this which has been mentioned is that this procedure would tend to collect more potential problems than could be coped with by the services available. In the matter of clinics it seems best at present to concentrate on the setting up of exemplary special clinics which may at a later date have their function taken over by general paediatric, psychiatric and school clinics. Probably, however, the appropriate expertise can best be cultivated in special clinics at present.

Pre-school facilities
Perhaps the most unsatisfactory provision at present is that for the

pre-school child. As Tizard points out, more efficient help at this stage might well avoid long-term admission to hospital. The parents of young retarded children have a great need for moral and material support. Health visitors could do more in this direction but the tradition of separate departments and service dies hard. Many efforts are now being made to improve the training of health visitors to cover this area of work. So far as mental health workers are concerned, there are not enough of them, and they are unable to cope with the burden of work. Medical officers of local authorities have made heroic efforts in some areas but in others most of the younger retarded children are not known to them until they reach school age. Teams based on hospitals cope with a limited number of children.

Parents have done much to help themselves and there are a number of play groups organized in a co-operative manner on the initiative of branches of the National Society for Mentally Handicapped Children. Some private nurseries are available for those able to afford them, but there are very few day-nursery and nursery-school places for such children. More day nursery places are urgently needed and should be given priority. They are essential as an alternative to long-term care for families whose material or psychological resources are inadequate.

School age children

At one time Professor Tizard expressed the view that provision of places in junior training centres was approximately adequate. This may appear to be the case on paper, but in the writer's experience all local authorities seem to have difficulty in finding places. Most of them have a waiting list and many are apt to reject children on the grounds of additional handicap, disturbed behaviour, profound retardation, incontinence or for other reasons. Much more provision will have to be made if the new legal situation which came into force on 1 April 1971 is to be met. Parents are now entitled, as of right, to claim education for their children. There is still a saving clause in the Act which excepts children unable to respond to an educational stimulus. It is hoped, however, that this category will be interpreted narrowly, and that the present special care units, where they exist, will be included and developed in other areas. In view of the wide local variations in adequacy of service, an example can be taken from those authorities which have coped best in the past.

It has been estimated that for a population of 100,000 ninety places in a junior training centre would be required whilst the senior training centre would need 260 places. The majority of the children could be living at home whilst a children's hostel would accommodate some ten of their number. These figures give a realistic view of the relative size of the problem for adults and children. With existing trends, the average age of the seriously handicapped population is likely to increase, and there will be an even bigger proportion of adults in the future.

Teaching or supervisor staff
Those teaching the mentally handicapped in junior training centres have up till now been known as supervisors or assistant supervisors. Some of them have the qualification awarded by the National Association for Mental Health. Others have none other than experience. A few are nurses, a few have other qualifications, in occupational therapy, for example. Occasionally regular teachers have been appointed to posts such as head teacher of schools in hospitals for the mentally retarded.

Hospital schools for the mentally handicapped have in the past tended to be run quite separately from local authority training centres. The staff of the former are paid by their hospital management committee, and the latter by the health department of the local authority. Now they will both be the responsibility of the local education authority, so allowing some degree of integration. In principle, it would be good for children in hospital to go out daily to a local authority school, with transport provided. Alternatively, as a second best, it would help to break down the isolation of the hospital if children attended the hospital school daily from their own homes. Such arrangements have already been made on a small scale in some hospitals, but are exceptional.

Pauline Morris, in her survey of institutions, found that 67·5 per cent of the staff had no formal qualification. The Scott Report (1959) showed 2,149 staff, other than domestic and escorts, employed in training centres in England and Wales. Of these, only 363 held the National Association for Mental Health diploma and forty-two were qualified teachers. No fewer than 1,466 were thought to have no relevant professional qualifications. It is therefore perhaps remarkable that training centres manage as well as they do. It would also be surprising if the full possibilities for education latent in children attending these centres were realized. It is to be expected that much more will be achieved when qualified staff are employed for this challenging task. A policy has been worked out for the take-over of existing staff and for their gradual replacement by qualified teachers. It is possible that, even at this stage, there are those who might query the wisdom of this expenditure of effort and wonder how much return there will be. As argued elsewhere, this is a matter of self-interest for the community as well as being of broader humanitarian interest. If children in the range of ability below an I.Q. of 50 are adequately educated, the burden of their care will be greatly reduced and a majority of them will be able to make an economically valuable contribution when they reach adult life. Professor Clarke has recently reviewed some of the formidable array of evidence which shows the learning capacity of severely handicapped children and their response to instruction and improved conditions.

Speech is one aspect of development which is not too difficult to assess, and Lyle, comparing similarly treated children living at home or in institutions, found that speech was better developed in the former group. The Brooklands experiment, carried out in a small unit at Reigate attached to the Fountain and Carshalton Group, showed that speech again improved demonstrably with better conditions and a better staff ratio (including an enthusiastic teacher). Many different approaches have been made to the problem and the term 'operant conditioning' is now familiar to those working in this area. It has been shown by those using this technique that regular responses can be obtained from handicapped children to carefully arranged systems of stimuli, and in this way useful learning can be achieved. It has likewise been demonstrated by Hermelin and O'Connor, among others, that mentally handicapped children, while slower to learn, retain what they have learnt relatively well. This most important cue shows that longer periods and more repetition are necessary to acquire a particular skill. If 'one step at a time' is the usual educational slogan, then, for the severely handicapped, the steps taken should be much smaller.

Interesting psychological work has also been done on generalization of learning in the severely mentally handicapped. Ordinarily such children learn in a practical and concrete manner. It is of no use employing a largely verbal approach to them. However, once they have mastered a particular exercise, they are better able to do another but similar one. In other words 'transfer of training' does take place despite the severity of their handicap, and they are able, in the class situation, to learn from experience. The need for skilled and qualified staff is emphasized by these and other findings. In his work at Hull University Professor Clarke has shown that—within limits—if handicapped children are presented with a difficult task, they learn more than if they are given something which is easy for them. He adds: 'Needless to say it would be equally profitless to place children in a situation so complex that they acquired nothing.'

Every credit must be paid to those teachers who have coped with unreasonably large classes of handicapped children, often in totally inadequate premises and, despite their lack of training, have achieved praiseworthy results. Yet it must be said that all too often instruction has fallen into one of the two extremes indicated by Professor Clarke. On the one hand, some children have continued year after year to repeat exercises which they already knew and which had ceased to offer any challenge. On the other hand, they were often given complex verbal instruction, were talked at, or given material ridiculously inappropriate to their capabilities. Incidentally, it goes without saying that in addition to the great need for trained teachers, if possible with additional specialist training, it is essential to have clinical or educational psychologists associated with the work of these schools.

Numbers attending training centres
Figures are available for the numbers attending training centres in England and Wales and also for the total number of the mentally handicapped under the care of the local authority services. For 1968 the number attending training centres was just over 42,000, whilst the total number of those in the care of the local authority services was just short of 100,000. In regard to children under sixteen, the figures are approximately 20,000 and 28,000. For all the reasons mentioned above the 'ascertainment' is inevitably far from complete. There is considerable variation from one area to another, depending primarily on the adequacy of staffing of the local authority departments concerned. Even with these limitations, which make the figures quoted a considerable underestimate of the real problem, it would appear that a large number of children and many more adults are not attending training centres and are presumably, for the most part, unoccupied. Thus there is an urgent need to expand the provision of training centres for adults, and much leeway to make up for schools for children.

It is true that there has been a rapid growth in the training centre provision since the Second World War, and that many excellent premises have been provided to take the place of unsuitable church halls and other makeshift facilities. Those attending training centres in 1961 numbered 22,000, that is, little more than half the 1968 figure. The number of children was some 12,500, which again shows a striking growth in seven years.

Another way of looking at the available figures gives a far less satisfactory impression. The number of people per 1,000 of the population attending training centres is 0·9 for England and Wales as a whole. However, if we look at individual local authorities there is a remarkable difference. One authority has 1·5 people attending and at the other end of the scale is an authority with only 0·2 attending. Apart from these extremes, there were twenty-one authorities with 0·6 and ten authorities with 1·3 or over twice as many. It seems likely that if as many as ten authorities were providing for 1·3 per 1,000 people, then it would be reasonable to set this as an intermediate target for all local authorities until the real need is established. This would involve making almost half as much provision again as is now available. Unless this is done many children and many more mentally handicapped adults will languish at home. This situation is one of the principle reasons for the demand for residential care. It may be reasonable in most cases to expect a family to provide care for a child or an adult, if he goes regularly to school or an occupation, but the provision of twenty-four-hour care is an unreasonable burden for most families.

Home teaching
Some children who have been considered unsuitable for education in school have been provided with home teaching. This arrangement is unsatisfactory by every criterion. It is seldom possible for the teacher to be in the home for more than a brief period each week. It is difficult to attract suitable staff. The arrangement is expensive and wasteful in travelling time. The chief objection is that it fails to educate the child in the broader sense of the term. A prime objective of school attendance is social development. This means learning to be a member of a group, to function in a broader setting than the home can provide, to learn to relate to other children and to adults other than the parents. Many homes may be indulgent to the child, and others may be restrictive or poor materially and in developmental opportunity. Facilities for social development can be provided in the school to complement the advantages that the majority of children have in their own home—security, affection and a known base from which to explore the world.

Special care units
The majority of mentally handicapped children are only mildly handicapped. A smaller proportion are more seriously retarded, and of these a majority have moderate or severe mental retardation or roughly, an I.Q. of between 20 and 50. This group has been regarded as 'trainable', and most junior training centres have provided for them. There are still certain minority groups for which provision is often

not made, though some local authorities are able to arrange for these children also to attend training centres. These minorities are: (a) the profoundly retarded child with an I.Q. below the 20 mark, (b) the severely physically and mentally handicapped child, for example, the immobile spastic, and (c) the severely disturbed child. Whether or not these children can be fitted into the training centre will depend on the number of places available, how much selection is available, the number of staff, the suitability of premises (for example, steps or stairs versus ground-floor accommodation with ramps) and above all the attitude of the staff and the authority.

Some authorities have specifically recognized this problem and have provided 'special care units'. Where these have been deliberately designed they provide for smaller groups and for more generous staffing. The premises are suitable, with adequate toilets and facilities for washing incontinent children. They are on the ground floor with ramps and doors wide enough for wheelchairs. It is particularly desirable that there should be available to such units facilities for physiotherapy, advice in regard to suitability of chairs and other apparatus and for attention to various physical handicaps. In general such units which will be included in the school system should have the service of a speech therapist for assessment as well as treatment. Such children will also need more attention in regard to deafness and visual defects. There need to be facilities for keeping glasses and hearing aids serviceable and making sure that they are used appropriately as well as any other aids and apparatus. Appropriate equipment is also needed. For example, some grossly physically handicapped children can become mobile given a coaster, whilst others only see the world from an appropriate angle if they spend part of the day in a suitable chair.

There are still only a small number of such special care units. A few authorities have made provision for all children without special regard for degree or type of handicap, and this arrangement has worked very well but these authorities are the exception. In a majority of areas, it is very difficult to arrange day placement for such severely handicapped children. Parents who might be quite willing to care for their doubly handicapped child if day care five days a week were provided may be compelled to ask for residential care. Others shoulder an oppressive burden which severely restricts their life and social activity as well as their earning capacity. The National Spastics Society and other voluntary bodies have made day provision available at their centres, but only for certain areas. Some parents are fortunate in that their local authority provides for weekly boarding. But families with profoundly handicapped children need help at week-ends, in the evenings and for holidays. A modicum of provision of this kind is needed in each area.

Day hospitals
While day hospitals are well accepted for the mentally ill, very few day hospital places are available for the mentally handicapped. Where such exist they can be extremely valuable in the situation described above. There seems no good reason why the local authority service alone or jointly should not provide everything which is available in hospital. In fact it does not do so as a rule. If such day hospitals were more widely available they might well combine the functions of the special care unit described with those of assessment, diagnosis, educational appraisal, parental counselling and therapy directed to behaviour disturbance, to hearing difficulties, speech and other special areas. In the writer's experience such arrangements have proved most helpful to parents and to local authority staff.

In this connection a plea may be made for more co-operation between local authorities and hospital authorities. It seems remarkably easy to arrange television and other public debates in which each side blames the other for the inadequacy of facilities. It is, of course, quite true that if there were more hostels and community facilities generally then the situation in the hospitals would be much improved. It is equally true that if the hospitals were able to absorb their waiting lists, the immediate worries of mental health workers and community doctors would be eased, though this would be in the writer's opinion, an incorrect solution. So long as there is a division of expenditure between that from the national treasury and that from local rates it is all too easy for this to become an area of petty political bickering at the expense of the service to the retarded child and his family.

It must be evident to any impartial observer that what is needed is co-operative effort by the different branches of the public service. There are excellent examples of this, and since the central government furnishes a large share of the funds for local expenditure it should have no difficulty in guiding further developments along these lines. Hospital staffs should on no account function in closed institutions, they should be conducting clinics, as many of them already do in general hospitals or children's hospitals or on local authority premises. The facilities of the institution should be available for day hospital use or for short-term stay, either to help parents or to assess or treat particular problems. There is often a difficulty in getting suitable premises for junior training schools or other such units, and regional hospital boards often have land attached to hospitals which would be suitable for this purpose. These could be any type of hospital. This need not imply hospitalization of the unit, which can be situated apart from the hospital proper and with a separate entrance. It should mean that the facilities of the hospital would, however, be readily available to the educational unit. There is no reason why hospital and local authority schools for the mentally handicapped should be kept separate. It is particularly desirable that if children are to be resident in hospital, perhaps until residential children's homes can be improved, they should go out daily to school. However, there are many possible permutations on these themes, depending on local circumstances, and co-operation between the different authorities concerned can hardly fail to improve the service to the child.

Residential provision
The greater part of this chapter has been taken up with consideration of the community services. It is suggested that if these were generally as well developed in all areas and in all aspects as they are in some then the demand for residential and hospital places would be greatly reduced. It would not so often be necessary to resort to hospital admission, and the institutional population could first be balanced and then reduced. This would enable hospitals like St Lawrence's at Caterham, which struggles gallantly along with 50 per cent overcrowding in its male wards, to decongest these and to reduce the present wholly unreasonable size of the groups of patients.

A major joint effort by local and central government in the provision of new hostels is needed on the lines modelled by Dr Albert Kushlick in the Wessex Hospital Region with the backing of the Department of Health and Social Security. This would bring the problem of mental handicap into the twentieth century, and would gradually enable the closure of the most objectionable of the old institutions and relief of overcrowding in others.

Residential régimes
Raynes and King carried out a study of hospitals and children's homes and found that the régime in the children's home tended to be 'child orientated' and that in the hospital 'institution orientated'. In most cases in our society a child living in its own home has a very flexible environment. Some attention is likely to be paid to his wishes as expressed by gesture or by word. It is therefore worthwhile for him

to make his desires known. In an institutional environment this may not seem worthwhile. There is a very big turnover of staff on any given ward, so that a particular nurse may never get to know a particular child sufficiently well to understand his likes or dislikes. There is usually a fixed diet for all children from a central kitchen, so there is little point in asking for something different. The children may regularly all be toileted at the same time, so there is little opportunity for initiative in this respect.

These and similar considerations tend to stunt mental growth in the institution. It is agreed that, for almost all children, they do best in their own home with their parents and with the opportunity to be introduced gradually to the wider community through school and other means. For those without families, or whose families cannot manage them, the happiest solution is a small children's home with an informal régime, a stable staff and every opportunity for family grouping. Meanwhile, modification of the régime in existing institutions is feasible but it would need a radical alteration in training and attitude.

Chapter 8
Care: some parental problems

Management is the core of the problem of mental handicap. This is the main question on which parents want advice and the most difficult one to answer. There is, in fact, no simple answer; everything depends on the individual situation. The same general principle, mentioned above, applies; treat the handicapped child as much like an ordinary child as possible. It is often surprising to compare similarly retarded children living at home with those in an institution. Some parents have managed to take severely handicapped children out for meals in restaurants and to mix socially in such a way that they are quite acceptable, whereas many of those who have lived apart from the general community and lack social experience would behave in an unacceptable way. One colleague likes to quote the case of an adult mentally handicapped patient living in hospital who was very proud of her new denture, and took it out to show to any stranger she met. Although this naïve behaviour is part of the childishness associated with mental handicap, it could easily be replaced by a more sophisticated approach and an understanding that strangers might not care for this kind of behaviour. Another patient, a young man, went out from hospital to work in a store, but lost his job because he was in the habit of begging cigarettes from everybody he met, including customers. This also is something which might have been altered had he been more sophisticated through living in the general community.

Different difficulties arise at different ages with backward children as they do with intelligent children, and it is perhaps useful to think about mental age rather than chronological age. Given one of the standard batteries of tests, a child of twelve may do as well as an average child of six or have an I.Q. of 50. She can then be said to have a mental age of six. In fact, many parents, especially those who have several other children, are able to make a very good estimate of the mental age of a retarded child. When they are asked how far the child progressed, and how he or she compares with the other children or what sort of age level she has reached, they often give an answer which fits quite well with the formal assessment. It is useful to put this question to parents and to discuss with them any differences between their estimate and the formal result. This helps them to think again about their child in a somewhat different way, as this kind of approach gives them more information than just thinking in terms of an I.Q. In fact, an I.Q. for a particular child does vary from year to year, and in some cases very considerably. However, for most children the expectation is that it will tend to remain about the same. Tests are, in fact, so designed. Parents often do not know this and are disappointed if the quotient has not risen. They may interpret this as meaning that the child has made no progress. In fact, if the I.Q. remains constant it does mean that the child *has* made progress but that, relative to his real age, he is doing as well as before.

If parents can think of the child mentioned above as being at about a six-year level of development then their expectations may be more realistic. They will not demand too much of her but on the other hand they will not expect too little, especially in the way of behaviour. One mistake would be to make her nervous and anxious by expecting her to read as well as a normal twelve-year-old. It would be equally mistaken to over-indulge her and allow her to get away with behaviour which would not be tolerated in her six-year-old sister. Whilst there are some parents who just cannot accept that a child is retarded and are unreasonable in their demands, these are exceptional. Much commoner are those who, because the child is handicapped, give way to every whim and allow quite unacceptable patterns of behaviour to develop. In some such cases the child uses a temper tantrum as a weapon and, especially in public, will throw himself on the ground and scream till he is blue in the face, if unable to get his own way. This is extremely embarrassing to the mother, who promptly gives the child the ice cream or whatever he demands, so ensuring the same behaviour next time. In this respect the retarded child is just like any ordinary child who has been made neurotic by over-demanding parents or spoilt by the over-indulgent.

Development
Whilst in general a retarded child should be treated like any other child of the same mental age, there are some obvious differences. A girl of twelve with a mental age of six may be bigger than her six-year-old sister, though smaller than an average twelve-year-old. She may also be near puberty and show breast enlargement. She may be a little more self-conscious than a six-year-old and a little more aware of boys and interested in dress and cosmetics.

A big difference between such a child and the ordinary six-year-old girl will be in her speed of learning. She will take about twice as long to learn anything as the ordinary six-year-old, although she may have quite a good memory. She may also have acquired some wisdom in finding her way about and in other respects, having lived twice as long as the normal six-year-old. If such a retarded child is set a new task, like helping to lay the table, she will have to repeat it many times more than her six-year-old sister before she can do it perfectly. Once she has mastered the technique, she is likely to remember it quite well.

In the generalization of instruction, the normal six-year-old is also likely to be superior. Once she has learnt to count out four knives and forks for four people, she may, without further prompting, be able to get four saucers and cups on her own initiative. Her handicapped sister, however, may have to be told to count four cups and four saucers, even though she has already counted the knives and forks correctly. It may also be necessary to adopt a more concrete approach. The normal child might be told to lay the table for four people, and this would be sufficient instruction for her. But the handicapped child might have to be given a separate instruction for each item: 'Get the cloth out of the drawer. Put the cloth on the table. Now unfold it. Now put it straight. Now a little bit more this way. Now smooth it. Open the knife and fork drawer. Take out four knives. How many have you got there? Yes, that's three. Take one more. Now count again. Good, that's four. Now, put them on the table....'

The use of words

Most backward children are more behind in speech than in other ways. The exceptions are those with cerebral palsy, whose speech may yet be quite good. Speech is essential for communication and elaborate social relations, and, as we have seen, is more retarded in children who live in institutions than in those who live at home. This is because children living at home are more exposed to speech, to the meaningful use of words. In hospital, for reasons which have been mentioned—shortage of staff, large ward groups, hospital routine —nurse may be too busy to talk to the individual child. Because of a big staff turnover on the ward she may not even get to know all the children by name. At home the mother, the father, perhaps other children in the family, neighbours and the milkman will all have time for a little conversation.

The child living at home, if he learns to use words meaningfully, is able to command with them. They have a kind of magic. In this way words are 'reinforced'. If a child says to his parent 'carry' and his father or mother carries him he is motivated to use the same word again next time he feels tired, or would like to enjoy the pleasure of contact with his mother. In the days of clockwork toys, the phrase 'Wind it up' could produce the desired result long before he had learnt to do this himself. In this situation there is a concrete incentive to continue to use words and to learn new ones. With words, as with other skills, the ideal is to present the child with just the amount he can take. At the start, efforts should be made to teach him words that come readily and which can be linked with things that are important for him—'Mama, Dada, Nana, drink, cup', and all the simple day-to-day items. This is as true for the retarded child as for the bright one. The major difficulty is that the retarded child is slow, and the parent may despair. But most retarded children *do* learn to speak, even if late. It is only, as a rule, those who are profoundly retarded who fail to do so, and they make up less than one quarter of the seriously retarded. If the mother is disheartened she may give up trying. It is most important that she should continue her efforts to get the child to speak. Attendance at the day nursery and later at the training centre may help and encourage her. She can have a period of rest and try again with renewed enthusiasm. Sometimes parents too readily anticipate the needs of a backward child and give him what he wants immediately he points to it without allowing him the opportunity to ask for it. Without frustrating him by waiting too long the desired word should be pronounced clearly by the parents, followed by a pause to allow him to try to say it before he is given the apple, ball or whatever it is he wants. If he does say the word, then getting the thing he wants will be its own reward, but it should be supported by the mother's smile, by 'good boy', by a kiss or a cuddle. All this will happen naturally with a quick child, but not every mother will do as much for the one who is backward. She should be encouraged to do so.

In fact, the mother may be depressed. If she is, it may be difficult for her to encourage her child as she should. Children are in part motivated to speak by a copying process, by the pleasure at the sounds they make, and by being rewarded by the mother's smile and change in expression. When they copy, they tend also to copy the change in facial expression. and the intonation of the voice. If the mother is depressed, her face may be expressionless and the voice flat and without intonation. Help from a sympathetic neighbour, her family physician, the social worker or the teacher in regard to the retarded child may help to dispel her depression. If it can be arranged so that she does not have the care of her child for all the twenty-four hours in a day this will permit her to relax, and to see something of her friends, relatives and neighbours. In some cases, such a mother feels much better if she can do a part-time job to give the social contact which she has been missing.

Verbal control of child
While language serves for communication, it is more specifically used for giving instructions. Mothers continually use this form of control, and the attitude expressed in the classic *Punch* cartoon, 'Go and see what baby's doing and tell him not to' has become proverbial. It is obvious that ordinary children ignore many instructions of this kind. But, by and large, they do serve to shape and control the child's behaviour. A younger child will turn to his mother when she addresses him, and will decide by the look on her face whether she is serious or whether he can persist in what he is doing without the risk of serious displeasure. Often the mother's cry of warning will halt him when he is about to step into danger, on the kerb, near the fire, the stove, the teapot, etc. A child who does not respond to verbal instructions may be said to be out of control.

A major difficulty in communicating with many backward children is that of first gaining their attention, and this was Itard's preoccupation in his classic work. In some cases efforts to control a backward child by verbal instruction may fail because the instructions are too complicated and are not rewarding. Such a child, therefore, has developed the habit of ignoring adult speech because it is meaningless to him. If we say to a child sitting in a chair on the other side of the room by a table, 'Bring the book here and look at it with me', he may not respond to show he has heard. If we now say 'Stand up!' he may do so, depending on his mental level. It may be necessary to repeat the command several times, perhaps to say it loudly and firmly, and perhaps to accompany it with a gesture. Having got the child standing we can now attend to the next instruction: 'Pick up the book!' This may be accompanied by nodding, smiling indicating the book by pointing. This can be followed, if successful by 'Come here', and so forth. At the beginning of speech development, a few words, spoken clearly, supported by gestures and generously rewarded when the response is correct are much more likely to be successful than elaborate instruction. Whereas with the ordinary child results might show in a few weeks, in the backward child persistent effort over months or years may be necessary. Sessions of this kind should be short, especially if success is limited. Do not annoy, exhaust or antagonize the child by trying to push him faster than he can go.

All instruction of backward children should be concrete and built on what they know already. Most children like nursery rhymes. They enjoy the jingle and any pantomime on the part of the parent that goes with it. 'Ride a cock hoss to Banbury Cross' appeals because it is accompanied by bouncing on the mother's knee. Such rhymes give an opportunity for copying and for playing with sounds, but they have very definite limitations. Most young children do not know what they mean at first, and they learn them by heart, parrot fashion. Much more important for speech and for every other kind of learning is concrete learning, that is, learning from something that the child can see, hear, feel or experience.

Concrete learning involves the simultaneous use of different senses. If a child is given an orange he can feel it: the roughness of the skin is different from the feel of an apple. He can try to hold it in his hand, and feel the quality of roundness. If he pushes it, it will roll. It is firm but not hard like stone, but not so soft so that he can push his finger into it. Then it has a characteristic smell. If he bites it, the skin has a bitter flavour, but if it is peeled for him he can taste the juice and the acid sweetness. He can see the shape and the colour. All these become linked together in his memory with the reward of the pleasant taste. Further experience with oranges will lead to a liking for them. If the word 'orange' is used by the mother when he is having these other sensory experiences it will also become linked with them, and eventually the question 'would you like an orange?' may produce salivation and interest. In due course the child may himself say 'Orange', and if he does, and if the word is rewarded by giving him an orange, this word is now very firmly built into his vocabulary in a useful and meaningful way. These principles apply to the education of the ordinary child, but are particularly important for the backward child. The bright child will probably 'muddle through' in some way and get the right answer.

It has already been mentioned that many children who are quite markedly retarded none the less have a good memory. Parents are often pleased because they have taught their backward child to count, but this and similar exercises are of very little value in themselves. If a child can use numbers meaningfully, this is a different matter. If he can reliably distinguish between one penny and two pennies, then this is a real achievement. But the child who can count up to twenty by rote may be quite unable to use this knowledge, and he is really being taught the wrong way round. He should first learn the numbers of things that he can see and touch, counting with them, a step at a time, many times over, before going on to abstract concepts like numbers in themselves.

Social problems
Like learning problems, social problems cannot usefully be discussed in the abstract. Advice will depend very much on the social background and personalities of the parents. Many social difficulties are only incidental to the backwardness of the child (for example, inadequate housing). In particular cases, however, the child's disability may be very important. A very few retarded children are extremely noisy at home. This never seems to be a problem once they are in hospital, and it probably results from some reaction between the child and other members of his family. Children, no matter how backward they may be, like attention. If, every time a child screams, he is picked up and nursed, he may develop a regular pattern of screaming. This may keep the family awake at night, leading to the father being tired and late for work, tempers becoming frayed, the elder daughter being sleepy at school and her work suffering. Neighbours may complain and the landlord may want the family out. The neighbours may call in the National Society for the Prevention of Cruelty to Children, believing that the child is being cruelly treated.

According to conditioning theory, which has proved very successful in shaping behaviour in backward children, desired behaviour should be reinforced and undesirable behaviour not. This is, in fact, the way we usually learn. In the particular case of screaming it is important to nurse and fondle the baby when he does *not* scream. When he does scream, always provided he has no good reason for screaming, he should be ignored for as long as the family can tolerate the sound: which does not mean that he should be left lying with a pin sticking into him! It only implies that regular and persistent screaming without good cause in a well-fed and well-cared-for baby should be treated in this way.

Destructiveness
Destructiveness can be tackled in a similar manner. A few children are unbelievably destructive. It is not suggested that all these cases can be cured by behaviour therapy and commonsense, but many of them can be much improved. For big robust children who are very retarded, small fragile toys are of little value and the parts can be dangerous when broken. A swing, on the other hand, is always a source of pleasure. Many parents can make robust toys or an ordin-

ary wheelbarrow will serve, though the use of such things implies the existence of a garden or play space. Flats at the top of tall buildings are entirely unsuitable for housing an active, destructive child. Sometimes it is possible to arrange an exchange through the housing department for a home on the ground floor, preferably one with a garden. Destructiveness in the home may be treated by what the Americans call the 'time out' technique. If there is a garden, as soon as the child smashes something, or is otherwise destructive, he should be put either into a special bare room or into the garden, weather and conditions permitting. It is important that this treatment should *immediately* follow the behaviour it is desired to remedy. It will have no effect if an interval is allowed. The child should be given time out for a limited period of time only, say, five minutes. On the other hand, he should be rewarded, if he is not destructive, with sweets, kindness, smiles, cuddles, whatever is appropriate for him. Such treatment must be adapted to the individual child. Time out will hardly work, for example, if he enjoys being in the garden.

Unless some active method of dealing with destructiveness is evolved the results are sometimes devastating. One family, occupying married quarters belonging to the army, faced a bill for several hundred pounds for damage caused by their mentally handicapped child. Some parents are able to deal with and prevent this kind of thing. Without being aware perhaps of how exactly they do it, they use a behaviour-shaping technique. A withdrawal of favours immediately follows destructive activity; reward follows the absence of destructiveness. The attention-seeking element is very important in the home, and children often get pleasure from some prohibited action because this is a way of gaining the attention of the parent. Even if the mother is annoyed and distressed, this is better than just being ignored. It may therefore be very important for the parent to avoid an outward show of feeling. In such cases, if daily attendance at a training centre fails to improve the situation a period away from the parents may make all the difference; perhaps a spell with relatives, if any are available who are willing to take on the responsibility, or a short period in hospital.

Destructiveness often results from boredom and lack of suitable positive occupation. The writer remembers one large retarded boy who had become a specialist in the destruction of furniture. He would lie under a table and arrange himself between the legs so that, by pushing with his feet and his back, he could remove them in a few seconds. He had developed this pattern of behaviour in a large hospital ward which had few staff, no imposed pattern of behaviour and no playthings. With a great deal of patient effort and individual attention it is possible to get such a child to do constructive things. In general education, there has traditionally been an avoidance of industrial work in schools. This attitude resulted from a desire to avoid any suggestion that children were being exploited. With retarded children in what used to be called the 'trainable' range of intelligence, or, earlier, the 'imbecile' range, this objection seems no longer valid, particularly for children whose behaviour may be difficult. Given individual attention by the use of conditioning techniques, very difficult older children can be involved in industrial-type routines, and seem to enjoy this kind of productive effort. Hours of such work for them should, of course, be strictly limited, and there should be plenty of opportunity for recreation including gross movement, i.e. running, jumping, swinging. All junior training centres should have an adequately equipped playground. The children's hospital on which the writer is based has the advantage of a heated swimming pool with the shallow end sloping up to nil depth—a facility very much enjoyed by the retarded children. There can be little doubt that patterned activity of the kind suggested with opportunity for periods of play is the right answer to most forms of difficult behaviour, including destructiveness.

Drugs
There is a tendency in some institutions to use considerable amounts of sedative drugs for dealing with difficult patients. At one time large quantities of paraldehyde were used in mental hospitals, and the writer's early experience is inseparably linked with its smell. Surprising though it may seem in view of its highly unpleasant taste and smell, some patients became addicted to it. At present, tranquillizers are more in vogue. Occasionally patients have been on very large doses of such drugs for long periods, which is liable to have a bad effect on their general health and to render them more prone to pneumonia and other illnesses. Another disadvantage of some sedative drugs is that the patient may seem perpetually 'drunk', and his behaviour may be more confused and difficult than when he is not on drugs.

Studies by Dr Michael Craft and others—carried out on a careful 'double-blind' basis—showed no improvement in behaviour of groups of mentally retarded patients on treatment with a variety of drugs. The term 'double-blind' implies that neither staff nor patients knew which group was having the real tranquillizer and which a dummy medicine. Usually in such experiments there is an improvement in behaviour of both groups, presumably as a result of the interest of the staff and the increased attention paid to the patients. It is the writer's view that there is only a very limited place for the use of sedatives and tranquillizers in the treatment of the mentally handicapped child. I continue to be impressed by the extent to which the behaviour of the most difficult patients varies with the individual staff who are caring for them. It has already been remarked that children admitted to hospital with a reputation for noisiness, constant screaming, sleeplessness or other difficulties are often no problem at all in these respects in the ward. Likewise, children with a bad reputation in one hospital or one ward suddenly lose this in another. Remarkable changes for better or worse can take place with a change of nursing personnel. Some respond to a male nurse with a liking for strict order; others to a motherly type. We are all familiar with the child who wets the bed at home but has a dry bed every night when staying at grandmother's (much to the chagrin of mother). Almost all these forms of difficult behaviour in most backward children are much more influenced by the type of care and management than by drugs. Sometimes quite a little change in the situation can have a big effect. Over-anxious parents may never have tried allowing a backward boy to sleep in a separate room, though to an outside observer he seems capable of doing so. Being in the same bedroom as the parents he disturbs the parents at night and causes difficulties and arguments in the family. Moving him into a separate room, where the parents have such, may make all the difference.

Life expectation
Parents with a backward child may like to make plans for the future. Some are content to cross their bridges when they come to them. Others are more anxious, or more prudent, as the case may be. Generally it is not expected in Britain at present that the brothers or sisters of seriously mentally handicapped children will have to care for them. Some parents take this into account, and whilst they are not anxious for their child to go into the larger type of institution, they try to make arrangements for him to go into one of the smaller units in the event of their own death or illness. This is at present very difficult, though increasingly it is becoming a possibility. There are, of course, various private organizations such as the Rudolf Steiner villages, which are prepared to take mentally handicapped individuals above a certain level of development. This also applies to a number of convents. In a majority of cases, the private organization expects the cost to be met. Usually this may be arranged with the

local authority, and it involves application to the Director of Social Services, for adults.

One question which parents may ask in the case of a severely handicapped child is how long he will live. This cannot be answered precisely for any particular child. Sometimes parents have been led to believe that he will live only for a very few years, whilst twenty years later he is still with them. This is partly because of the improvement in life expectation of children generally, in which the severely handicapped have shared. There are quite a few people of pensionable age in hospitals for the mentally handicapped. The life expectation of the mildly handicapped is little different from that of the general population. For the moderately and severely retarded, the life span is appreciably reduced, and that of the profoundly much more so. It has been mentioned that half of the children with Down's syndrome still fail to reach the age of five years or thereabouts, and the mortality in spina bifida is even greater. The loss of cases of profound retardation before five years is also probably greater, though reliable statistics are not available as only selected groups are recognized and studied. This is not to say, however, that the individual profoundly retarded child will not reach twenty, thirty or more years.

A few retarded children suffer from a progressive disease of the brain. Some of these have been mentioned (lipidosis, disease of the white matter of the brain, progressive encephalitis). Patients with Hurler's syndrome (gargoylism) and similar conditions tend to go downhill very slowly. In such cases some sort of guess as to life expectation can be hazarded. Some families may understand this problem because there will have been other cases in the family. In Tay Sachs disease (a form of lipidosis), life expectation is usually only a few years, but there are exceptions to most rules. It is the cases which obey the rules which find their way into the medical textbooks.

These progressive cases which are likely to die within a few years are very exceptional. With most retarded patients, the abnormality in the brain does not get worse. The commonest cause of death is inflammation of the lungs. This may be due to infection, but is more commonly caused or aggravated by inhalation of food. Spastic patients are at a disadvantage in that they cannot cough properly and thus cannot clear the airways. Often when they are in hospital a sucker has to be used to do this. Another cause of death which is not uncommon is known as 'status epilepticus'. A child who is liable to fits will sometimes have one fit after another, and some children die in such a state. In such a child the condition may be brought about by an infection such as influenza. In status epilepticus the temperature may rise to a very high level and so do further damage to brain. The condition demands immediate admission to hospital, sir in the home facilities for clearing the airway by means of suction will not be available. The epileptic state can be interruped by a variety of drugs. Until recently paraldehyde injected into the muscle was used, but other preparations such as valium are now likely to be employed. For the management of such a condition the services of an anaesthetist are very valuable.

Apart from abnormality of the brain, mentally handicapped children may have disorder of other organs; for example, abnormality of the heart which is common in Down's syndrome and in the rubella syndrome. In these cases it may be the abnormality of other organs, rather than that of the brain, which is responsible for the death of the child. For example, in spina bifida, control of the bladder is often defective. This may lead to retention of urine and back pressure on the kidneys, and such children may die of kidney failure if the faulty bladder cannot be corrected. Sometimes the control of the bladder can be improved by surgery, and efforts are also being made with an artificial 'pace-maker' to substitute electrical impulses for those which are normally supplied by the nervous system.

Incontinence

The development of clean toilet habits is a social convention and a hygienic necessity. Profoundly retarded children may never achieve this, but the great majority of the mentally retarded do so, though often much later than more intelligent children. Exceptions are those with spina bifida, who may have special difficulties due to the fault in the spinal cord rather than in the brain. Teaching clean toilet habits follows the same pattern as all other forms of social training. The bladder and the bowel empty by reflexes. When they become full, the distension of the wall stimulates nerve endings which trigger off a reflex through the spinal cord, causing a contraction of the smooth muscle in the wall and a relaxation of the sphincter muscles. This permits the organs to empty. As the baby develops, information about the state of the bowel or bladder is fed to the brain, and he becomes aware of the need to pass urine or faeces. At a later stage, he becomes able to inhibit the action of these organs for a certain time. At first this is difficult, but later it is easier and he can hold his water or motion until it is convenient to relieve himself. In due course, the activity comes largely under voluntary control. Control can be lost again as, for example, during an epileptic fit, and young children may be unable to control diarrhoea. If a child is anxious or excited for some reason, wetting or soiling may take place. Usually control is better by day when the child is fully awake. Bed-wetting may persist much longer than wetting by day.

Sometimes bed-wetting may occur in older intelligent children, or even adults. The reasons for this are not clear. In some cases it is a neurotic symptom only occurring when the child is under stress of some kind. In other cases, it seems to run in the family and it may be that in such cases that part of the nervous system which deals with bladder control has been slow to mature. It is perhaps some consolation to parents that most children do eventually become dry and clean, though some much later than others. There is some class difference in social expectations of cleanliness, the children of unskilled workers and the less well off tending to become clean later. During the Second World War, when large numbers of children were evacuated to country areas from London and other large towns, there was considerable surprise among those who received them as to the large proportion who had not yet developed clean toilet habits. Likewise, among army recruits were quite a number of young men who still wet the bed at night. Something may depend on family size and the amount of parental time available for each child. Something will also depend on facilities, whether there is an indoor toilet and bathroom, whether the house is warm at night, whether perhaps the toilet is shared between a number of families. The expectation and attitude of parents is all-important. If they are indifferent to the problems of toileting, then cleanliness will be achieved later. If they regularly and gently encourage cleanliness, this will be managed sooner. If they are over-anxious or punitive, they may well cause the child to have a neurosis about toileting. Thus one father, who was very religious, believed that his little daughter's dirtying herself was a sign of wickedness. Eventually she went to a boarding school, where she was happy. But after a few years, the father said he thought she had been punished enough, and that she might now go to day school. Fortunately such cases are rare. Possibly in that particular case the little girl's persistent dirtying was due to the attitude of the father.

Toilet training is another example of how we learn by conditioning. The basic reflex is encouraged by some things, inhibited by others. The feel of the rim of the pot must become a positive signal if the child is to react to it. So, at a later stage, must taking down the trousers or seeing the toilet. There is a natural reward in toileting in the form of relief when the bladder or bowel is emptied, but this is reinforced by the mother in normal toilet training. She looks pleased or makes sounds of approval after the child has used his pot, or withdraws approval or makes disapproving sounds when he has wet or dirtied himself. If this pattern is persisted in sufficiently long, even quite retarded children may become clean. The best time for training is after a meal, when the gastro-colic reflex normally operates. In this reflex a message passes from the full stomach to the lower bowel causing it to contract.

Some mothers of retarded children get discouraged when they fail to achieve cleanliness in their children. In a few cases the child uses soiling or wetting as a means of getting attention from the mother. When this situation develops it is most helpful if someone else can help to get the child trained. This can often be done in a day nursery or junior training centre, or, if all else fails, during a temporary admission to hospital. It is unfortunate that some training centres refuse to take incontinent children, since toilet training should be part of the teaching of the child where this is necessary.

Residential care

The tendency in the past was for many moderately and severely mentally handicapped children to be automatically recommended for admission to long-stay places in hospital, and there are still some professional advisers who advocate this. But most parents and workers in the field now realize that the majority of children fare better in their own homes if the family is able to manage. An important practical consideration is also the shortage of residential places. Perhaps partly due to increased life expectancy, the proportion of mentally handicapped who have been in hospital for five years or more has increased from 69 per cent in 1954, to 71 per cent in 1963 and 75 per cent in 1968. The age distribution was, naturally, very different 13 per cent for five- to ten-year-old children and rising to 48 per cent with the ten- to fifteen-year-old group. For fifteen to twenty the proportion was 57 per cent and 71 per cent between twenty and twenty-five. However, the numbers of patients under twenty in hospitals for the mentally handicapped fell quite noticeably both in actual figures and in proportion to the total population. For all ages, the numbers of resident male patients fell from 145 per 100,000 population in 1954 to 137 in 1968. The corresponding figures for females were 119 and 108. For ten- to fifteen-year-olds the drop per 100,000 population was from 172 to 139 for boys and from 117 to 93 for girls. These changes are almost certainly due to better community care.

It may be useful, in considering residential care, to look at profoundly retarded children as a separate group. Such children are less affected by their surroundings than others, but the writer has the impression that they live longer when cared for at home because they are always fed by the same person. But their psychological development is little affected by the extra love and care which they get. Their I.Q. is roughly below 20, but this is admittedly difficult to measure precisely with young children. Such children are not numerous and are less than one in 1,000 of seven-year-olds. Parents find them a heavy burden, and residential care should be provided as a priority if desired. With the more numerous moderately and severely retarded, the benefit of home care will be more obvious.

Short-term care in hospital
Another very important change in the function of the hospital for the mentally handicapped has been the great increase in the numbers admitted for short-term care or assessment. This is reflected in the total number of discharges from such hospitals year by year. The figure was 1,275 in 1954 and rose steadily each subsequent year until 1960, when it reached 3,165. By 1964 the number was 8,709, and in 1968 had reached 9,599.

Short-term admission on an informal basis had been provided for in a ministerial circular of 1952, but since 1959 hospitals have been free to admit or discharge as they please without legal ceremony. The numbers described as admitted for 'social reasons' (presumably for short-term care) rose from 4,901 in 1964 to 6,039 in 1968. It would appear that facilities for short-term care by hospitals are now well accepted and used. This increasing practice has altered the outlook of such hospitals in increasing their links with the general community. Short-term admission enables many families who might otherwise have given up the struggle to continue looking after a handicapped member. Parents often seek such admission for a few weeks during the summer to enable them to take a holiday alone or with the rest of the family. This aid is also valuable if the mother is having another baby, if she becomes ill and has to go into hospital, if she has become exhausted or depressed or just needs a rest. Apart from so-called social reasons, these periods of hospital admission can be used for assessment, checking physical diagnosis, trying the child at school, help in toilet training or dealing with particular problems such as control of epilepsy, hyperactivity, soiling, destructiveness or other special difficulties. It would appear that considerable use is made of this facility at all ages, but in 1968 the biggest number was in the five- to ten-year-old range, 1,572

Care: some parental problems **151**

children being discharged from hospitals for the mentally handicapped after a stay of less than three months and a further 1,024 among the ten- to fifteen-year-olds. A disturbing feature which is notable in all other aspects of the service for the mentally handicapped is the very great variation between different hospitals and regions. One hospital admitted six patients in 1968 per 10,000 catchment population, whereas twelve hospitals only admitted one each. The variation in admission rate per 100,000 population between hospital regions was between thirty-three and thirteen. These figures suggest that there is scope for much better provision in many areas.

Hostels
There has been a sharp improvement in the amount of residential accommodation provided by the local authorities. The expenditure under this head has risen from £166,000 in 1960 to over three million pounds in 1968. Over the same period the numbers accommodated rose from 598 to 5,091 (broken down about equally in 1968 as between persons described as severely subnormal and those classified as subnormal). Of the severely subnormal, 1,116 were children, whilst, of the subnormal, only 226 were children. The reason for this is that if the children were 'subnormal' and residential care was essential, they would usually be placed in a residential school for the educationally subnormal. Despite the increase in these figures, it is clear that much more expenditure is needed if overcrowding in the hospitals is to be relieved and the modern concept of care in a homelike environment realized. Parents who reluctantly face the fact that it is becoming difficult for them to care for their handicapped son or daughter will be pleased to know that he or she can be placed in a contemporary type of hostel. For the majority this is not yet possible, and they will have to make do with the local hospital which is of considerable age in some cases, and which may be overcrowded and understaffed.

Hospital provision
There are certain to be considerable differences between hospitals in the type of patient cared for. These, however, are not adequate to explain the great difference in level of service provided as judged by available figures. Some hospitals have as little as one psychiatric medical staff member per 500 patients, whilst another may have one per 100. Since as many as twelve hospitals have managed to achieve one for 200, this might seem to be a reasonable intermediate target to be reached by the hospitals which have less than this. Similarly,

there are five hospitals with thirty nurses per 100 resident patients and thirty-six which have much poorer staffing than this. If hospitals could be brought up to strength in these and other respects there would be more resources to devote to advisory services for patients living in the community. There is a very wide variation in this respect between hospital regions, the best figure for attendance of new out-patients being thirty-five per 100,000 of population compared with one for the worst, with attendances for the same population varying from 150 to six. The same kind of variation applies to provision of day-hospitals for the mentally handicapped, attendances ranging from 609 to twenty-two per 100,000 population.

If a greatly increased effort is put into consultative services, training centres and hostels it seems likely that conditions in hospitals will improve greatly in the near future. This should lead to parents being more willing to make appropriate arrangements for residential care when they themselves are no longer able to cope. Meanwhile, it would appear that the major problem in the management of the mentally handicapped is not so much the difficulty of the task as that of making adequate provision for routine needs for the majority. There is a very difficult and disturbed minority, but all the evidence suggests that they too would be much more manageable if the resources were adequate. The remarkably meagre provision of social workers in hospitals for the mentally handicapped may be singled out for special mention. The best region achieves something like one per 500 patients, and the worst something of the order of one per 3,000. In this situation it is not surprising that there is much stagnation in hospitals, and neglect of opportunity for rehabilitation and return to the general community.

Other forms of care
Local initiative has shown that there are many little explored possibilities for the care of the mentally handicapped. It is usually considered that for adoption a child must be as near perfect as may be. In fostering, experience has shown that there are many foster-parents who are willing enthusiastically to take care of a handicapped child. Many potential foster-parents do not know of this possibility, and the effort devoted to seeking such is limited. With adolescents and patients at present in hospital but working out, there has been considerable success in some areas in finding suitable lodgings and landladies who are willing to give a little extra help and supervision or advice. If possibilities of this kind were explored, the total size

of the outstanding social problem of mental handicap would be reduced.

Advice

In this chapter it has been possible to touch on only a few of the problems of management of the mentally handicapped child. Often parents would like detailed information on a wide variety of problems. Often, too, they would like reassurance that their child will not grow up to be delinquent, sexually abnormal, anti-social or violent. Many such fears are quite unreal, but these parents need sympathetic reassurance. They can get this by mutual exchange of information and by joining the local branch of the National Society for Mentally Handicapped Children (Head Office, 86 Newman Street, London W.1). They can seek advice from the National Association for Mental Health, 30 Queen Anne Street, W.1. Advice may also be had through the local authority's health department, from the office of the Medical Officer of Health, the school medical officer, the Social Service Department, the health visitors and the local authority children's clinic. It is taken for granted that parents will already have consulted their general practitioner and that they will keep him informed of any action that they are taking or contemplating. Through him they can apply for help to the hospital service and can be referred to appropriate clinics which may be held in their area.

Chapter 9
Education

We learn from books, from lectures, from advice given by others. In the traditional village school, much learning was by rote. Multiplication tables were repeated with a sing-song rhythm *ad nauseam*. It is appreciated nowadays that children learn more by seeing, by being shown how to do things, from practical instruction, visual aids, models, pictures, films, television, and watching experiments. Actual experience is worth far more than repetition of material which is often poorly understood because there is no practical basis for it in the child's experience. Mark Twain in *Tom Sawyer* gave an excellent account of the old style of teaching, which made children learn verses of the Bible off by heart. They were also often taught elaborate prayers, the language of which was much too complicated for them to understand. Often they would turn the words of the prayer into a homely language which they could understand, and the result would have greatly surprised the teacher, had he heard what the individual child was saying.

Even more fundamental and important than being shown, is learning by doing, by trying, by experiment. This is the basis of all learning, and without this it is of very little value going on to the other stages mentioned above. The old style of elementary school tended to copy the grammar school in a simplified way, and to concentrate on 'the three Rs'. The teaching was often academic, and divorced from reality. Today the importance of practical activity is better appreciated. These principles are of vital importance in the education of any child, and are particularly important for backward children. Such children remain longer at the practical stage of learning through direct experience, come late to the stage of learning by being shown, and still later to the stage when they can learn through words. They may never reach the stage of learning from the printed word, for each of these stages involves a further abstraction from reality. A cat is a living animal that can be seen and touched and stroked. It responds to stroking by purring, to rough handling by scratching. It drinks milk, and if milk is offered it will come. If it is annoyed it will wag its tail. It is a long way from this reality, which the young child can experience, to the picture of a cat. A bright child can bridge the gap fairly quickly, but for the retarded child a much longer interval may be necessary. At a stage, say three years, when the ordinary child much enjoys looking at coloured pictures of animals or cars, the handicapped child may pay them no attention. If given a book, he may discard it immediately, he may hold it upside down, or he may be interested only in its mechanical properties, turning over the pages. Incidentally, there are few picture books which are suitable for young backward children. When a child is just beginning to take an interest in pictures, these should be simple and in bright colours, showing primarily one object in the foreground. Complicated pictures with too much detail, stylized pictures, cartoon characters of animals in human clothing, all have little value in early teaching of picture recognition. However, some good children's picture books with clear illustrations on good stiff board are available, and these can be used. Better still, individual books can be made from pictures of interest to a particular child, of food or clothes for example, to encourage and enhance his vocabulary.

Hand regard
Babies in their cots show what we call hand regard. At a certain stage when left to themselves they begin to hold up their hand and look at it, moving the fingers to form a changing pattern. They often accompany this form of play with cooing and sounds of pleasure. They may move the hand against a background of trees or other objects near the pram or cot. This activity on the part of the baby is essential to all future learning. When he moves his hand and looks at it, he learns to link the sensations derived respectively from eye and hand.

It is customary to speak loosely of our five senses; vision, hearing, taste, smell and touch. In fact, it is possible to break these down into many more. There are nerve endings in muscle, bone, joints and tendons, and the 'feedback' from these is essential to all muscular activity. As the baby moves his hand, he gets messages from all the nerve endings which inform his brain of what is happening in the hand. As he moves his fingers nearer to and further away from his eye, he not only sees the movement, but also registers the feeling in the fingers, the head, the arm. In this way is born an eye–hand coordination which is the basis of all future psychological development. These movements are also a first measure of space and time. The units of length still employed in this country are based on the parts of the body, the inch, foot, yard. As the baby's tiny hand moves, it provides a visual basis for comparison with the background of objects which surround him outside his own body. At a later stage, he learns to roll, crawl, sit, stand, walk, and increasingly he has the opportunity to explore his environment in depth with his own body and hands.

The profoundly retarded child of any age may, if he has nothing better to do, still be seen engaging in hand regard. Even when fully grown, he may hold up his hand in front of his eyes and occupy himself with what are, at that age, known as 'digital mannerisms'. The same movements which the little baby makes in his cot have, in the case of the severely mentally handicapped child, become stereotyped, and may be complicated by play with a bootlace or some other object dangled in front of the eyes for hours at a time.

Sensory training
Much special training and education has been influenced by the Montessori methods of sensory training. These recognized the importance of sensory input, and the fact that children, especially the poor learners, learn primarily from the evidence of their senses. This was, in fact, a big advance over the traditional verbal approach in education, and permitted enrichment of sensory experience through stimulation of the appropriate nerve endings. Normal children with an adequate material and social environment get most of the experience they need through play. Learning through play has a fundamental role in laying a basis for all future aspects of education. The normal child proceeds from the stage of play with his hands to play with other parts of his body, and then from things which are near (clothing, rattles, etc.) to play with more elaborate toys, play with other children, and then to constructive and imaginative play. But with the retarded child, each stage may be much delayed, and as in all his training, he can learn only by activity appropriate to the stage which he has reached. A child who has begun to show exploratory play like the small baby, should be encouraged to extend this and to experience the properties of different objects. If his efforts are encouraged, he may eventually proceed to social and imaginative play, but at this stage he does not respond to them.

Verbal and practical learning
Many, if not most, scholars are much occupied with words. The historian, the philosopher and their colleagues read, lecture, write,

Education 157

and enter into verbal discussion and argument. Most of their learning is of a verbal nature. Contemporary educationists recognize that this is dry stuff for children, and try to teach history by pictures, visits to places of historical interest, the use of museums, re-enactment of historical events and other visual and practical means. For the retarded child, words are an abstraction and history is nothing for him when he has little grasp of the distinction between today and yesterday. On the other hand, he may be ready for a great deal of practical learning, provided it is set at his level and pace. For him, learning may be learning to walk on a narrower base than his original waddling baby gait. For him, being led by the hand along a plank and avoiding falling off may be a major achievement. This may pave the way to the tasks which are eventually going to be within his competence. Professor Clarke and his wife have shown that quite markedly retarded people are capable of relatively refined practical tasks, such as soldering television components, if they are given suitable training. They would be hard put to it to explain in words exactly what they were doing, or how they were doing it. To some extent they explain by gestures, but in practice they are able to do the given task reliably and have built up a pattern of activity which they can check by feel and vision.

Sensory dominance
Vision and hearing tell us about events happening at a distance. Touch and taste inform us about our immediate surroundings. All these, and all their sub-divisions, are necessary for normal existence. Touch is a word we employ loosely to cover a variety of senses which include fine touch, discrimination between hardness or softness, pain, fine assessment of temperature and the feeling of very hot or very cold stimuli. It has been suggested that people of very low intelligence do not have some of these sensations—that of pain, for example. This is not, generally speaking true. They react somewhat differently, and more slowly, but they do not like a pin-prick any more than ordinary people. There is the very rare exception in which the sense of pain is missing, and such individuals rapidly become increasingly disabled because withdrawal, the normal protective reflex to pain, is absent, and they are hence unable to protect themselves from dangerous contacts. They develop arthritis and sores, break bones, cut themselves, and die at an early age. There are, of course, the better known and far commoner cases of association of blindness and deafness with mental retardation.

Babies like to explore everything by touch, taste and smell. In some very retarded children the habit of smelling everything and putting objects to the mouth to investigate them persists for much longer, and they may never lose it. Most adults rely very considerably on vision and hearing. It seems, however, that retarded people may make a somewhat different use of the senses. Hermelin and O'Connor carried out some experiments in which retarded workers were compared with people of normal intelligence. Working in the ordinary way—using vision to check hand movements—the normal group did far better than the retarded group. But when both groups worked with their hands through a screen so that they could not see but only feel what they were doing, the difference was less. In other words, retarded people are not as a group so handicapped when they work by touch as when they work by vision. (The word 'touch' is used loosely here. Most of the information about the work in this experiment comes from 'kinaesthetic' sensation, that is, from nerve endings in joints, tendons, muscles, etc.)

These results reinforce the suggestion which has already been made—namely, that to obtain results with the retarded it is necessary to employ all the senses, particularly those which might be regarded as more primitive. The backward child, if he is to be able to look after himself, to play and later to do industrial types of work, must learn through testing the properties of objects by touch, by kinaesthetic sense at the same time as he sees them or hears words applied to them. A severely retarded child may never learn the concepts of 'Left' and 'Right'. If he is told to turn to the left or to the right, he will not know what to do. However, if he is shown in doing a particular task that he must fold the left side under the right, he may learn to do this reliably. He learns this by seeing and feeling, and may be able to correct others if they are doing the task wrongly. This learning is, however, fairly specific, and lacks the potential for generalization which mastery of the concepts of 'left' and 'right' gives.

Incidentally, the work by Hermelin and O'Connor shows that in this respect patients with Down's syndrome are in a somewhat different category. Whilst other handicapped people fared relatively well in tests of kinaesthetic ability, they did not. As we know, they are 'floppy', that is, they have hypotonia, or low muscle tone, and it is relatively easy for them to put one foot behind their head. Perhaps this low muscle tone is connected with the fact that they are not very good at working by 'feel'. This is not to say that they are not able to do good work: many of them in fact do so. Unfortunately, they also often have eye defects. Squint is very common among them, so are refraction defects such as short-sightedness. They often have a degree of cataract, and a few have nystagmus (wobbling eye).

Here it should be said that efforts at education may be wasted in the presence of sensory defects, especially of hearing and vision, unless every effort is made to correct them. Similarly, a child with a cleft palate will be unable to shape sounds properly, and so is deprived of the experience of hearing his own speech sounds in a normal manner. To make the best of a child's potential for education, he must, for instance, be supplied with the right glasses if these are needed, and gently coaxed to wear them. They must be kept carefully and repaired if damaged. Whilst play with other children must by all means be encouraged, effort should be made to see that glasses or hearing aids are not damaged during this, and they may be temporarily removed if necessary. Unfortunately, in hospitals with large wards it is difficult to ensure the safety of such appliances, and they tend to be removed permanently and stored uselessly. In the writer's experience, the arrangement whereby the hospital speech therapist has special responsibility for the care and maintenance of hearing aids has worked very well. Unfortunately not every hospital has a speech therapist, but making this work the responsibility of one individual should be helpful.

Cataract is not uncommon in association with mental handicap, and in certain conditions—rubella damage, Down's syndrome, galactosaemia—it may be part of the condition. Treatment may improve educational potential. Cataract is operable, although operations are by no means uniformly successful. There are two possible operations, one is removal of the cataract and the other is needling, which allows the watery fluid from the front part of the eye to get into the lens and dissolve it. The second is more often performed on children. Another operation which may be necessary is partial iridectomy, that is, removal of part of the iris, the coloured membrane which shields the eye. Cutting of a window in this may allow light into the eye, bypassing an opaque area. After a cataract operation there is, in effect, no lens. Therefore the child needs very strong magnifying lenses to compensate. Without them, everything is blurred, he can just distinguish light and dark and vague outlines. However, even a little vision is of great value to the child. Many children whose cataract operation has been only partially successful are able to see a certain amount by turning their head in the right direction. Only minimum vision is required to orientate by the window, to avoid bumping into the furniture, to see that somebody is standing in front of us. It is surprising how much use can be made of this limited information.

Hearing loss
Whilst it is desirable to cultivate the other senses in retarded children, hearing remains of fundamental importance in education. A number of conditions which cause mental handicap, however, also carry with them the implication of deafness including children damaged by jaundice soon after birth, and babies whose mother suffered from rubella in the early part of pregnancy. At least one of the diseases belonging to the group of Hurler's syndrome (gargoylism) predisposes to deafness, and the few thalidomide-damaged children who were retarded were also likely to be deaf. Deafness in itself may be a major cause of educational retardation unless the communication barrier can be overcome. The old term 'deaf and dumb' implies this, since it indicates that deaf children were also thought to be dumb. As we know, this is not so, and if appropriate methods are used they can be taught to talk. With intelligent but profoundly deaf children, this tends to be done by relying on lip-reading and persistent effort. Signing as a mode of communication is today out of favour, since children may find this too easy and neglect to make the more difficult step of learning to lip-read and vocalize. It may, however, be unrealistic to expect as much from backward deaf children and, whilst every effort should be made to encourage speech, communication by signing is for them a big advance. Deaf children become very disturbed if there is no adequate communication with others. They do not develop social contact and the constant exchange and modification of behaviour that comes from this is lacking. If they can be taught at least signing there may be a dramatic improvement in behaviour. This is best done by the teacher of the deaf, or a speech therapist able to devote the time necessary. Failing this, and in any event as a supplementary measure, it is desirable that parents, other teachers, or nurses for those in hospital, should learn an appropriate sign language if they have the care of retarded deaf children.

Hearing aids come in a variety of shapes and sizes. Commonly the deaf child is not completely deaf, nor is he uniformly deaf on all pitches. The cochlea—the spiral of the inner ear—is more easily damaged in that part which serves the high tones, so these are more often lost in the diseases mentioned above as well as generally in cases of deafness. The writer remembers a boy who had suffered from jaundice of the newborn owing to rhesus incompatibility. When the word 'house' was said to him, he looked at his trousers in an embarrassed manner, evidently thinking they were perhaps undone. On looking at the words 'house' and 'trousers' it will be seen that the sounded vowel is the same and that, as written, 'ouse' occurs in both. Vowels are pronounced at a lower pitch than consonants, which is how we distinguish words with a common vowel sound from one another. The person with high-pitch deafness may fail to do this, unless the sound is much amplified. It will be apparent that, if the deafness is selective, there is no need to amplify all the range of sounds, as ordinary hearing aids do. Those which give selective amplification are more complicated and costly.

It may be difficult to decide on the correct aid for a particular child and even more difficult to get him to use it regularly. Many retarded deaf children are too disturbed or too retarded to cooperate in charting an ordinary audiogram giving the extent of hearing loss for each level of pitch. The usual practice with cooperative children is gradually to reduce the volume of sound fed in through earphones, and to rely on the child saying when he can no longer hear. This is done, for example, at frequency 256 (middle C on the piano), 512, 1024, etc. Various attempts have been made to make this procedure more interesting for the child—for example, the 'peep-show' technique, in which a display appears if he presses a button when a tone is sounding, but not otherwise. This is a conditioning technique, with the picture as the reward. Often with disturbed children it is necessary to rely on producing sounds of known volume and pitch at an appropriate distance, screened from the child's vision and having an observer in front of him to watch his reaction. He is scored as hearing if he turns or stills. Stilling is indicative of attention to a new stimulus, and is part of what Pavlov called the 'What is it?' reflex. Other approaches include getting the child to do something like dropping a disc over a ring when he hears the sound. Where more elaborate methods fail, rough tests include rustling paper near to the child's ear but out of visual range. It is worth asking the parents if he responds to the rustle of sweet paper. The rustle of paper has a high pitch, and if the child can hear this, he probably has adequate hearing for speech.

While, for the deaf child, a hearing aid may be essential for education, he also needs to be educated in the use of it. A few deaf children are so delighted at being able to hear that there is no trouble, but supervision remains necessary to ensure that other children do not remove the aid. Initially, for most children, introductory sessions will be necessary, with the child using the aid and the speech therapist acquainting him with sounds he hears through it. Small groups of deaf children may be formed, and these can share the teacher of the deaf or speech therapist. The classroom can be wired for sound, so that the children are free to move about but are still receiving sound at a controlled volume. There are insufficient school places for children with multiple handicaps. The proper procedure would be to find out how many children need special education and then to arrange facilities accordingly. At present, admission for children has to be sought at particular schools where there might be a vacancy. The child is then selected only if he is thought to fit that particular school. He may be rejected by a school for the deaf if he is considered too retarded or disturbed, or if he has some other defect, such as athetosis (in glossary).

While limited facilities exist for those few children who have the double handicap of blindness and deafness, the unit organized by the Royal National Institute for the Blind at Condover Hall has done very valuable work in this area.

Preliminary psychological assessment of children with special handicaps such as blindness, deafness or cerebral palsy for education can be done by the psychologist. Where there seems to be any possibility of response to an educational régime, the child should have the benefit of the doubt. The trial should last for at least a year to produce conclusive results, and the final test of ability will be his response to appropriate education. It is wrong, in principle, for a child who might be deaf to be rejected out of hand on the basis of a single assessment. Quite often, authorities have been shown to be wrong in their judgment of the role of deafness in retardation, and such cases are extremely difficult. Objective techniques now being assessed include the evocation of potentials to sound shown in an electroencephalogram, but even this may not be conclusive evidence of an ability to perceive speech sounds. This test is done by attaching electrodes to different parts of the head, from which leads are then fed into a delicate amplifier, so producing an ordinary electroencephalogram. The pattern of the brain waves is changed when sounds are made within earshot of the normally hearing subject, but these are difficult to detect. Therefore the current technique is to utilize a computer analysis of the brain waves before and after emission of sound.

Conditioned reflexes
At the present, various techniques of behaviour therapy, behaviour shaping and operant conditioning are in vogue, and have shown good

results in improving the behaviour of particularly difficult retarded children. They rely on the general principles of conditioning as developed by the Russian physiologist Pavlov, whose work now tends to be referred to as 'classical conditioning'.

On the basis of his animal work, Pavlov evolved a general theory of learning. He did much to take psychology out of the realm of metaphysics and to join it with biology, and it has taken the greater part of a century for his ideas to be properly appreciated. He applied the general rules of excitation and inhibition, which Sherrington had demonstrated as applying to the lower parts of the nervous system, to the activity of the higher nervous system. Like Watson, he showed that the only sound basis for work in psychology is the study of behaviour, and his prime contribution was the notion of the formation of 'temporary links' in the brain. At first sight, this seems very similar to the explanation of learning as an 'association of ideas'. In fact, Pavlov's contribution was of a much more fundamental nature, since he was able to account for learning at a basic level before ideas had been formulated, and then to show the physiological basis of idea formation.

In brief, Pavlov showed how learning proceeds in a step-by-step manner on the basis of satisfaction of instinctual drive. He studied inborn or instinctual responses as 'unconditioned reflexes'. If sugar is put into the baby's mouth, he salivates. When he feels the nipple in his mouth, he makes sucking movements. These responses are inborn and unconditioned. At a later stage, and after a certain number of repetitions, the same response can be produced by something which did not elicit it before. If sugar is often given to the infant, he will begin to salivate at the *sight* of it. Since he regularly sees the breast just before being fed, he begins to make sucking movements at the sight of the breast before it comes into contact with his lips. In these situations the sight of the sugar or the breast have the same effect as the unconditioned stimulus. They are active signals which produce the same effect. They have become conditioned stimuli. A link has been formed in the nervous system between the sight of these objects, as reflected in the visual areas of the brain, and the stimuli to the mouth, as reflected in the gustatory area of the brain. But the links are temporary and conditional, and the response can be elicited by quite a different stimulus given appropriate conditioning. This demands that the object to be conditioned must be presented as a stimulus a short interval before the 'reward', or the unconditioned stimulus. There is no automatic or inborn response to a feeding bottle, but after appropriate conditioning, the baby responds to the sight of it as he would to the breast.

Pavlov did most of his practical work using salivation and oral stimuli. Skinner, who developed 'operant conditioning', used mainly motor responses, or actions. In his experiments, an action produced a reward, so motivating the individual to carry out the action. In due course, the activity was carried out automatically in the appropriate conditions; a conditioned response had been elicited and a temporary link formed. A simple illustration of this principle can be found in a device used for assessing the perceptual and learning capacity of children. A sweet is hidden under one of three cups. On lifting the cup, the child will have the sweet and be 'rewarded', that is, in Pavlovian terms, the activity has been reinforced. He has now learnt to lift the cup in the course of developing this simple conditioned response. If the sweet is always placed under the left-hand cup he will, unless too retarded, in due course, immediately lift this cup without trying the others. Thus, a slightly more elaborate set of conditions has been established and further learning has occurred.

Once a given stimulus has become conditioned, it may itself serve as a reward. There is then no need to use the unconditioned stimulus immediately as a reward. This principle was well illustrated in the case of mentally retarded people employed in an industrial unit. They were given halfpennies (these were then current) as a reward for their work. Having finished one unit of work, a halfpenny was immediately paid, and this produced a rapid improvement in output. The reason for using halfpennies was that, in accordance with conditioning principles, the reward must follow soon after the stimulus to be conditioned. In this case, the feedback from the work of production constituted the stimulus to be conditioned, and the halfpenny was the reward or reinforcement. Clearly a halfpenny is not an unconditioned stimulus. There is no natural response to it. But once the subject has been conditioned to money, which gives access to sweets and other good things, it can in its turn be used to condition other stimuli. Pavlov thus conceived of all learning as being made up of chains of conditioned reflexes.

If conditioning techniques are to be used in teaching, those who use them must be familiar with the rules governing conditioning. In fact, good teachers often use these principles without being aware of the fact, but it is useful to have some knowledge of the theory of conditioning [which is based on thousands of experiments carried out basically by Pavlov and his colleagues, more recently by workers in the United States and many other countries]. One principle concerns the size and strength of the stimulus. The Clarkes showed that retarded people asked to copy a simple pattern consistently ignored a small detail placed beside the main item. This would not have been expected in more intelligent subjects. In order to produce a response in the mentally retarded the stimulus may need to be a little bigger, a little more definite, a little clearer than for ordinary people of the same age. At the other end of the scale, it has been shown by Pavlov that excessive stimuli can produce unexpected results, even, in some cases, a neurosis. It is undesirable, as a rule, to shout continually at a backward child in the hope that in this way he will be induced to respond when an instruction given in an ordinary voice fails. Backward children bullied in this way may panic, or become nervous or anxious.

Lovaas in the United States has used a conditioning technique to discourage undesirable behaviour. In this connection he uses a painful electric shock. It is open to question whether this type of stimulus is appropriate, and it would certainly not be appropriate for an educational approach. It seems generally contrary, to the contemporary approach to such problems, to use painful stimuli of this kind. It is possible that, by doing so, a neurosis may be generated, though there is little doubt that the immediate objective may be gained. It would seem preferable to use techniques such as 'time out' or withdrawal of favours, mentioned earlier. By the same token, the use of corporal punishment would seem to be highly undesirable in the case of the mentally retarded.

The complexity of the stimulus was another matter which was extensively investigated by Pavlov's school. If dogs were set the task of distinguishing between two stimuli which were very alike, they became neurotic if the task was too difficult. It was mentioned above that Professor Clarke's results suggest that if the task is too easy, little learning takes place. This suggests the commonsense conclusion that in teaching backward children, they should be set tasks within their competence, difficult enough to present a real problem but not so difficult as to distress or fatigue them excessively. All teachers know that giving easier problems initially induces confidence on which basis more difficult tasks may be set.

The number of combinations of the conditioned stimulus with the reinforcing stimulus is of cardinal importance in conditioning. In some cases, a single combination is sufficient. It is said that 'the burnt child dreads the fire', and this applies to many retarded children who, after accidentally hurting themselves, avoid the cause of the trouble. Here, however, we are dealing with a relatively simple avoiding reaction. On the other hand, in the case of learning to dress, the matter may need endless patience. Garments are complicated; they can be put on back to front or inside out or in the wrong order. The child should be encouraged to try the simplest garment each time that dressing takes place. He should at first be assisted, and then the help should gradually be reduced. Efforts should be rewarded by praise, by a smile, by verbal encouragement, and a success can be rewarded by a sweet or by any other stimulus appropriate for that particular child, that is, by anything he particularly likes. It may take six months for a child to master one garment, and the mother may feel that success will never be achieved. She may console herself in the knowledge that the skill used in the process of learning the first step may be generalized or transferred to putting on the other garments.

Learning from others
A major advantage in school attendance as distinct from home teaching is the opportunity it presents for exchange with other children. The child becomes, perhaps for the first time, a member of a group. In view of today's small size of families he may well be the only child at home. In the school setting, the child has an opportunity to learn about social contacts and gradually to shape socially acceptable behaviour. He should learn the principles of group play and group work. This implies some sacrifice of individual freedom, some inhibition of his own activity. He must learn to give up a toy to a playmate, to take turns, to help others, to be gentle. He has to learn that his own wishes cannot immediately be realized, that he must wait a little for satisfaction. If the mentally handicapped child can acquire group discipline he is well on the way to social acceptability, and this may be more important for his future than more formal learning. Play and work at school should therefore be so designed for the mentally handicapped so that there is every opportunity for group and joint activity. Much play apparatus based on the see-saw principle, which is quite safe at nursery level, is now available and this constitutes a point of departure, since it cannot be managed by one alone. Many variations on this theme are possible.

In this connection we can raise the whole question of special nurseries, special care units, junior training centres, schools and classes for the educationally subnormal, screening in primary schools and comprehensive schools. If the teacher is viewed simply as an instrument for feeding knowledge into children who are all in competition with each other, then the case for separate educational provision is good. But in real life when he leaves school the individual has to mix, work and co-operate with people of all levels of ability. If he has always been separated throughout his school life into an artificial stream he may lack the capacity to understand or to work with others with different intellectual endowment. As has already been indicated, at present there is a specific advantage in the special school or class with smaller numbers and teachers with appropriate qualifications and experience. It seems, however, reasonable to expect that in future the numbers of children in ordinary classes will decrease, and that there will be a general increase in teachers with experience and qualification. There is also a move towards comprehensiveness in general education. If a class is so organized as to promote co-operation rather than competition, and if the role of the teacher is to stimulate joint and group work, it may be an advantage to have a group of pupils with varied talents. The basic principles of an exercise may be built up by the least talented, the theme elaborated by those more gifted and critical appraisal made by the most able. Suitable pairing or grouping could give better endowed children the opportunity of helping others, which, at the same time, provides an admirable opportunity for checking their own knowledge. An attempt to explain a problem to others, no matter how simple the exercise, gives an opportunity for clarification and illuminates fresh facets of the problem. The difficulties encountered by less able pupils may, when analysed, prove extremely instructive to both teacher and child. Exposure of the less able to the more gifted can be of mutual advantage in the learning situation.

Incentives
Contemporary schools are much more interesting places than previously. A majority of children seem quite glad to go to school, somewhat to the surprise of the older generation. It is seldom now a question of 'creeping like a snail unwillingly to school'. Many school activities are intrinsically interesting, now that there is more use of visual aids, practical activities, free play and other forms of educational activity which may blur the distinction between play and work. There has also been some change in parental attitudes. In the first decades after the introduction of compulsory general education there was a tendency for poor and less literate parents to resent the loss of family income resulting from school attendance. This is less likely to be the case at present, and there is increasing realization of the values of instruction, of literacy and a certain amount of scholarship, however limited. There has also been a considerable change in the classroom atmosphere and in the atti-

tude of teachers. The element of competition is less in evidence, and formal ranking of children in class places is less frequently employed. Although corporal punishment is still permitted, it appears to be less in evidence as a reality or as a threat, and the attitudes which went with it also appear to have changed. School refusal (truanting) seems rare among retarded pupils, and where it does occur there are usually special reasons. A child seen recently by the writer alleged that local boys had laughed at him because he attended the 'daft school' (E.S.N. school). In fact, it emerged that he was a member of a very large family with an extremely low income, and his main motive in absenting himself from school was to earn money on a milk round to help his mother. Incidentally, the blurring of distinctions between different types of educational provision should help to overcome the tendency for the more fortunate group of children in the present system to make derisory remarks about others whom they may regard as inferior.

Classical work on incentives for seriously mentally handicapped individuals was reported by O'Connor and Tizard in 1956. Much has been done since, notably by the Clarkes, but the original findings remain valid. If the retarded subjects were divided into three groups and were given a routine task, the results were found to vary markedly according to the type of encouragement given. Those who were just left to get on with the task scored low, those who were given encouragement in the form of praise did much better; and those who were shown goals in a visual manner did best of all. Once a certain tempo had been achieved, the retarded individuals tended to keep to it, even if less encouragement was given. The work reported also showed the importance of 'social' success. It would appear that, like ordinary people, the seriously retarded react very much to public opinion in the group situation. O'Connor and Tizard summarize the findings of some of the work which they quote by saying that 'defectives' do respond in an essentially normal way to incentives. Contrary to usual clinical opinion, it also appears wrong to assume that defectives, because of low intelligence, can be left to do simple uninspiring tasks similar to those suggested by Tredgold and Lewis, for we have seen that under similar conditions to these they lose interest and their performance deteriorates.

One further reference to O'Connor and Tizard's publication may be made. This concerns the restructuring of a unit so that imbecile and feebleminded patients were paired together. As the authors say:

> The imbeciles, instead of only working with other patients of

the same grade, now found themselves co-operating with high-grade patients on terms of equality, making a manifestly important contribution to the total job. For perhaps the first time in their lives they were able to actually see that what they were doing was useful and to understand how it was related to a finished product. Even the patients with Binet I.Q.s in the 20s developed a sense of pride in the work of 'their team'.

These references and quotations refer, of course, to an industrial type of setting or to an experimental situation with young men. The principles are, however, applicable to any age. For very young children, motivation for behaviour-shaping is likely to be provided primarily by the parents. Later, the range of contacts increases, and as the mental age grows, children become susceptible to the influence of other children. Reverting for a moment to conditioning theory and practice, it should be remembered that consistency of conditions and patterning of the surroundings is essential for the technique to be successful. Because retarded children take longer to learn, it is all the more important for them that there should be consistency. An attempt to reach this situation can be made by co-ordination of the efforts of a team, but it is highly desirable that relationships with adults and with other children should be as long-lasting as possible. In a normal household, the members of the family provide a constant background. At school, in the early stages, the relationship of a particular teacher to a group of pupils should be maintained for as long as possible. There is also an advantage in keeping classes as units. In other settings, such as residential schools, children's homes or hospitals, the same principles apply. Children in hospital are particularly at a disadvantage here, owing to the constant turnover of staff which has become built into the system. This strikes at the root of the educational process. The child is at school for a limited number of hours each week, and what happens in his home or substitute home may determine the success or failure of his education.

Responsibility for education
'Who does what' disputes are not confined to industrial workers, and there may be differences of opinion among some of the professions responsible for the care of handicapped children. By and large we need more attention to the problem, better facilities and more staff. Perhaps the question of who precisely makes the decisions will be less important when facilities are no longer in short supply. If a special

unit for deaf children has only fifty places and there are a hundred applicants, then fifty must be refused. It may not matter greatly whether this negative decision be taken by a doctor, a psychologist or a teacher. The important thing is to provide places for the other fifty children.

Within this general principle, there is still room for useful discussion on who should make decisions about children's education. So long as handicapped children were excluded as being unsuitable for school education they remained the responsibility of the health authority. Unfortunately many doctors brought to bear on the problem a clinical judgment and were somewhat less interested in behaviour or the possibility of its modification. It might have been felt that since severe retardation was an incurable condition then there was little to be done about it other than 'supervision and control'. It is unwise to read too much into names, but perhaps the use of the term 'supervisor' in regard to 'occupation centres' typified this attitude, though we all know that such supervisors have often done a very good job of teaching. Until the present one of the functions of the assistant medical officer of health or the school medical officer has been to decide which children were unsuitable for education in school and to arrange for their exclusion in due form. Since this function will shortly disappear together with this form of categorization of children the edge should be taken off the argument as to who accepts responsibility for decisions. All children should then be treated in a similar manner. It should be recognized that the prime responsibility for teaching lies with the teacher. In practice it will be he who gets results, or fails to do so. The psychologist and the doctor with special experience in this field should be in a position to advise, but always on the basis of classroom findings as well as on the results of their own examination of any particular child. When special problems arise with a retarded child in school, the social aspect may be of decisive importance. Such cases will be the subject of case conferences with participation of the teacher, the psychologist, the social worker, the doctor and other professions who may be concerned, not forgetting the parents. They should be primarily educational conferences, and not be converted by the prestige of the doctor into clinical conferences. Similar considerations apply to special training of teachers, which should be practical and relate primarily to teaching. Some understanding of clinical and psychological problems is essential, but the aim should not be to turn the teacher into a diagnostician or specialist in the measurement of I.Q.s, but rather to improve his teaching skill.

Chapter 10
Growing up

Ordinary adults often behave in a childish way, and this applies at all levels of intelligence. Growing up is, for the mentally retarded, slower and even more patchy. People grow up differently in different social classes and in different countries, and we use the expression 'growing up' in many different ways. What we have in mind is not so much a question of learning or intelligence, as of social behaviour. Children are naïve and unsophisticated; adults have had more experience, and are less impressed by the unusual. Retarded people, like those who are more intelligent, tend to become steadier and more settled as they grow older. They are less overactive, more set in their ways, and their enthusiasm may be more difficult to kindle. They are less distractible because they are more accustomed to things which distract children. On the other hand, the mentally retarded remain more suggestible, more gullible for those who make fun or take advantage of them. They are also more biddable as a rule than people of ordinary intelligence, and less inclined to assert their individuality or independence. These are generalizations, however, and there are exceptions.

It is usually considered that potential intelligence does not increase after the age of sixteen. This can only be an approximation to the truth, but it is a useful convention which serves as a basis for calculating an intelligence quotient. On this assumption an I.Q. is calculated by dividing the mental age by the chronological age below and up to sixteen years, but thereafter sixteen continues to be used no matter how old the person is. For example, if a child of eight has a mental age of four on tests, then his I.Q. is expressed as 50. The tests are so arranged that the average is 100 for the population on which the test is standardized. If the subject is sixteen and his mental age is eight, the I.Q. is again 50. If we then assess a person of sixty and find a mental age of eight, once again the I.Q. is 50. We do not expect a person of sixty to be more intelligent than one of sixteen. In fact, the reverse is the case, and there is a slow decline of intelligence with age, for which allowance is made in calculating the results of such tests as the Wechsler scale for adults.

Intelligence is, however, different from wisdom and experience.

Most people gain these during the course of their lives, and the backward are no exception. Their store of knowledge and experience may be quite limited, but it serves them in good stead and enables them to cope with their particular circumstances. Often the degree of adaptation is quite surprising, and a few people with an I.Q. below 50 have managed a paid job satisfactorily. Others of limited intelligence—perhaps with a formal I.Q. a little above 50—have managed a home or have brought up a child satisfactorily. In dealing with everyday situations, temperament seems to be even more important than intelligence within certain limits.

The mentally retarded as mothers
Work carried out by Dr Mary Sheridan with neglectful mothers at a Salvation Army Home especially allocated for them and their children illustrates this point. She found that the results gained from a period of residence and instruction in the home varied with the intelligence of the mothers. On the whole, the less intelligent improved more in child care as a result of their stay in the home than did those who were more intelligent. This result seems at first sight strange, but on reflection it is understandable. If mothers of low intelligence neglect their children, it may be because they do not *know* how to look after them properly and need instruction. On the whole they are willing and able to benefit from this. On the other hand, women of good intelligence who neglect their children do so for other reasons—perhaps from lack of motherliness, perhaps because they are mentally ill or temperamentally unstable.

It is important to remember that, when we speak of the mildly mentally retarded, most of these people are not specifically identified. They are not known as being mentally handicapped, and do not appear in any list. They pass as ordinary people, though those who know them well understand that they are not very clever and may often need a bit of help. Their fertility and marriage rate tends to be lower than average, but many do marry and manage to live normal family lives without great trouble.

Marriage
Assortative mating is a well-known phenomenon. People are influenced by many considerations in their choice of husband or wife, but generally it has been found that like tends to marry like. We may think the opposite to be true because we remember couples who seem to be very ill assorted, but we do not always notice those who

are very alike. This tendency to assortative mating also tends to apply to intelligence, so that if people of lowish intelligence marry they tend to marry people of a similar level. There are exceptions, and in such cases there tends to be a division of labour. If the wife is brighter, she tends to do all the paper-work in the home, settle the accounts, reckon the money and take charge of the budget. If the husband is more intelligent then he is more likely to do the planning. This kind of arrangement seems mutually satisfactory in many cases. People do not always like to have an equal for a mate, and they may like to protect or to be protected, as the case may be.

These remarks apply particularly to the mildly mentally retarded, or to those who were previously feebleminded Among them it is those with a higher intelligence and without additional physical disabilities who are more likely to marry, though a high proportion do not do so. The question of marriage is unlikely to arise with the more seriously handicapped who have an I.Q. of less than 50.

Mrs Brandon reviewed in 1960 200 women discharged from two units at Streatham in London. These were all in or above the mildly retarded range, judged by the results of the Wechsler-Bellevue test, though a few were a little below this on the Terman-Merrill scale. Of this total, forty-six were married and thirty-one had had children. The group's I.Q. covered a wide range and a number of them were in the dull normal range. The question of the competence of such former patients as mothers, wives and housewives has been much discussed. Mrs Brandon quotes E. O. Lewis, in his time a leading authority in the field of mental handicap, as saying: 'Defectives make inefficient parents; if only for social reasons they should not have children.' The opposite view was expressed by Michelson, who stated: 'From results one concludes that with the exception of those with I.Q.s between 30-49 the degree of the mother's retardation has no relationship to the adequacy of child care.'

To elucidate this point, Mrs Brandon arranged for independent assessment of twenty-three of our ex-patients by an experienced social worker. They were rated separately for their ability as mothers, wives and housewives. As a group their score was in fact, slightly above average, for the neighbourhood in each of these three areas of competence. Of those rated as wives, two were separated from their husbands and three were unhappy, but still together. Seven seemed average for their social group, seven rather happier than average and three extremely contented. It was felt that in some of the less happy marriages, the difficulty lay more with the husband.

Several women were working as well as running a house, and in two cases were keeping the husband whilst he was ill by doing domestic work. An attempt was made to break down this rather small group of married mentally retarded women into two groups—those doing well and those doing less well in their marital capacity. There was no difference in the intelligence of the two groups. It should be emphasized here that most of the 200 women discharged from the Streatham units had been transferred from other hospitals where they had been judged unsuitable for outside employment. It was considered that at that time these women were representative of those in other institutions who had been classified as feeble-minded. They would now, if they were in hospital, be regarded as 'subnormal' or mildly mentally retarded.

Children

Most mentally retarded women are fertile. More is known about their children than those of mentally retarded men. In the past a number of very definite opinions have been expressed about the children of the mentally retarded. Once again, the case of those parents with an I.Q. below 50 may be looked at separately. There are, in practice, very few of these. Unless the parents have some specifically transmissible condition there is no special reason why the child should be affected. The case of Down's syndrome has already been discussed, as has that of tuberous sclerosis. These make up a minority.

Most children born to people regarded as mentally retarded are born to parents who are either mildly retarded or dull normal in intelligence. In her study, Mrs Brandon looked at 150 children of seventy-three 'certified mental defectives'. The average I.Q. of these children was 91·3. Those children who were brought up by their own mothers seemed to do better, and only four of the children achieved an I.Q. lower than 65 (3·7 per cent of the total). These results fit in with a general observation that has been made about the intelligence of parents and children. Where parents have unusually high or low levels of intelligence there is a tendency for their children to 'regress to the mean'. This implies that if parents are very bright or very dull the children are likely to be nearer the average than themselves.

In the Streatham survey, limited information was available about the husbands of these ex-patients or about fathers of illegitimate children. In the fifty-four cases where information was available, there was a wide scatter of occupations (three rating as highly skilled, eight skilled, twenty-one semi-skilled, thirteen unskilled, six casual labourers and three 'certified defectives').

The average age of the ex-patients was forty, and many of them were unlikely to have further children. They had had 150 children, of which 109 were living—an average of 1·5 live children each. This does not fit in with the widely held notion of excessive fertility among the less intelligent, though it should be mentioned that many of these women had been detained for long periods of time. The high death rate in the children is striking. If those born earlier are compared with those born later, there is a marked difference. It would appear that the general decline in infant mortality has had a clear-cut effect here, and it should be remembered that, as a group, these women not only had low intelligence but also were under-privileged, coming from poor homes or in many cases being themselves illegitimate. They had also spent considerable periods in overcrowded hospitals.

Gain in intelligence
It is not to be expected, as a rule, that there will be much gain in intelligence quotient as children grow older. The standard tests are so designed as to reduce the size of variation. It is, however, generally recognized with young children that their performance on standard tests is a poor guide to the future because of unevenness of development and the testing of different abilities in the very young from those assessed later. Not until they reach the age of about seven do their test results give a reliable guide to probable future development. With very retarded children, however, even at a young age a poor performance on standard assessment indicates a poor outlook. But, with mild retardation, the conclusions are the same as for the ordinary range of intelligence, and the results obtained for young children in this range should not be taken as a firm guide. At the age of four or five, however, they may indicate the need for admission to a special observation and diagnostic class, if such exists in their local school system.

It has been mentioned above that cultural factors may have a marked influence on test performance. With individuals who have been under-stimulated and under-privileged, a definite improvement in test quotient can be observed after a period of suitable stimulation. Results published by Hilliard, Mundy and by the Clarkes illustrate this fact. Although sixteen is taken quite arbitrarily as the point of cessation of growth of measured intelligence, this may not be correct for certain people, especially those with a poor home environment.

The Clarkes describe changes occurring in a group of 'high-grade' patients over a period of eighteen months. The range of changes in I.Q. in this group was from an increment of twenty-five points on the Wechsler-Bellevue scale to a loss of five points. To verify these findings, they tested a further fifty-nine patients by the Wechsler scale after an average interval of twenty-seven months. The average gain in I.Q. was 6·5. The authors concluded that, for many of these patients, the improvements 'did not represent the total change which the individual had made or would make in the future'. When these patients were divided into two groups, depending on whether or not they had come from poor homes in every sense of the term, those from poorer homes showed an average improvement of 9·7 points and the others 4·1. This difference was judged to be statistically significant. It was suggested that these findings indicated the effect on the individual of a poor home in early life, and how this might stunt the growth of intelligence for a long time to come. On the other hand, this stunting appeared not necessarily permanent.

Attention has been drawn by Bowlby and others to the undesirable effect which an adverse early environment might have on young children. It was suggested that this, especially deprivation of normal mothering, might impede or distort normal psychological development. These views received wide attention and led to improvements in residential care for children. They also carried the implication, however, that the ill effect was necessarily permanent and could not be undone in later life. So far as intellectual development is concerned, the work of the Clarkes and others emphasizes that this is not wholly true. It would appear that appropriate measures of rehabilitation may do much to make good the leeway in the development of the under-privileged. At the same time, there is a wider implication that if conditions for children were improved, then this form of retardation could be largely avoided. Those particularly at risk include the illegitimate child, the institutionalized child, the slum child, members of large low-income families, children with mentally ill parents, children in 'problem' families and those from poor areas. More day nurseries, remedial classes, social workers, better housing —all these could help, but if the economic tide sets against such communities then the little good done can easily be washed away. As mentioned, this problem of mild and potentially remedial handicap is a much bigger and economically more important one that than of severe mental handicap, which affects a much smaller number of people.

Emotional maturation

Retarded children develop emotionally at a slower pace than those who are more intelligent. Sophistication comes more slowly and later. They do, however, stabilize, given the opportunity, and as a rule, take on the pattern of behaviour and emotional reaction of those about them. There has been much discussion about sex education and advice on contraception for the mildly mentally retarded as for the more intelligent. It has been the writer's experience that, if this subject is mentioned, however tactfully, to mentally retarded young women living in an open hostel, they tend to react as many more intelligent women would, with indignation and an implication that unpleasant suggestions are being made about their behaviour. This still applies even when it seems almost certain that they have run the risk of pregnancy. To be fair to them, however, in work reported by Hilliard it was not until over a hundred such young women had been placed in the community that the first unwanted pregnancy occurred. This might suggest that the mentally retarded are less at risk here than their more intelligent sisters.

Retarded people tend, like others, to show a dual standard of morality. They have a public image of themselves which they are anxious to defend. They know the kind of behaviour expected in a given situation and will claim to have conformed to this. On the other hand, many deviations from the approved pattern are revealed in confidence between each other. Young retarded people are unwilling to take advice if this is offered in a formal manner. In hostel conditions, the best approaches seem to be in group discussion or informal chats with someone whom they know and trust. Question-and-answer group discussion provide both a remedy for ignorance and an acceptable forum for advice. It is interesting to note that in such group discussions it rapidly becomes evident that there is a group moral code for the unit, and that individuals who transgress this are exposed to heavy criticism from their fellows. This applies to sexual behaviour, to questions of individual property, to behaviour generally. The girl who stays out late at night and disturbs staff and others on her return is likely to be extremely unpopular, and her subsequent behaviour may well be modified by this fact. It should be emphasized that the particular hostels to which reference is made here are used by people who are disturbed as well as retarded, so that they are more demanding than most young retarded people in hostels would be.

Another example of a group code of conduct which applied to extremely retarded patients came to light when Professor Stengel carried out his investigation into pain perception. He examined all 600 patients at the Fountain Hospital and found that they were all normal in this respect, contrary to suggestions which have been made in the literature. The technique used was simply that of a light pin-prick, followed by observation of the reaction. In one ward a number of boys failed to show the usual response. It was then realized that the charge nurse in that ward was fond of drilling the boys in a semi-military fashion, and had succeeded in convincing them that it was unmanly to show pain, and for that reason they had reacted so stoically. For the majority of the retarded there is no real difficulty in getting compliance with an accepted code of conduct. There are exceptions, but these are also numerous among the more intelligent population!

A major difficulty about some of our more overcrowded hospitals is that limited space and facilities make it difficult to develop a normal régime; therefore patients who have lived in such conditions are unable immediately to adjust to the style of living in the general community. In hospital there is little mixing of the sexes, and people who have been accustomed to this style of life may not know how to behave in ordinary society. In ward conditions it may be that more than fifty patients have to dress or undress at the same time, and there may be no locker space for storing clothes. There may also be no privacy in toilet and ablutions. It would not be surprising if, after living in such conditions, people who moved into the general community fail at once to appreciate the usual social taboos.

Mention is often made of a 'permissive' Western society. This notion, however, is curiously mistaken when it is a question of everyday living. There is still a great deal of rigidity and lack of minimal tolerance. The slightest deviation from expected behaviour by a retarded person will arouse intense indignation. As an example, a teacher in a school for the physically handicapped complained of the behaviour of a thirteen-year-old spastic pupil. She said that he had put his hand under her skirt. The item of apparel was only a few inches long, and the boy was unable to walk. She would, therefore, have had to move close to him in order to permit the alleged offence. Had she made her displeasure clear at the time, and avoided too close an approach for the future, presumably all would have been well. Clearly the teacher expected as high a level of conduct from this physically and mentally handicapped boy as from any ordinary pupil. Neither, apparently, did she feel that undesirable behaviour on the part of a member of her class was a reflection on herself, or that it was part of her duty to teach correct behaviour.

The headmaster asked for the pupil's removal from school and admission to hospital.

Much of the shaping of behaviour which takes place in retarded as in normally intelligent children and adolescents is taken for granted. Neither those who provide the example nor those who copy patterns of behaviour may have thought out any definite strategy. The copying and passing on of codes of conduct and attitudes is seldom expressed or clearly formulated. When codes are stated, they are often fragmentary and mutually contradictory. It might be thought that, so far as the retarded are concerned, their limited intelligence would make it difficult to alter their behaviour in a desired direction. Yet all the evidence is to the contrary, suggesting that the majority are more biddable than people of ordinary levels of intelligence.

Psychotherapy
Specific behaviour-shaping techniques dependent on conditioning principles have already been mentioned (pp. 162-6). There is, however, evidence that less formal approaches can be very helpful with young retarded people. The group discussion approach with hostel residents was referred to above. In order to assess results a careful experimental design is required, such as used in the study reported by O'Connor and Tizard. Here a group of seven young men took part in a 'non-directive' discussion on 32 occasions in a period of six months, and were compared with two similar control groups. There were changes in work diligence and in recorded intelligence, but there was also a marked improvement in behaviour and verbally expressed attitudes. There was a significant improvement in expressions indicating appreciation and zest, whilst there was a reduction in attitudes indicating sadism (cruelty) and masochism (self-punishment). The authors felt that even this limited experiment indicated the possibility of improving psychopathic attitudes and tendencies over a relatively short period. With unstable, mildly retarded people, they suggested, too often the current manner and behaviour is accepted as permanent. All the evidence is to the contrary, suggesting that in the great majority of cases improvement is possible, which would in turn make adjustment in the general community easier.

Over-protection
Attitudes to retarded children, especially the mildly retarded as they grow older, will vary according to the family background. In a poorer, larger family the mildly retarded member may be accepted on equal terms without too much trouble and get as much or as

little opportunity for self-expression and development as the others. Paradoxically, difficulties associated with growing up often arise in families who have provided a good standard of care. Quite often it is difficult for them to accept the fact that the backward member of the family is able to be semi-independent and to take his rightful place in the community.

In the United States the Group for the Advancement of Psychiatry in their booklet on mild mental retardation quote the case of John, a twelve-year-old boy, the son of a judge. The parents enjoyed a high social position and were proud of it, but John was adept at and enjoyed farm work. The parents were distressed by this, since they felt that such work should be done by individuals from a lower social level. However, with advice from their physician they allowed him to become successful in farm work, even though at first it hurt their pride. This is a very common picture. Unfortunately in the absence of such advice the retarded son and particularly the daughter is likely to remain at home, doing very little of positive value and undergoing a gradual atrophy of drive and interest. The problem is likely to be particularly acute in mixed cultures. A daughter of a family who had been missionaries in China eventually returned to Britain. By this time she was in her forties, and was of dull normal intelligence. As all the other members of the family had been so much more intelligent it had never been accepted by them that she could do anything of value. Furthermore in China she had been waited on hand and foot by servants. On arrival in Britain she was quite incapable of any useful effort beyond engaging in chat in a somewhat affected voice. The situation of the occasional family from South Africa who have sought advice about a mildly retarded member is even worse in view of the very sharp division of labour there between black and white. It appears, in fact, to be quite difficult for a retarded white person to get a manual job in that country.

The booklet by the Group for the Advancement of Psychiatry also briefly discusses some of the unfounded anxieties which parents may have about mentally handicapped children. At times parents become abnormally preoccupied with the future: 'They may begin to worry about the sexual behaviour of their children whilst they are still infants, perhaps because society has had an exaggerated image of the sexual potency of the retarded.... The retarded are no more likely than ordinary individuals to indulge in sexual activity. In many ways, despite their limited intellect, they may be more moral than persons of greater intelligence. Certainly there is no evidence of increased sex drive on the part of the retarded.'

Delinquency

It is rare for the severely mentally handicapped to commit crimes, and if they do these may only be petty or inadvertent. A seriously retarded person might be in trouble for passing urine in the street and be accused of indecent exposure. Usually their efforts at committing misdemeanours such as stealing would be so obvious that they would be forestalled, as one would a small child. With the mildly retarded the situation is different, and considerable numbers may be at present in prison. However, as pointed out earlier with reference to Woodward's study, much will depend on assessment. Very often young offenders have a poor scholastic record, and if a method of assessment is used which penalizes them because of this, then there will seem to be a large number of mentally retarded among them. Allen, writing in Washington D.C., was interested in test results obtained from prisoners, and found that a variety of tests are used by correctional institutions. These are often administered (sometimes to large groups of inmates) and scored by untrained persons. As an example of the difficulty of the problem, he mentions one state where the Otis test is used. On that test the mean I.Q. of the supposedly retarded prison inmates was 61·8, but special retesting by the research team gave a mean I.Q. of 77·8, with only one inmate in the sample scoring below I.Q. 70. He refers to an earlier nationwide survey which elicited replies about 200,000 prisoners (80 per cent of the total) and which suggested that 9·5 per cent had I.Q.s below 70 and 1·6 per cent below 55. These figures would be subject to the reservations mentioned above.

In Britain, if the mentally retarded commit offences, these are likely to be of a very minor kind. Allen reports an anomalous situation in the United States, where the commonest crime committed by those identified in a survey as mentally handicapped prisoners was first-degree murder. He qualifies this by pointing out that the institutions concerned were, in a majority of cases, maximum security prisons and, therefore, quite unrepresentative. Again, it should be pointed out that in the United States murder is commoner than in Britain, and the availability of firearms is very different. More than two-thirds of the prisoners tested in the survey reported by Allen had committed their crimes alone. In this respect they were different from prisoners who were not retarded, who had committed their crimes as members of teams.

Certainly in Britain parents need not be worried that their retarded children will commit major crimes (if, of course, they were allowed to play with lethal weapons the situation might be different).

There is no particular reason why the retarded should commit minor offences, provided they have the advantage of a good home.

The old notion of moral deficiency has now been abandoned in favour of a more sociological and scientific approach. When careful studies such as those reported at some length by O'Connor and Tizard are done, there seems little to choose in point of intelligence between delinquents and similar control groups drawn from the same social class and having the same social composition. While there are a few exceptional individuals who may be described as 'psychopaths', and who seem to have relatively fixed anti-social trends, very few of them are mentally retarded. The case of Straffen is a notorious example of a child murderer who was supposedly mentally defective, but the probability is that he would not have scored within the mentally retarded range if he had been assessed by contemporary methods.

Leisure

The over-protected and under-stimulated young person with limited intelligence may spend all of his spare time looking at television or just doing nothing. Such cases are exceptional, however, and where there is a job to be done or a senior training centre to be attended, these usually tend to bring friends and society in their train. Joining a youth club should be encouraged, and if the parents belong to the local branch of the National Society for Mentally Handicapped Children they will know what leisure facilities are organized locally. The Society and other voluntary organizations arrange summer holidays for mentally handicapped children as well as for older people. Some retarded young people are drawn into social activity through their church, Scouts or other local youth organizations. Senior schools often help in this direction. It is essential that parents should encourage the development of friendships, have other young people into the home and facilitate visits to friends.

Although the mentally handicapped do not usually excel at sport there are exceptions. Some have done very well at swimming and others have become competent skaters. Horse-riding has been organized for handicapped people generally of late, and hospitals for the mentally handicapped traditionally have effective cricket and football teams, though these usually involve only a very small number of patients. Much good work has been done in some hospitals by physical training instructors, since mentally handicapped people, even if they have no particular physical handicap, often seem to walk in a very clumsy way and to have poor muscular co-ordination. This is much improved both by physical work and by physical training. Most of these remarks would apply equally to the ordinary population, but these considerations should not be forgotten in the case of the mentally handicapped.

Attitudes of brothers and sisters
Where parents have been able to give the right lead, the attitude of brothers and sisters to the handicapped child will be positive. Problems sometimes arise when the sister has a boy friend or the brother a girl friend. If the matter has been handled openly and frankly by the parents, the brother and sister need have no major problems. They will not regard the presence of the handicapped brother or sister as a guilty secret. They will not be afraid to speak about him. It would, in any event, be unwise to attempt to hush up the existence of the affected member of the family. The unknown is always worse than the known. Gossip soon gets around, and if the girl friend were accidentally to hear from some third person about the backward brother she would take it less kindly than if she had heard about it from her boy friend himself. If, as sometimes happens, the parents are embarrassed and self-conscious about their handicapped child, it is likely that their normal children will be also. They will be reluctant to invite any boy or girl friends to the home, with resulting difficulties and stresses. Any doubts about the wisdom of marriage into an affected family are best dealt with frankly and openly. If expert advice is required, there should be no difficulty in obtaining this.

Legal rights
Apart from formal legal rights, when they reach adult years the mentally handicapped should be treated as much like ordinary people as possible. They should not be spoken down to, as they may resent this. Often in hospital they are referred to at any age as boys and girls. This is a bad habit. It should be remembered that their needs are those of adult men and women, though somewhat modified depending on the degree of retardation. If in doubt they should be addressed as Mr or Miss, as the case may be. If you shake hands with other members of the family, then shake them by the hand as well. If their future is being discussed in their presence—which is very desirable—then they should not be spoken about as though they were not there. If possible, they should be drawn into the conversation, and most will understand that it concerns them. According to their level of understanding, they should, if possible, be told clearly what is

proposed, and they should be invited to express an opinion if they are able to do so. They should be coaxed and persuaded rather than ordered to do things. Often they will say no to an abstract proposition—for example, joining a youth club—not knowing what it implies. If, however, they are taken on a visit to the club, they will understand better and may become enthusiastic.

Broadly speaking, the mentally handicapped have the same legal rights as ordinary citizens, though these are curtailed in the case of the minority who are compulsorily detained in hospital. If their legal competence is called into question on account of mental handicap, each case is open to be judged on its merits. Since there has been no formal statutory ascertainment of the mentally handicapped in Britain since 1959, the question of mental handicap will not be raised in regard to legal matters, unless the handicap is obvious. In case of doubt, it would be for an expert to decide whether the degree of handicap was such that there is legal incapacity. This would apply, for example, to persons charged before a court, to know in the first instance if they understood the nature of the charge and were able to enter a plea, and then to determine the degree of responsibility for their actions. In other cases the ability to enter into a contract may be in doubt or testamentary capacity, the ability to give reliable evidence in court, eligibility for juror service and so forth. In a majority of cases of mentally handicapped, their names will appear on the list of electors as a local resident, and there will be an entitlement to vote: but this does not apply to residents in psychiatric hospitals.

It has already been mentioned that if the mentally handicapped appear before a court charged with some minor offence and if they are recognized as being mentally handicapped, they are very likely to be dealt with as such and sent to a hospital. This may be done by the court formally or informally. It can happen in such cases that the individual faces a long period of detention in hospital for a very minor offence which would have been best dealt with by probation. The court will be influenced by the presence of a relative or friend who is able to vouch for the handicapped person. In the absence of such and in the event of an overburdened probation officer's unwillingness to take on this responsibility, it should be exercised by the local authority's mental health worker, whose task should be to rehabilitate the retarded person and to ensure, if possible, that he is kept out of mischief or bad company.

Special hospitals are provided at Rampton and Moss Side in Britain for mentally handicapped persons thought to show dangerous, violent or criminal proclivities. While these make up only a small fraction of the total number of mentally handicapped, in the past the road into these hospitals has been much easier than that into Broadmoor, the special hospital and erstwhile criminal lunatic asylum used for persons found to have committed some major offence and thought likely to remain a danger to the public. Many, if not most, of those admitted to Rampton or Moss Side are there because they have proved difficult to manage in the appropriate local hospital. It appears to the writer that many of these are patients who have relatively good intellectual capacity and who might have been rehabilitated in more propitious circumstances. Many have an unfavourable background. As a result of some petty offence, they may have found themselves detained in hospital. Faced with a long period of detention, and in the knowledge that many patients appear to be serving 'life sentences', they have become increasingly rebellious. Unsuccessful attempts to escape may have led to them being recaptured and brought back to hospital. The resulting process, whereby a person with an already difficult character is subjected to increasing repression and restriction, can lead to an explosive reaction, and grievous bodily harm to the staff of the hospital, where the patient has by now acquired notoriety. In these circumstances he may well be sent to Rampton or Moss Side. It would appear that if local hospitals were less over-crowded, better serviced by social workers and run on less authoritarian lines a number of such cases could be avoided at the outset.

Death of parents
A large proportion of the mentally handicapped who survive infancy can be expected to outlive their parents, to whom knowledge of this expectation is sometimes a source of anxiety. Parents can familiarize themselves, through the National Society for Mentally Handicapped Children and their local authority, with the local resources for residential care. The mildly retarded should, so far as is possible, be maintained within the general community. They may be able to find lodgings in the ordinary way if they are no longer able to live at home, and for some, residential hostels may provide an answer. For others who have spent the whole of their lives in the general community and have reached old age, the ordinary community provision for old people will be appropriate. There is no reason for segregating them at this stage. Their needs will be the same as those of other old people.

Chapter 11
Employment

The employment of the mentally retarded cannot be considered in isolation. The situation varies from time to time and from one place to another, dependent on general economic considerations. There is an accelerating rate of change in this field. As an example may be taken the relative value of labour and material. At one time labour was cheap and material was valuable. At present in the developed countries the opposite is increasingly true. At one time there was a considerable demand for the tinker's skills, whilst at present practitioners of this art would be difficult to find. After the Second World War when O'Connor and Tizard were carrying out their survey at Darenth Park, a large hospital for the mentally retarded, they found many patients still employed in cobbling. Footwear from other establishments maintained by the London County Council was sent to that hospital, as well as to others of its kind, for repair. Increasingly it is becoming less realistic to devote valuable man-hours to repair of foot-wear and a 'wear and throw away policy' is gradually extending to this category of article of consumption. O'Connor and Tizard's chief objection to the use of cobbling as a suitable occupation for the mentally handicapped was, however, of a different nature. They pointed out that the skills involved were too elaborate and too demanding for a majority of patients. The results were certainly very often extremely unsatisfactory. The work régime inside the institution seemed to have become fossilized, whilst changes in light industry generally were proceeding at a rapid pace. Shoe-mending is now outdated, even under institutional conditions, as a major source of employment for those of limited intelligence.

Against this general background certain principles may be set out for guidance in finding employment for the mentally handicapped. The job should be relatively simple; it should be manual rather than clerical; it should be suited to the physical capabilities of the individual and take into account any additional disabilities which he may have; it should be, in the main, repetitive rather than varied and demanding constant adaptation and judgment; it should be supervised and, as a rule, should be undertaken in the company of others rather than in isolation. If possible the work should be undertaken alongside workers of normal intelligence and should attract standard rates of pay; it should not demand an unrealistic tempo; it should not involve a team bonus, which could cause resentment of the retarded individual by his workmates because of the risk of his reducing the output of the group. The work should not carry an element of risk such as would be increased by limited intelligence.

Protected work
For the foreseeable future there will always be a need for protected work for the more seriously handicapped, that is, subsidized work in which the employee does not fully earn his keep. In the case of the mentally handicapped this can be arbitrarily defined as meaning below an I.Q. of 50 in present conditions. It seems possible that increasing demands for technical training may increase this level. On the other hand, the increasing semi-automation of many tasks takes away an element of skill and renders them suitable for people of lower intelligence. Heavy capital investment in standard products may also leave room for relatively simple production methods for products which command a short-term or seasonal market. For example, one of the contract jobs undertaken by units for the mentally handicapped is making Christmas crackers. This work could presumably be fully automated in the factory producing a standard Christmas cracker. However, in view of the desire for variety and novelty, there is a potential demand for a product with a short-term vogue, and for this kind of work simpler forms of production may be competitive.

As suggested earlier, although at present senior training centres and other industrial units for the mentally handicapped are usually located in separate buildings owned by municipalities or hospitals, there is no particular reason why this should be so. Workshops for the severely mentally handicapped could, if agreement was reached, be created within industry. These would be protected workshops in the economic and technical sense. Payment would be according to work done as at present with contract work undertaken by local authorities and hospitals. There would be generous provisions for training and induction. Processes carried out would demand a level of skill appropriate to the mentally handicapped working there. It might be necessary to introduce more intelligent workers for certain key processes. On the other hand, by the use of special jigs and adaptations it is often possible to bring a task within the competence of a severely handicapped worker. For example, in the preparation of articles for sale by the dozen, it is necessary to count out twelve items and put them into a plastic bag, securing it. This process can be automated, but with seasonal or novelty goods it is economic to undertake it by hand. But the patient may be unable to count twelve reliably, though if he is given a board with twelve depressions he may learn to fill *all* of them with, for example, marbles, or whatever the product may be. He can then throw them from the board into the bag.

If such work were kept within industry instead of bringing it out into the separate training centres as at present, the facilities available in the centre would need to go with it. For example, there must be adequate toilets and ablutions, and good access for wheel chairs. A reasonable degree of supervision should be provided to ensure work discipline and safety. The appropriate professional staff must also be available, and it should be the task of a psychologist to review the cases of all those working in protected conditions to consider whether any of them could work in open employment. No doubtful or borderline case should be prejudged, and several trials may be necessary since normal young people often need to try several jobs before they find one that suits them.

One of the writer's patients expressed a desire, very common among girls leaving school, to look after animals or children. She wanted to work in kennels and care for dogs, and a job in kennels was arranged, but to her chagrin she was given the task of looking after cats. This seemed to be beneath her dignity; presumably the attitude was conveyed to her by those working in the kennels, where there must have been a 'cat and dog' hierarchy. It was therefore arranged for her to work with dogs. Soon after she was bitten by a dog, and left the job! Although this little history sounds rather simple, it seems unlikely that attitudes of more intelligent school-leavers are any less easily influenced by trivial incidents and passing fancies. Some people object to working in a laundry because it is too hot. Others have a strong desire to work in the open air and nothing else will satisfy them. Two of the writer's patients were young men, one of whom liked garden or farm work. As they were friends they wanted to go to the same place to live. They were offered the opportunity of living in a new hostel provided by one of the London boroughs. This was very elegant, but was set in a clearance area of dilapidated buildings. The two young men stoutly refused to leave the hospital, situated in pleasant country surroundings, for the new hostel. It will be seen that intelligence is only one of many factors to be considered in rehabilitation, a task which calls for great skill, tact and persistence on the part of the social worker, nurse, employment officer or physician who undertakes it.

In protected work, the main considerations are the simplicity or otherwise of the task, and work satisfaction. A tradition of art and craft work has grown up in regard to the handicapped whether for the blind, the palsied or the mentally retarded. The modern tendency is towards a more industrial type of activity, which brings the more severely handicapped more into line with the general community. It provides many jobs well within their competence, and, by a degree of work rationalization and the use of appropriate machinery, an increased output can give them more job satisfaction and more earnings. They should always be paid for work done, no matter how small the amount. They also need attention and praise. Art and craft work need not necessarily be wholly discarded, but a correct balance should be achieved, and this kind of work may be done as a leisure occupation and for pleasure. Knitting, embroidery, rug making are all things which the more severely handicapped like to do, partly because of the pleasure they may get from knowing that the article is destined for a particular person, and will be received by that person with pleasure. The least skilled workers will be paid a minimum reward, which will exceed the value of the work done, but an effort should be made apart from this to relate the amount paid to the work achieved, and this should be clearly distinguished from 'pocket money'. As with ordinary workers, money rewards can be a powerful incentive, even when the amounts are relatively small. All values are relative!

A worker who has produced a complete item by his own efforts for example, a rug—derives a great deal of satisfaction from it, and is glad to show it or have it included in an exhibition. In industrial work the finished product may be less in evidence, and there is a greater need for monetary and psychological rewards. A team may be built up depending on the levels of ability in individual workers. They may have a task of making cardboard boxes, which could, among other operations, be broken down into cutting, folding, glueing and checking. The team could be composed of four workers. The checker might fetch the material, ensure its distribution and the flow of work, check the product and take it away; the cutter would have to work to a design and so would have to acquire the necessary skill; the tasks of the gluer and the folder might be more easily acquired. The most able worker might act as checker, and for him this might be a prelude to promotion into open employment.

Consideration should always be given to frequent revision of the work which any individual is doing. For younger people there is a certain advantage in trying several different kinds of work so as to broaden their range of skills, though this tactic should be used with discretion. There are some disturbed patients who need concentrated individual attention over a very long period for the establishment of work habits. In the ordinary way it might be said that they cannot be occupied and that they are hopelessly withdrawn, antisocial, destructive or self-destructive as the case may be. Recently the use of conditioning techniques has shown that some at least of this minority group of very disturbed individuals can have their behaviour improved. This is, initially, costly in terms of the teacher's, psychologist's or physician's time, but as a result of prolonged effort such patients can often establish a useful work routine and lose the undesirable features of their behaviour. It might, however, be tempting fate to alter their routine—once this was satisfactory—without very careful preliminary thought. For the majority of young severely retarded people there is, however, considerable possibility of improvement of skills. Change should be moderate and not too frequent. New patterns must be learnt, one step at a time, and old patterns must be inhibited, otherwise they will persist into the new work and cause confusion.

Care must always be taken to advance to more skilled and more responsible work whenever this is possible. The writer remembers a group of women patients in a large hospital before the Second World War, who worked in a sewing room. Some were doing work by hand, others by machines. The number of machines was limited, and the best patients were allocated to them. This became a matter of prestige, of intense rivalry and jealousy. A patient demoted from machine to handwork 'lost face' and would complain bitterly. In the restrictive circumstances of the time, she might well react by breaking windows or, a favourite gambit, smashing the fire-alarm glass. A more liberal régime and better planning should eliminate such situations and reactions.

Protected workshops should be restricted to the severely handicapped and others who are very unlikely to make the grade in open employment. These include some young retarded people with additional disabilities such as blindness, deafness, cerebral palsy or frequent fits. It should not automatically be decided that, because youngsters have an additional disability, they are unfitted for open employment. There may well be a place in light industry at bench work for the mildly retarded with lesser degrees of cerebral palsy.

The intelligent deaf and blind can be employed, and jobs for those who are mildly retarded may also be found.

Epilepsy
Epilepsy should not automatically debar an adolescent from work any more than it should stop a child attending school. In the first place, it is necessary to know a little more than just that the candidate for employment is epileptic. This may mean much or little. Some epileptics have not had a fit for several years, and in their cases the risk can reasonably be ignored. Epileptics have an undeserved reputation for being fractious and difficult. Some are, but they are only a small minority. Some only have fits at night, or when they become sleepy or very bored, and are unlikely to have an attack if they are busy working. Others have an 'aura', a warning of the attack allowing them time to sit down, lie down or get to a place of safety. There is an outdated notion that epileptics are not safe with machinery. Most modern machinery is adequately protected, and is indeed very safe unless the safety device has been tampered with. For those epileptics who have fairly frequent major attacks by day, even when busy, open employment may be difficult to obtain. They need supervision, acceptance of some responsibility by the employer, and a little care, if they do not have warnings of attacks, to make sure they do not fall onto sharp objects or into acid or any other dangerous material which might be used on the job. Naturally, such epileptics are not employable as window cleaners, steel erectors, builder's labourers or in similar work. An epileptic liable to attacks in the street or on public transport should always be accompanied, and for hospitals and hostels it may not be difficult to arrange for two such patients to travel to work together.

Temperamental difficulties
A young person may have sufficient intelligence for open employment but may fail several jobs because of a difficult temperament. It should not be accepted that this is necessarily permanent or irremediable. Age has the effect of settling people, and a young man of twenty may be much more stable and employable than a boy of sixteen. It is also possible to study the individual and to find out the weaknesses and reasons for job failure. The fault may lie with the nature of the job, with the other workers, with the foreman or it may be that the preparation was insufficient. The young person may have lost his way, or not taken sufficient money for his bus ticket, or he may have answered back or sulked when reprimanded for late-

ness. Others have difficulty in accepting or understanding criticism. If their work is bad they may not like being told so and may feel that they are being 'picked on'. These are also difficulties which can be overcome by good management. The individual who is not very bright may become aware that people are liable to make fun of him, and as a result may develop a 'chip on his shoulder'. In his case, criticism should be precise and constructive. General criticism may be meaningless to him. He should have the faulty work shown to him and be helped to put it right, to do better, in a simple manner. Such disturbed youngsters can only succeed with a foreman who is patient and good at handling difficult people.

The length of trial is important. Difficulties may arise almost immediately, but if the initial problems can be overcome a suitable work routine can be established. Sometimes results greatly exceed expectation. One young man with limited supervision because of home problems was able to get up at 6 a.m., make his breakfast and a cup of tea for his ailing mother, and then travel by bus and train across London to arrive for work at 8 a.m. He continued this routine for several years until the branch of the firm where he was working was closed. His intelligence was at the lower end of the range of mild mental handicap, but he had the advantage of a stable temperament.

Open employment
There is still considerable inhibition about recommending people who are recognized as mentally handicapped for open employment, that is, competitive employment in the open labour market. Where this is the case, it may be a disadvantage to be recognized as having low intelligence. The person who is not recognized often gets a job without too much bother despite his limited ability. The mildly retarded tend to come to notice because they have character difficulties or additional physical disabilities, or because they have no effective family or friends. In these circumstances there is a real danger that they may be kept in a closed industrial unit in a hospital or hostel for an indefinite period. A definite dynamic programme is required if such people are to get into open work. Some solve the problem for themselves by finding their own job. In the present system this may involve running away from the institution where they are to look for a job. In the past, they would have been recaptured and brought back to hospital, but fortunately more and more of those in authority over such in-patients recognize that action of this kind taken by the patient may be in his best interests. The job they take may sometimes seem unsuitable, like the retarded

young lady who found herself work off Piccadilly washing up in a café with a somewhat doubtful reputation. Yet she kept this job for some years, seemed happy and never got into any personal difficulties.

It is most important that mildly retarded people in institutions or attending senior training centres should have their cases reviewed and be given every opportunity to fit into a job. Predictions of working capacity are very 'hit and miss', and it is very easy to underestimate the possibilities of the individual or the capacity of the work place to fit him in. Unless, therefore, an actual trial is undertaken it cannot be said for certain that a particular individual is incapable of employment. For those who are over-confident, an early trial and failure may often have a sobering effect and help to spur them on to further efforts in training. On the other hand, a common problem is that of the individual who lacks confidence. This is particularly the case with the patient who has been in hospital for a long time. They will tend to be frightened of the prospect of work, of the work place, of workmates. Such people may need a lot of coaxing and encouragement. They may need to be accompanied on the journey several times, to be introduced personally to the foreman and to be given some personal encouragement by him in their efforts.

A critical phase in habilitation of the mentally retarded is that of school leaving. Those leaving a special school are likely to get special help in finding a job suited to their level of intelligence. Those leaving ordinary school will not necessarily have this advantage. The great majority of those leaving special schools do, in fact, enter gainful employment. It is likely, however, that the youth employment officer may have reservations about some of the candidates for employment from special schools which will be reinforced by doubts and anxieties expressed by their parents. In some cases, there can be little dispute that these doubts are valid. In others they may lead to lost opportunities and to the individual adapting all too easily to a routine below his level of potential. The writer recently interviewed a young man in hospital who had been in open employment earning some £15 a week. In hospital he was getting about £1·50 for his labour, which was light. Asked if he did not regret the loss of his previous earnings, which were, of course, reduced by the amount he paid in hospital for his keep, he replied that he did not mind. He had his collection of records which entertained him, and seemed to have very limited ambition. He had, in effect become institutionalized; this is not only a way of life but a state of mind.

Whilst there have been considerable improvements in the expertise in finding suitable employment for the mentally handicapped, the situation has changed for the worse in a number of directions. A survey published in 1944 showed only 23 per cent of E.S.N. school-leavers doing remunerative work at ordinary rates of pay, while no less than 17 per cent were admitted to hospitals for mental defectives, 13 per cent having been excluded from school as ineducable and 4 per cent living at home and doing no paid work. These figures give a partial explanation for the present overcrowding in institutions for the mentally handicapped. Since that time, there has been a great increase in the numbers attending E.S.N. schools. Finding employment for them was easy during the Second World War, but has recently become almost more difficult than at any time since 1939.

The position varies greatly from one part of the country to another. In the London area, at the time of writing, suitable jobs can be found even for patients who present difficult and complicated problems. This may demand great tenacity of purpose and infinite patience. For the more difficult cases, it is desirable to find a social worker whose special province this will be and who has the ability to gain the confidence of the patients in question. At the same time, the person undertaking this task must have a good knowledge of local industry and employment potential, as well as being versed in hostel and other residential or lodging possibilities. She must keep a list of potential employers with work likely to suit her patients. She will need a good knowledge of transport facilities, and be able to work out ways in which a candidate for employment can get to the place of work. She should be able, without being too obtrusive or giving an employer the impression that the candidate cannot stand on his own feet, to give moral support on first entry into employment. She will need to be available for a whole series of inquiries about health and insurance cards, pay slips, organization of budget, purchase of clothes, payments for board and lodging, post office savings books, boy friends and girl friends, leisure activities, youth clubs and many other aspects. The strength of the contact between the mentally handicapped person and the social worker or other person who acts in this role will in many cases determine the success or failure of open employment. These remarks apply, for the most part, to those of the mentally handicapped who have failed initially to find employment on leaving school and who are in hospital or hostels. Those living at home will have the support of friends and relations, though they also may need professional advice, especially if the parents are over-protective.

Suitability for employment

It has already been suggested that there is a critical level of intelligence at about the 50 mark on the Wechsler scale. This is by no means absolute, and is in any event conditional on the employment market and other variables. It is now generally agreed that, apart from the question of intelligence and additional handicaps, prediction of employability is extremely difficult and that the best way of finding out if a person can do what appears to be a suitable job is to try him at it.

In their review of prediction of occupational success, O'Connor and Tizard pointed out that, in people of ordinary levels of intelligence, neurosis (minor mental disorder) is not necessarily disabling. They also remind us that while it is possible to use a scale for measuring neurosis in an individual or a group, the results vary considerably in the course of time. In other words, there is no good reason to suppose that, because an individual is unstable at one point in time, he will always be so. The young in particular show a tendency to settle with time as they approach more stable years. In their survey the same authors reached the conclusion that the limiting factor in employment for the mildly handicapped was not so much lack of intelligence or skill but rather emotional difficulties. They concluded, however, that only a minority of mildly retarded patients in hospital were affected by such a degree of neurosis as would impair their working capacity, and that these were eligible for treatment.

Traditional occupations

It was often considered that suitable forms of employment for the mentally handicapped were domestic service for women and agricultural work for men. This has not been our experience, and it is probably no longer true in contemporary Britain. On the other hand, a number of women ex-patients from institutions have been placed satisfactorily in domestic work in hospitals, in old people's homes, children's schools and other places of this kind. The position with private domestic work is very different today from what it was a hundred years ago. There are even less openings, and those that there are demand considerable versatility of talent. The domestic worker may still in some cases be expected to mind the baby, do the cooking, answer the phone, pay the milkman, operate the washing machine or the vacuum cleaner, do the shopping and a great variety of other jobs. She may be on her own for much of the time, and have limited supervision. Her mistress may be exacting and may demand excessive hours of working for a sub-standard wage. On the other hand, domestic work in a hospital is paid at a standard rate, there is good supervision, reasonable living quarters are provided, the hours are regulated, and there are usually opportunities to make friends and take part in social life. The work itself is more like work in light industry, inasmuch as there is a set routine with little variation and a limited number of different tasks. This gives the slow learner a chance to cope, and after much practice she will be able, hopefully, to produce the correct response to a given set of circumstances. In the writer's experience it has been found undesirable to take patients onto the staff of their own hospital since their status may suffer. They will still be regarded by the staff as patients. If they are to do hospital work, they should, therefore be employed in a general hospital.

On the whole it is preferable for most of the mildly retarded to find posts in light industry, though the problem of residence will have to be faced. The advantage of domestic work in a school or similar post is that residence will be provided. The advantage of industrial work is that the individual becomes a member of a close-knit team. She can see what the other workers are doing and will be affected by their tempo and industry. There will also be verbal and emotional exchange, and this will affect her working speed and attitude to work.

Work in agriculture has also seen big changes in recent years. During the Second World War the National Association for Mental Health in Britain ran some very successful agricultural hostels for the mentally retarded. There still is a place in agriculture for some young men of limited intelligence, and the Rudolf Steiner villages and similar organizations include agricultural activities in their régime. As a matter of policy, however, most hospitals for the mentally ill and the mentally retarded have decided to shift the emphasis from farming onto other forms of employment.

Farm work, especially on a smaller farm, tends to imply an even greater need for versatility than in domestic work. The very nature of agriculture demands constant adaptation dictated by the vagaries of the weather. Even a simple task, like hoeing turnips, demands skill to judge the right interval between the plants that are left and to distinguish between turnips and weeds. In contemporary agriculture, the emphasis is increasingly on machine work. Unlike factory machines, farm machines tend to be poorly protected, and are frequently a cause of accidents. For this reason alone they may be unsuitable for the mentally handicapped, unless there is careful supervision, and in the majority of cases this will, in fact, be difficult to provide. On smaller farms there will be little opportunity for team work. The individual may become lonely and, without the stimulus provided by supervision and emulation, he may work at a very slow pace and be regarded as unsatisfactory. It is self-evident that for farm work the individual should be reasonably robust, as he should for work as a builder's labourer. Some ex-patients have found jobs as nursery hands, or as jobbing gardeners or in public parks. These have less of the disadvantages of farm work mentioned above. In the park, however, it may be difficult to arrange adequate supervision, and there is limited teamwork. The nurseryman's job approximates more to light industry and there is an opportunity for teamwork and supervision with much repetitive activity, for example, in the potting shed.

Other forms of employment
The availability of local employment will determine choice, but many jobs that tend to be stereotyped, such as washing up in a large restaurant, are usually within the competence of most mildly retarded. It is worth repeating at this point that success or failure within a whole range of work will depend very much on the supervisor or foreman, on the way he handles relationships between the retarded person and other employees and on the way he tackles training and deals with any difficulties such as spoilt work, lateness, etc.

A number of parents have a small business of some kind, and some of the considerations which apply to employing ex-patients in their own hospital will be relevant here. If a son or daughter is employed in their father's business, or to do housework in the home, the parental expectation will usually be low, discipline will be slack and quite often there will be a revolt against parental authority. A handicapped youth may be doing minor jobs such as sweeping up and making tea which do not extend his capacity, and he may take advantage of being the 'boss's son' to waste time and to behave irresponsibly. Problems of automation have been illustrated in connection with employment in a particular firm manufacturing sweets. Prior to full automation, the kind of packing job offered by such a firm seemed very suitable. Full automation has greatly reduced the number of these unskilled jobs, but a few are still to be found. Another example is that of a gas-mantle factory, still actively in business at the time of writing. Some of the retarded employees in this factory sit at a long bench with a conveyor belt, packing the finished product. Others have at times done various jobs, such as operating a machine which trims the mantle, shaping it onto the support, or putting strips of impregnated material on racks to dry and pushing them into a cupboard. The fact that this place of employment has done well in employing the mentally retarded is due to the excellence of the forewoman.

Another type of work which still offers the advantages of simplicity, repetitiveness, supervision and teamwork is occupation in a laundry. For this the worker will need to be robust, if she is employed on lifting and handling linen and clothing. A number of workers are employed on sorting and folding, others on feeding items into or removing them from the calender. A proportion of people from hospitals for the mentally handicapped have been able to take paid work of this type. Many others are employed in the laundry in the hospital where they are patients. Those in open employment, however, receive the full wage for the job, whereas those who are in-patients in a hospital will receive a small reward for their efforts, though the contribution they make may be very similar. There may be a somewhat slower tempo in the hospital laundry. The principle difference is, however, in the relative levels of tolerance. The hospital laundry can take on the more severely handicapped and organize them so that the work is broken down for them. It may employ those who suffer fairly frequent fits or who have temperamental difficulties. Workers can be employed in the hospital unit who might have difficulty in finding their way to work by public transport, in paying for their ticket, in managing their wages and their budget, in completing forms, in asking for advice at work if they were not sure what to do, and in other forms of social adaptation.

From what has been said it will be clear that the main problem is often not in the job itself. It is possible to give a long list of suitable occupations, but this would not be very meaningful without precise specification of what was involved or what the exact circumstances were. The description 'van boy' might mean a youngster who travels on a van with a driver and who delivers parcels to private addresses. This would be a suitable task for a mildly mentally handicapped person. It would be much easier for him if the driver read the addresses and told him where to deliver, though he would soon learn a regular round. If, however, he were to be asked to collect money for the parcels, he might rapidly run into difficulties. Driving presents a special problem. The writer would not, as a rule, recommend a person with a Wechsler performance I.Q. of below 70 to drive a vehicle. But he has had in his care in the past a number of young men then considered to be mentally defective who were referred to hospital because they had been charged with taking and driving away motor vehicles. Similarly, examining recruits for the army showed a number of lorry drivers who had been driving for years without any apparent problems and yet who had quite low scores on intelligence tests. It may be that in driving, as in other activities, qualities other than intelligence are important—such as prudence, lack of undue aggression, steadiness.

Clerical activities appear by definition to be unsuitable for the mentally handicapped. There is, none the less, still room in some offices for a messenger or runner, and this duty may be performed by someone of lowish intelligence. There is no reason why simple filing and sorting routines should not also be carried out. This has been done in practice in hospital, and the resulting service proved very satisfactory even though the persons concerned were of a lower level of intelligence than those likely to be tried in open occupation. Here it is interesting to note that some people who have not learnt formal reading are yet able to distinguish individual items out of a series with reliable accuracy, for example, names of addresses, case papers, etc. This is presumably done by learning a minimum number of cues which make distinction possible.

One problem in deciding the suitability of employment for the mentally retarded is that both special schools and hospitals accept many individuals who are not strictly retarded in terms of measured intelligence. For example, a patient of the writer's at a time when a completely different régime from that applied at present was frequently returned to hospital from his employment in a public house. His problem was that he had acquired a taste for alcohol, but, in retrospect, his intelligence must have been at least average. He was returned to the hospital, not on account of mental retardation, but because no other solution for his problem had been found. Another ex-patient from a hospital for the mentally retarded has been employed for the past twenty years or more in a private home, where she can, if necessary, assume full responsibility for most activities. In her case, also, early deprivation was the problem, and not want of intelligence as such.

Preparation for open employment
O'Connor and Tizard, as we have seen, criticized the types of training they found provided in hospitals in 1952. Their argument, in fact, favoured much closer liaison between training units and open industry. They pointed out that large numbers of high-grade defect-

ives were employed on carpentry, book-binding, envelope making, box making, brush making, needlework, painting, building, wood chopping and bundling and shoe repairing. The names of the occupations gave little idea of what was actually done by the workers. The teaching methods, equipment and techniques were extremely old-fashioned and bore little relationship to the outside world. They suggested that, at that time, equipment in use in such units was so outdated that it actually cost money to use it, and the work learned in this way bore little relationship to the sort of job that the patient might expect to learn outside hospital. This situation related in part to the age of the institution, its limited budget and its isolation.

Shortly after the Second World War the writer was serving in a military psychiatric unit situated in a civilian mental hospital which was a prominent local landmark. He was summoned hastily to a fatal accident in the boiler-room. A patient had fallen from a gallery into the main pump and had been horribly mangled. It was understood that, had the premises been open for inspection under the terms of the Factory Acts, the arrangements would on no account have been tolerated. It was also suggested that the Science Museum in South Kensington would be interested in acquiring the pump for exhibition in view of its historic value. This incident is aside from the immediate theme, but it illustrates the total problem faced by existing outdated psychiatric institutions.

Adult training centres and industrial units run by local authorities do not have this problem, since they are, for the most part, new. They have, however, only recently been promoted from being occupation centres. It is important not to confuse the issue here by trying to bring terminology up to date. The function of such training centres is to improve by all possible means the level of skill and social competence of the severely mentally handicapped. There will come a point, however, when a reasonable level of skill relative to the age and potential of the individual will have been attained, and what is then required is, indeed, regular occupation. This should be as productive and as socially valuable and meaningful as possible. In the course of psychological research on motivation in industry, some workers, presumably of normal intelligence, were given a task and their speed was studied. The task was artificial in the sense that it consisted of packaging goods which were unpacked when the experiment was over. By some means the workers discovered this fact, whereupon they are said to have lost all interest in the work. There is no reason to suppose that the mentally handicapped would not react in a similar manner. Even at a very simple level, they have a lively appreciation of the social significance of products.

On the other hand, senior training centres also carry a certain number of the mildly mentally handicapped and are attempting to fit them into a job in the community. In present circumstances it is not certain whether these units are the best place for such training. It is certainly true that people of doubtful suitability for open employment will be far better off attending such a centre than vegetating at home, but it is also the case that the centre may have difficulty in providing training and experience strictly relevant to the kind of job for which the individual might qualify, or which he wishes to do. Retarded people, like ordinary people, often have very definite ideas about the job they want to do. Sometimes these views may seem illogical or based on prejudice, but unless a job is really entered upon voluntarily, there will be little prospect of success.

In view of the radical changes at present taking place in the organization of services for the mentally handicapped, the time seems ripe for an urgent review of facilities for job placement and training. It would seem logical that there should be some youth employment officer on an area basis who could collect information about local firms with work suitable for the mentally handicapped and maintain liaison with foremen and supervisors who have been successful in making placements. They would then be in a position to supply this information to their colleagues, to hospital social workers and to headmasters of special schools. They could also act as consultants for specially difficult cases. Various schemes of this kind have been undertaken, but the information is not generally available.

The policy of existing industrial training and rehabilitation units, whether under departmental or private control, should be reviewed at the same time. Some of these units have excellent facilities, but have been reluctant to take on the training of the mentally handicapped. An intensive course at such a unit with a realistic tempo, approach and equipment might be of much more value to the person marginally suitable for employment than spending a long period in a senior training centre geared primarily to the needs of the more severely handicapped.

Leisure
There is little enough provision for leisure in institutions where grown men and women are often put to bed at an early hour, like

infants. The situation in the home may be little better, though it will be eased by the incidental diversity of ordinary life. Retarded adolescents are like those of better intelligence in the sense that their minds are still developing, still fresh and receptive to new experiences and opportunities. Opportunities are needed for learning household skills, such as simple cooking, for overcoming illiteracy on the least ambitious scale, for finding a suitable hobby and for engaging in sport. These are some examples of what is necessary; these needs have been met here and there in a fragmentary manner. The education authorities and voluntary bodies could do much more. Whilst the handicapped resent open patronage as much as the rest of us, it should be possible by tact and skill to interest many more existing voluntary bodies in including retarded young people in their activities and consciously helping them to attain full citizenship.

Chapter 12
Research

This is the age of technology. Man has succeeded in sending his own kind to the moon and bringing him back again. It is possible to destroy the whole population of New York in a few seconds or to kill a single man with one drop of 'nerve gas'. Vast crop-producing areas of Vietnam have been turned into deserts by the military use of defoliants. Drugs have been invented which can cripple the human mind. Despite all these and many other scientific achievements, man knows little of the forces which control his destiny, or which determine his intellect, his motivation, his behaviour. The tiny brain of a pigeon conceals more mysteries than have yet been revealed by all the electronic engineers and atomic physicists.

Apart from threatening to destroy himself in the short or the long term, man has done much to better his own lot in the interval. He has greatly lengthened the span of his life, has brought under control most of the important infectious diseases and has enormously increased food production. He has created science and art. If a small fraction of the budget which directs knowledge, skill and inventiveness to the perfection of weapons and the exploration of space were to be devoted to an understanding of the human brain and its imperfections, many of the tragedies with which this book it concerned could be averted. Brain damage and malformations are just as capable of being understood and, therefore, of being controlled as smallpox. It will take longer, it will need more effort, but it is possible. The stunting of the human intellect by unfavourable circumstances is, in principle, avoidable and presents no insuperable technical problem. If the resources and privileges accorded to the Registrar General's Class I were extended to all the other classes this aim would largely be achieved. The task is one for the economist and for the commonsense of ordinary people, when it is possible for this to be expressed.

It is not necessary to demand the astronomical budgets spent on preparation for war or on investigation of space. Just a fraction of the money spent on alcohol, tobacco, betting and cosmetics would be ample to promote a research programme which would radically change man's understanding of himself in general and, in particular, could set him well on the way to controlling and preventing mental handicap.

Britain has at present no major research unit which has as its brief the investigation of all aspects of mental handicap, its causation, prevention and amelioration. Many of the advances which have been made in this field have occurred almost by chance or as a by-product of other work, and were not primarily directed to mental handicap. Much progress has been made as a result of the interest of gifted individuals who have temporarily influenced the direction of work of the team of which they were members. When Professor Penrose (author of the classic Colchester survey) was at the Galton Laboratory at University College, London, he was able to organize a whole series of productive researches into this field. This applies similarly to the studies which have emanated from the Social Psychiatry Unit of the Medical Research Council at the Institute of Psychiatry during the term of office of Tizard and O'Connor in that Unit. Since then they have been able to influence other workers in academic establishments to apply themselves to the field of mental handicap. The results have been very valuable, and doubtless much further information will emerge from what appear to be chance discoveries or from the inspiration of individuals. However, the size and urgency of the problem is such that it cannot be left to chance and individual effort alone. During the Second World War, concentrated and organized effort solved, in a remarkably short time, complex problems of malaria and scrub typhus infestation. Concentration of effort on mental handicap could produce similarly gratifying results.

Only a quarter of a century ago, my colleagues and I at the Fountain Hospital set out at a scientific meeting the proposition that mental handicap should be a matter of public health, and could be tackled by strategies similar to those already in use in preventive medicine. This view was met with frank disbelief by those in authority at the time. Today, however, there is little need to argue the case. It is readily accepted by government departments and by a majority of the professions concerned. Despite this, the logical conclusions have still not been drawn, and there is no organized effort to tackle the problem of mental handicap on the scale it deserves.

Recent developments
A brief outline of some of the advances in relation to mental handicap may help to illustrate the possibility of further progress. Inevitably, work in this field is related to wider scientific and social progress.

What is lacking is consistent effort to utilize the advances made in other sciences.

Cretinism may be used to illustrate some of the principles involved. This is a rare condition today in South-east England, but it does occasionally cause mental handicap, sometimes severe. It is now known to be the result of the absence or faulty function of the thyroid gland in the neck. If this gland is not working properly in the adult, it leads to a condition known as myxoedema. In this condition there is premature dementia, loss of intelligence. If thyroid function is not properly established in the infant, the result will be cretinism and a failure of brain function and the growth of intelligence. Inorganic chemistry was sufficiently advanced in the nineteenth century to show that there was more iodine in the thyroid gland than any other part of the body. It was then appreciated that thyroid disorders, such as goitre or 'Derbyshire neck', occurred in limestone areas away from the sea—areas where there was a shortage of natural iodine intake. It is only during the present century that the need for supplementing deficient diets with iodine in salt has been appreciated.

There is plenty of experimental evidence from work with animals to show that if the thyroid gland is not working properly there will be dwarfing and failure of brain development as well as other effects. Organic chemistry then revealed that the active principle of the thyroid gland—the 'hormone' or 'chemical messenger'—is a substance known as thyroxin, and that this contains iodine. Experimental therapeutics showed that this substance would return function to normal in organisms deprived of a thyroid gland. Long before this, however, it had been realized that giving thyroid gland to cretins by mouth greatly improved their growth and appearance. It was later appreciated that the diagnosis must be made at a very early stage if damage to the brain was to be prevented. The giving of fresh or dried thyroid was an effective way of replacing thyroid function. Exact dosage was necessary, since excess of thyroid is poisonous. But it was not until pure active thyroxin was available that the dose could be accurately standardized. This substance has now replaced the crude gland preparation.

Our present understanding of this form of mental handicap derives from these pioneer studies by chemists, clinicians, workers in experimental medicine, pharmacologists and psychologists.

It was gradually appreciated that there were several forms of cretinism. Anatomical studies showed that some cretins were lacking a thyroid gland, and that others had a gland in the right place. Then the development of the use of radioactive isotopes greatly facilitated studies of the action of the gland. If a small dose of radioactive iodine was given, much of it was taken up by a normal gland. If the neck was then monitored for radioactivity, a significant amount was detected. On the other hand, if the gland was absent, most of the radioactive element would be excreted by the kidneys and the radioactivity detected in the urine. In this way physics, and atomic physics in particular, made a useful contribution to clinical science.

There are certain disadvantages in principle to the use of radioactive substances in the body if this can be avoided and biochemistry provides a very acceptable method for testing thyroid function. The amount of cholesterol in the blood may be a useful guide, as it tends to increase in thyroid failure. More specific is the amount of iodine in the blood. This is usually assessed as 'protein bound iodine' since the free iodine is not active as thyroxin. Recent work has shown that in a few cases this measure can be misleadingly low because in some individuals with a normal thyroid function there is a failure of the mechanism by which iodine is bound to protein. But such cases are rare, and the broad principle of the method stands. A great advance in this connection and in similar biochemical investigations has been the development of micro-methods. Fifty years ago, most methods of analysis demanded a large amount of blood from a vein. This was impracticable in the case of babies. Nowadays half a millilitre of blood obtained from a finger, heel or ear prick is sufficient for many purposes.

Further light was thrown on the complicated problem of cretinism when it was understood that in some cases, although the thyroid gland was present, it did not function normally. There may or may not have been enlargement (a goitre) but the hormone thyroxin was not properly formed. There are several ways in which this substance may be chemically malformed, so there are several different chemical varieties of cretinism. Chemical reactions in the body go in chains. One is followed by another. A block anywhere along the line may cause a hold-up and an undesirable accumulation of some substance combined with a shortage of others which should be formed. In cretinism, it is the shortage of active thyroxin which counts. In phenylketonuria, it is the build-up of phenylalanine and other substances which interferes with normal chemistry. Each link in the chain of chemical processes calls for an appropriate enzyme. Unless this enzyme is formed under the guidance of the particular gene responsible, the chemical reaction will not take place.

In general since the various chemical forms of cretinism are hereditary, more than one case can occur in a family. However, there are substances such as those in which thyroid hormone is involved, which interfere with the action of chemical processes. One of these is thiouracil, a drug used to counteract excessive thyroid activity. Some people suffer from Grave's disease or hyperthyroidism, a condition in which the heart beats too fast, the body burns energy too rapidly and the eyes may protrude. Thiouracil may be used in such cases. If a pregnant woman suffering from overactivity of the thyroid is treated with thiouracil, this may interfere with the function of the thyroid in the foetus and disturb its development.

It was a century ago that Langdon Down's clear description of Down's syndrome made it possible to distinguish this condition from cretinism. During the century which has elapsed many sciences have contributed to a better understanding of errors of function of the thyroid gland and cretinism. As knowledge has accumulated, it has been applied only slowly in practice, largely because of limited interest in the subject and insufficient effort. If more resources were devoted to similar problems, the fertilizing effect of other sciences would be more readily brought to bear and better use would be made of existing knowledge. For a long time after the death of Langdon Down cretinism and 'mongolism' tended to be confused. For many years it was customary to recommend thyroid for Down's syndrome though benefit has never been demonstrated, and such children do not suffer any impairment of thyroid function.

It is often suggested that laboratory facilities are wasted if they are used in a 'blunderbuss' fashion for diagnosis. It remains true that requests for laboratory aids should be made with discretion by a wise clinician. Increasingly, however, as the reliability of laboratory tests improves, there is a field for regular 'screening' procedures. An example is the Guthrie test for phenylketonuria. Many children's centres will now include measurement of protein-bound iodine in the blood as a routine test of thyroid function in any infant who is making poor progress. One reason for this kind of approach is that not all cases of disease are typical. The clinician may recognize the obvious case at the bedside but fail to detect the unusual case. Another problem affecting disease involving the brain such as cretinism is that if diagnosis is delayed until symptoms are obvious, irreparable damage will already have been done. Lawson followed cases of cretinism which had been treated and found that results in terms of mental development were far from satisfactory. One reason for this is delay in making the diagnosis.

It is often believed that the older generations of clinicians were very wise and that because they lacked the aids which we take for granted they used their powers of observation much more effectively. This is nonsense. Although there were brilliant clinicians, like Langdon Down, whose wisdom and powers of observation enabled so many pictures of disease to be recognized, the great majority of doctors were able to recognize only a limited number of conditions. They therefore invented all manner of non-existent conditions to explain symptoms and made very frequent mistakes in diagnosis. There was a widespread tendency, perhaps particularly evident in the French school at the turn of the century, to attribute almost every evil to alcohol or sexual indulgence. Up till very recently and in the writer's own experience the role of syphilis in mental handicap was grossly exaggerated. The increased use of refined laboratory techniques has been most salutary because it has shown clinicians their mistakes. The author remembers one eminent and respected teacher of neurology expounding a case to his students as an example of a rare condition. Unhappily his houseman, in an audible whisper, told him after the exposition that the laboratory findings were characteristic of general paralysis of the insane. If the most distinguished and perceptive of clinicians could make such gross errors, there is no need for the rest of us to be ashamed of the free use of laboratory aids. Nor, indeed, is there any excuse for failing to make full use of laboratory facilities whenever these may be relevant to the detection and prevention of disease.

Cretinism is also an example of a condition in which diagnostic errors can often occur. One of the considerations about treatment of such diseases by 'replacement therapy' is that the treatment is not curative. If there is a genuine deficiency of thyroid activity, treatment must be continued throughout life. Many infants with no demonstrable defect of the thyroid have been subjected to long periods of treatment with thyroid, happily perhaps in most cases without too much ill effect. Phenlyketonuria was discovered in 1934 by a Norwegian biochemist named Fölling. Penrose found a number of phenylketonuria cases at Colchester (1938) and the condition was well recognized here but in the late 1940s the writer came across a brother and sister with this condition who had been treated at a teaching hospital as cases of cretinism. This kind of error implies no criticism of individuals but illustrates the lack of systematic study of infants at the time. The resources then available were not being routinely applied. This situation is being gradually remedied but the process is impeded by limited economic resources and, though to a decreasing extent, by the dogma that a mystic clinical 'sixth sense' will somehow substitute for laboratory screening. The accumulation of information in the course of such screening constitutes one kind of systematic research since it enables comparison to be made between what is observed in the clinic and what is found in the laboratory. The great variation in the manifestation of disease symptoms is thus exposed, and attention drawn away from the misleading typical 'text-book picture', which may be the exception rather than the rule.

Whilst the discovery of an effective treatment of cretinism was a great advance, it is obvious that the ultimate aim must always be prevention. Even with the most careful clinical study and the most comprehensive screening procedures, some cases will be missed until irreparable damage to the brain has been done. Of the several rare forms of chemical error causing cretinism, most are handed on indirectly in affected families. If the diagnosis is established, genetic counselling should be available. The risk of further children being affected appears to be of the order of one in four, and there are few patients who would be willing to take such a risk. As technical development proceeds, it should be possible to detect those members of the family who have only one of the abnormal genes which lead to cretinism, and who are therefore carriers. Such individuals may not be completely unaffected and may show minor signs of abnormality. This is certainly a field for further research. At this stage in technical development it seems unlikely that it will be possible in the near future to distinguish an affected foetus early in pregnancy by amniotic puncture. Doubtless, if such a project were made the subject of intensive co-ordinated research the problem could be resolved. It would then be feasible to terminate a pregnancy if the baby was affected, and to allow it to continue if not.

The cause of anatomical abnormality in those cases where there is no effective thyroid gland involves another branch of knowledge—immunology. It seems likely from the work of Blizzard and others that in a number of babies in whom the thyroid has failed to develop the mother has anti-thyroid antibodies in her blood. The reason for this is not at present clear. It seems likely that this area of knowledge may become increasingly important in understanding mental handicap. The best known examples of this kind of situation are those involving blood groups, especially the case where the mother has anti-D in her blood against the Rhesus positive baby with the D sub-group. Rarer examples are maternal immunity against the blood group known as Kell, and the ABO blood group incompatibility. At present it is not entirely possible to exclude maternal immunity to brain tissue as a cause of brain abnormality in babies. Such a state can exist and can be produced experimentally in animals. If they are given an injection of brain material they may develop a degeneration of their own brain. It seems theoretically possible that there could be such antibodies in some women, and these could interfere with the development of the brain in a baby. Certainly this is a field which is overdue for further exploration. The example of Rhesus antibody has shown how the formation of this type of substance may be avoided.

A very different kind of problem, but one which also concerns immunity, is posed by those cases of subacute encephalitis which are thought to be due to measles acting slowly over a long period of time. Measles is usually an acute disease and the fact that it can smoulder on in the brain in some children for years suggests that they are unable to react to it with normal defence mechanisms.

Antenatal care
The example of cretinism has been discussed to show how different scientific disciplines have contributed to growth of knowledge about this condition, how more could have been done sooner if there had been concerted effort, and what a great number of questions remain unanswered. We can now consider briefly how scientific research might help, and has already helped, in the care of the pregnant woman.

It is generally agreed that those women who receive antenatal care are more likely to have healthy babies. It does not require much research to show that illegitimate babies whose mothers are often slow to come forward for antenatal care, do less well. One way in which medical and nursing care during pregnancy can help is by providing various types of routine screening. The possibility of syphilitic damage to the unborn baby was recognized long ago, but it was not until the introduction of the Wassermann reaction and other blood tests that it became possible to check for this infection during pregnancy. Another test now regularly done involves blood grouping. This is useful for the mother if she requires an emergency transfusion at the time of childbirth, but it is also important for the baby, as it identifies those mothers who are Rhesus negative. These mothers, if they have a Rhesus positive husband, are at risk of becoming immunized at the end of their first pregnancy and so of developing antibodies to any subsequent Rhesus positive baby. In such women, therefore, it is important to check for antibodies and to estimate the amount present at intervals during the pregnancy. If they are present in a considerable amount, the baby may need an exchange transfusion when he is born, in some cases it may be decided to induce labour early, before too much damage has been done.

Considerable interest has been shown recently in 'small for dates' babies. It has long been realized that very small babies are more delicate and therefore more likely to die. Where they survive, as we have seen already, they run an increased risk of epilepsy, cerebral palsy, mental handicap and other forms of brain abnormality. They can be divided into two groups. There are those babies who are premature by date. That is, they are born well before the end of the ninth month of pregnancy. Another group, which tend to do badly are those babies who go to term but who are none the less small. It is not fully understood why this happens. In some cases there is something wrong with the baby. Many babies with Down's syndrome or with other chromosome errors or genetic abnormality are small, although born at term. In other cases there seems to be something wrong with the mother's ability to nourish the child in the womb. Why this should be so is not yet clear. If, after the seventh month of pregnancy, it is suspected that this is the case, and that the baby is failing to grow through being undernourished in the uterus, it may be in the baby's interest to be born earlier than term so that he can receive adequate nourishment in the outside environment as a premature baby.

Research is going on at present into various ways of finding out how well the placenta, or afterbirth, is doing in its task of nourishing the baby. We can measure various hormones and enzymes in the mother's blood to give us a guide to the placenta's activity. One of these substances is known as oxytocinase. If the value of this enzyme is low, the baby may be one of those 'small for dates'. A sudden drop in oxytocinase in the mother's blood is likely to spell trouble, which may take the form of an infarct—a blockage of a blood vessel with cutting off of part of the supply of blood to the placenta. At present this work is at an exploratory stage, but it has a potential value and may lead to better methods, helping to prevent the birth of at least some underdeveloped babies. One of the difficulties of this kind of screening programme on a large scale is that the laboratory work must be streamlined. In modern terms, this involves automation. Here again it is difficult to avoid casting an envious eye on the vast sums made available to space programme or the arms race. Meanwhile medical scientists are struggling with very limited resources to introduce automation into the laboratory. They have little support from commercial companies since this is not a financially attractive field for investment. The Department of Health and Social Security in Britain has given some help in the assessment of scientific apparatus, but has to cope with considerable difficulties because of the limited resources. If steady progress is to be achieved, there must be a different emphasis in priorities both in government and private spending.

Similar considerations apply to attempts to assess the work of the placenta by measuring the amount of other substances. These include the total amount of oestrogens (female hormones) put out in the urine during twenty-four hours and the serum cystine aminopeptidase. It was found that this latter substance, which is an enzyme involved in the work of the placenta, offers a useful guide to the efficiency of this organ. The amount of the enzyme rises as pregnancy proceeds and is abnormally low in small for dates babies. It is possible also that this kind of assay may be useful in pregnancies which carry additional risk for the baby such as those in which the mother suffers from diabetes. These methods will likewise have to be automated if they are to come into general use for screening during pregnancy.

Technical development

If progress is to be made in research into mental handicap, it is essential that scientists with a high level of qualification should be attracted. Most of those who take up or remain in this type of work do so at considerable financial sacrifice, since they could command higher salaries in industry. Every effort should be made to remove this disparity. At present, chemists, physicists and others who engage in medical work do so very much on a vocational basis. The structure of the service is such that scientists who are not medically qualified tend to be relegated to inferior position and status. Yet many of the necessary advances, as we have seen, will come from non-medical scientists. In the work on enzymes mentioned above it is necessary to have reliable methods which lend themselves to automation. At first many of the methods used for such assays were biological. That is, they were dependent on the use of living organisms. This applies to the Guthrie test, and, although this has proved very serviceable, it is likely that it will be replaced in due course by a method which is simply chemical and does not need the use of bacteria. In general this leads to greater reliability and ease of automation.

Another substance which is likely to prove very important in mental handicap is known as serotonin. There is not enough of it in babies with Down's syndrome and those with phenylketonuria if they are not treated. On the other hand, there is too much of it in some children with cerebral palsy. Attempts have been made to treat children with Down's syndrome by increasing the amount of serotonin to normal levels. It is doubtful whether this will in itself do much to improve the intelligence of these children, but it will doubtless add to our understanding of their handicap. It seems to remedy the tendency which they have to 'floppiness' of the muscles and brings back their muscle tone to normal. In connection with work on this substance it also proved necessary to measure the amount of an enzyme known as adenosine tri-phosphatase. For this purpose an extract was made from fireflies; it was essential to have Sicilian fireflies since the American variety do not contain the requisite enzyme. It is clear that different samples of biological material are likely to be very variable and also at times difficult to procure.

At one time chemical methods of assay of biological substances were revolutionized by the use of colorimetry. This provided for the matching of a colour against a standard. The matching was done by eye and had the disadvantage of subjectivity and human error. Considerable advances have been made by the use of objective spectroscopy, which involves automatic registration of the amount of absorption of light in different wave bands. A further development which facilitates more subtle and delicate analysis is the employment of fluorescence. These contributions—and many others—have been made by chemists. They will increasingly permit the supplementing of clinical observation by laboratory methods sufficiently delicate to reveal much information which cannot be obtained by ordinary methods of investigation.

Future developments
The prevention of mental handicap implies concern with all stages of human development; hereditary factors, maternal health prior to pregnancy, factors which might affect the sex cells before fertilization, the maturation of the egg cell, fertilization itself, implantation of the egg cell in the womb, factors influencing the embryo during pregnancy, delivery itself and events occurring about that time, the newborn period, the early years, childhood and adolescence, the home, the school, the social background and economic and psychological considerations. Technical developments are more likely to have a bearing on events in the early stages. Much of the work needed for prevention in the later stages relates to the application

of existing knowledge. Even here, however, there is a great need for the extension of the scope and depth of methodical research, for example, to see how lasting are improvements in the intelligence of the mildly handicapped when these have been brought about by opportunities for further development.

One example of the application of a technique uses the creation of fluorescence to render the male or Y chromosome visible. The substance mepacrine or atebrin, better known for its extensive use in malaria prevention, can be employed for this purpose. Even more successful is one of the 'mustard' type of substances, which have been used to destroy malignant cells in leukaemia. This technique renders the male chromosome clearly visible as a bright spot against a dark background, while female cells show no such bright body since they have no Y chromosome. Normal male cells will show one such body, but those unusual males (see page 40) who have more than one Y chromosome, will show two. It is not clear as yet to what extent this development will be important for the study of mental handicap, as this new technique is only a beginning of selective staining of the chromosomes.

Much work has already been done in the autoradiography of chromosomes. This technique involves the use of radioactive isotopes in chemical compounds which are absorbed by the chromosome in cell culture. This permits at least tentative distinction of one chromosome of about the same size from another. Further development of these and other initial approaches may reveal inversions and other structural changes in the chromosomes which are at present difficult to visualize. It is thus possible to anticipate a great extension of the present work on investigation into major and more subtle changes in chromosome structure. Such an advance could possibly make a considerable inroad into the yet as undiagnosed majority of cases of severe mental handicap.

A great many conditions have been described which are associated with mental retardation and others doubtless remain to be recognized. It is not at all certain if all of these can genuinely be regarded as separate conditions in the sense that they have the same cause. There are, for example, a few children with broad thumbs and big toes and who have faces which so resemble each other that they almost seem to belong to the same family. This condition has been labelled the Rubinstein-Taybi syndrome. So far the affected children have not proved to have anything wrong with their enzymes or their chromosomes. Another condition encountered from time to time is known as Amsterdam dwarfism, described by Cornelia de Lange.

These children are usually very retarded and dwarfed, have heavy brows which meet in the middle as well as other imperfections, and they also look very alike. In these and many other conditions, it seems possible that a common cause will be found if the search is sufficiently intensive. In other conditions the likenesses between the affected children may be purely coincidental.

Co-ordinated research

Most new advances in the understanding, prevention, treatment and amelioration of mental handicap involve teamwork. In the past some geneticists were occupied in studying family histories of congenital cataract, a condition not uncommonly associated with mental handicap. At that time many of the causes of cataract with which we are now familiar were not understood. We now know that cataract may be caused by German measles in the mother during pregnancy, by the disease known as galactosaemia, or, occasionally by a disease named after Lowe which affects the eye, the brain and the kidney. Congenital cataract may in all of these conditions be associated with mental handicap, and with a number of other defects. By using information derived from different specialists it is now possible to study the relationship between mental handicap and cataract in a much more meaningful way, and by genetic studies to follow the inheritance of the disease as a whole rather than in an isolated symptom.

Pooling of information

It is recognized that in the field of public health there is a need for central pooling of information. For this reason infectious diseases such as smallpox and typhoid are notifiable to the health authority. Arrangements are also made for registration of industrial diseases. In the field of cancer research, statistics and information are regularly collected. In regard to mental handicap, little work of this kind has been done. Statistics are collected on patients admitted to psychiatric hospitals, but these are limited both in scope and reliability, depending, as they do, very much on local interpretation and expertise. It would seem, particularly in the long term, desirable to have much more information of an epidemiological nature. Some attempt has been made to compile a register of phenylketonuria cases. There is evidence of local variation of phenylketonuria from one region to another, it being more common in Liverpool and Glasgow than in South-east England. This approach could be applied to other, rarer, conditions. Knowledge of existing cases should bring to light others in the family, though due regard must be paid to the confidentiality of information. A knowledge of identity of cases of metabolic disorders such as phenylketonuria which can be treated permits long-term study of the natural history of the disease and of the beneficial effect of treatment.

If proper planning of services is to be undertaken it seems very desirable to be able to follow the long-term trend of such conditions as Down's syndrome. There is no information at present as to whether the incidence at birth of this condition is remaining constant, is increasing or decreasing. If there is any considerable change, this would clearly be of the utmost importance in directing attention to the ultimate cause of the condition. Similar considerations apply to the pooling of information about new mutations, such as those causing tuberous sclerosis or Apert's syndrome. The possibility of local variation from one area to another, such as those found in spina bifida, is important and may throw light on the cause or predisposing factors. A pool of information about the rare conditions will also be particularly helpful in pursuing any special lines of investigation in cause or treatment.

Teamwork
The need for teamwork is better appreciated today but only limited use is made of the possibilities for research implicit in a multi-disciplinary organization. This is essentially because of restricted resources. In an example of the need for such an approach, it is possible to take diseases which are clinically fairly easily recognizable. One of these is known as dystrophia myotonica, a condition often associated with limited intelligence. It is rare, and is directly transmissible through a dominant type of genetic error. There is progressive muscular wasting of the face and other areas, and difficulty in relinquishing the grip. There may also be cataract, and in males the testes may be small. It seems almost certain that in a genetic condition of this type there must be a recognizable enzyme fault but this has not yet been discovered. It seems at least possible that a concentrated biochemical effort could break the deadlock, and possibly even lead to remedial treatment. If such a laboratory test for the disease could be devised, it might lead to the detection of potential cases, even before the symptoms had appeared, in families where the condition is present.

A comparison can be made here between diseases such as dystrophia myotonica, where the chemical error is unknown, and others such as Wilson's disease, in which more is known about the biochemistry. In Wilson's disease, as a result of co-operative efforts between clinicians and laboratory workers, there is now much more understanding about the relevant processes in the body. It seems that the mental retardation which develops in Wilson's disease is due to the accumulation of copper in the brain. A substance in the blood which normally carries copper is deficient, so that the metal is more easily deposited in the brain. Success has been reported in preventing brain damage in early cases of the condition by use of a drug which binds the copper and assists its removal from the body.

The introduction of the dietetic method of treatment of phenylketonuria is an excellent example of the success of a team method (see pp. 33-5). The initial approach was suggested by a biochemist who was able to obtain a suitable protein substitute containing only a limited amount of phenylalanine and supplemented as necessary with vitamins and other essentials. The clinical application was undertaken by a children's specialist and the assessment of the progress of the children treated was carried out by a psychologist. To obtain successful results many other specialists may also be involved —the dietician, the nurse and, in the detection of new cases, the bacteriologist, who has made a striking contribution in the shape of the Guthrie test.

On occasion, the introduction of a new discipline into a situation which has changed little over a long period will provide a fresh lead. This applies to the example of the use of telemetering to record evoked potentials in the brain as a means of assessing hearing or the application of the same technique to the transmission of information about changes in muscle tone as a result of auditory impulses. Research into the behaviour of children who are disturbed, overactive, non-communicating, destructive or anti-social can present special problems if their behaviour is to be observed objectively and an assessment made of, say, improvement produced by conditioning techniques. For comparison, it would be necessary to know how often a child has been hitting herself, banging her head, picking herself, tearing her clothes, screaming etc., before treatment. We can then make a similar record afterwards to demonstrate how much improvement has been achieved. The presence of an observer alters the situation and the child's behaviour. Use was therefore made in one research programme of a bird-watching technique, at the suggestion of a zoologist. A portable 'hide' was brought into the ward and from this regular observation could be conducted.

Sustained effort

Some research in the field of mental handicap has been specifically funded by parents of affected children who, as individuals and as a body, show a great interest in seeking remedies. This interest is largely altruistic, since in most cases any information gained would be too late to benefit their particular child. The Institute for Research into Mental Retardation, now well established, was made possible through the initiative of the National Society for Mentally Handicapped Children and has the full support of that body. The aim of the Institute is, however, to attract further support for this field of endeavour from academic bodies and government sources. It is hoped that the Institute will be able to establish its own premises and actively conduct research in addition to funding projects which are relevant to the problem. The Institute also acts as a forum in the field, organizing symposia and study-groups designed to promote research activities and also to provide a central source of information. It is hoped that the influence of the Institute will be such as to direct applied research into channels appropriate to an understanding of brain abnormality and child development. Such a body can act as a focus to stimulate the interest of specialists in different disciplines.

There is sometimes a tendency to distinguish between 'medical' and 'educational' research in this field. It is neither possible nor desirable to make any such sharp distinction.

It is possible to divide research into mental handicap into two broad areas, those of causation and those of amelioration. Even these overlap very much, especially with mild mental handicap. With more severe degrees of brain damage the fundamental research is biological—finding out why the brain failed to develop properly or why it became damaged. In amelioration we are concerned with a study of behaviour and efforts to adapt this to socially acceptable forms. If we accept that much mild handicap results from deprivation, then research into amelioration is also research into prevention.

The Hester Adrian Research Centre for the Study of Learning Processes in the Mentally Handicapped, directed by Dr Peter Mittler, is a part of the University of Manchester. As the name indicates, this centre exists specifically to deal with the particular problem of learning defects in the mentally handicapped, and will therefore continue to focus the attention of psychologists and others on this area. Its findings must necessarily be of great interest to teachers, psychiatrists, social workers and others concerned with the habilitation of less gifted children. One major difficulty in the past has been how we can best apply abstract and academic findings to practical use in the classroom, home or place of work. The work of Dr Mittler and his team should do much to bridge this gap.

These two institutions have been singled out for special mention because their designation and terms of reference ensure that they will continue to function in the manner outlined above. A great number of other Units make contributions which are extremely valuable but, as mentioned, the effort is not always sustained—it may depend on individual interest, or may be coincidental.

Whilst every advance in relevant sciences brings potential aid to the cause of the mentally handicapped, this may not be realized in practice unless there is someone with an interest in and knowledge of the problem, putting the right questions to other scientists. Experimental scientists may be quite happy to study the upbringing of monkeys and the problems of their family life, while for others rats are very absorbing. Much can be learnt from work of this kind, but it remains true that the study of man himself is more likely to be immediately fruitful in understanding failures and errors in human development.

It must be admitted that we tend to be so emotionally involved in our own kind that some truths become more obvious only when we study other organisms. Pavlov had to study dogs to discover how the human brain worked, for psychology at that time was fettered by armchair philosophy. Now that stage is behind us, however, we can fruitfully turn back to aspects of human studies which have often been neglected. It is possible sometimes to form an impression that human research is less well thought of, is held in lower esteem, is somehow considered less scientific, than work on some other organism. Studies by Tizard, Mittler, Hermelin, O'Connor, the Clarkes and others have shown not only how much can be contributed by interested scientists to an understanding of mental handicap, but also how much studies have helped in an understanding of humanity in general. A film by the Clarkes showing some of their earlier work with the mentally handicapped was called *Learning in Slow Motion*. It is a well-established technique to run films in slow motion and it is recognized that by doing so we can learn much that would otherwise pass unnoticed. In the very retarded, the learning process is, in fact, reduced to slow motion and to its simplest form, but it remains essentially human; every lesson learnt still has an application for education as a whole. This is true of all aspects of research into the mentally handicapped. The enormous volume of knowledge about the functioning of the normal human brain gained from the study of phenylketonuria alone illustrates this. The rapid growth of our understanding in the past decade of the tangled skein of human heredity derives almost entirely from a closer scrutiny of malformed babies.

The scientific investigation of our less fortunate children can be as intellectually rewarding as any aspect of science. It is particularly valuable in those areas of knowledge in which man is weakest: knowledge of himself. It is also emotionally rewarding, since every advance may help to prevent a tragedy for one family or bring to another the consolation of some improvement in their afflicted child.

Among the stories and pictures of wars which have come down to us across 4,000 years of history from Babylon and other ancient cultures, are accurate clinical descriptions of diseases, including those that afflict the brain causing stroke among other personal catastrophes. The pace of progress in the healing arts has been slow across the centuries, until our own days, when it has suddenly grown wings. In the interval, man has ceased to be a slave for barter. He is now, potentially, at least, his own master, on the threshold of a self-understanding which may save civilization whilst there is still time. It may yet be shown that a proper understanding of idiocy is the key to human genius. It is certain that our attitude to those who are weakest among us is a touchstone of the compassion without which mankind must perish.

Bibliography

Additional Reading

1 FOR PARENTS

1. Collins, J. *Help Your Child to Play.* Northern Ireland Region of National Society for Mentally Handicapped Children, Belfast, 1970.
2. Brinkworth, R. and Collins, J. *Improving Mongol Babies and Introducing Them to School.* Northern Ireland Region of National Society for Mentally Handicapped Children, Belfast, 1969.
3. Dobzhansky, T. *Heredity and The Nature of Man.* George Allen and Unwin, London, 1965.
4. Morris, P. *Put Away: a sociological study of institutions for the mentally retarded.* Routledge and Kegan Paul, London, 1969.
5. Furneaux, B. *The Special Child.* Penguin Books, Harmondsworth, 1969.
6. Hutchison, A. (Chairman). *Stress in Families with a Mentally Handicapped Child.* National Society for Mentally Handicapped Children, London, 1967.
7. Dybwad, G. *Challenges in Mental Retardation.* Columbia, New York, 1964.
8. Molloy, J. S. *Teaching the Retarded Child to Talk: a guide for parents and teachers.* University of London Press, London, 1965.
9. Duffie, O. *Help Your Child To Talk.* Northern Ireland Region of National Society for Mentally Handicapped Children, Belfast.
10. La Frenais, M. *Language Stimulus with Retarded Children.* National Society for Mentally Handicapped Children, London.

2 FOR TEACHERS, SOCIAL WORKERS AND OTHERS

1. Tizard, J. *Community Services for The Mentally Handicapped*. Oxford University Press, London, 1964.
2. O'Connor, N. and Tizard, J. *The Social Problem of Mental Deficiency*. Pergamon Press, London, 1956.
3. Tizard, J. and Grad, J. C. *The Mentally Handicapped and Their Families*. Oxford University Press, London, 1961.
4. Clarke, A. M. and Clarke, A. D. B. *Mental Deficiency: the changing outlook*. Methuen, London, 1965.
5. Rutter, M., Tizard, J. and Whitmore, K. *Education, Health and Behaviour*. Longman, London, 1970.
6. Carter, C. O. *Human Heredity*. Penguin Books, Harmondsworth, 1967.
7. Joffe, J. M. *Prenatal Determinants of Behaviour*. Pergamon Press, Oxford, 1969.
8. Clarke, A. D. B. *Recent Advances in the Study of Subnormality*. National Association for Mental Health, London, 1969.

3 FOR THOSE WHO WISH MORE DETAILED AND SCIENTIFIC INFORMATION

1. Penrose, L. S. *The Biology of Mental Defect*. Sidgwick and Jackson, London, 1963.
2. Hilliard, L. T. and Kirman, B. H. *Mental Deficiency*. 2nd Edn. J. and A. Churchill, London, 1965.
3. Crome, L. C. and Stern, J. *Pathology of Mental Retardation*. J. and A. Churchill, London, 1967.
4. Wing, J. K. (Ed.) *Early Childhood Autism. Clinical, Educational and Social Aspects*. Pergamon Press, Oxford, 1966.
5. O'Connor, N. and Hermelin, B. *Speech and Thought in Severe Subnormality*. Pergamon Press, Oxford, 1963.
6. Davie, R., Butler, N. R. and Goldstein, H. *From Birth to Seven*. Longman, London, in preparation.
7. Wortis, J. (Ed.) *Mental Retardation—An Annual Review*. Grune and Stratton, Inc., New York, Vol. I, 1969; Vol. II, 1970; Vol. III, 1971.
8. Standing Medical Advisory Committee for the Central Health

Services Council and the Ministry of Health. Ministry of Health, London, 1967.
9. Penrose, L. S. and Smith, G. E. *Down's Anomaly*. J. and A. Churchill, London, 1966.
10. Group for the Advancement of Psychiatry. *Mild Mental Retardation: A Growing Challenge to the Physician*. New York, 1967.
11. Standing Medical Advisory Committee for the Central Health Services Council and the Minister of Health. *Human Genetics*. Ministry of Health, London, 1967.

Glossary

Achondroplasia A form of dwarfism, with shortening of the limbs and normal size head.

Amino-acids The main end-products resulting from breakdown of proteins in digestion.

Amniotic puncture A method of obtaining for diagnostic purposes a sample of the fluid surrounding the baby in the womb.

Amsterdam dwarfism A clinical condition associated with mental handicap and reduced physical growth, described by Cornelia de Lange, a physician of Amsterdam.

Anaemia A reduction in the number of red blood cells or in the amount of haemoglobin they carry.

Anencephaly Almost complete absence of the brain, resulting in still-birth or early death.

Antibodies Substances formed in the body after exposure to a foreign agent, e.g. measles virus or Rhesus positive blood.

Antigen A substance which can evoke an antibody. Rhesus-positive red blood cells and measles vaccine contain antigens.

Apert's syndrome (acrocephaly-syndactyly) A congenital defect in which the fingers and toes are not fully separated and the skull is malformed.

Arhinencephaly Absence of that part of the brain thought previously to be concerned chiefly with smell.

Athetosis A form of cerebral palsy with writhing movements, interfering with voluntary activity.

Audiogram A graph showing the acuity of hearing in either ear at different frequencies.

Autism A state of withdrawal, with absence of normal social relationships.

Autosomes A term used for all the chromosomes except those specially concerned with sex, i.e. X and Y in humans.

Barr body A small mass of stained material seen in mammalian female cells outside the nucleus.

Binet test A system for assessing intelligence devised in Paris by Binet and Simon at the beginning of this century.
Biopsy The cutting out of a piece of living tissue, e.g. appendix or from the brain, for special diagnostic examinations.
Brain stem That part of the base of the brain which is the upward extension of the spinal cord in the skull.
Cataract Opacity of the lens of the eye, resulting in faulty vision.
Cerebellum The 'small brain', part of the hind brain, highly developed in man, concerned with fine co-ordination of movement.
Cerebral palsy Paralysis or loss of motor function due to abnormality of the brain; commonly spasticity.
Chromatography A technique for analysing constituents of fluid by allowing them to run through absorbent material and staining.
Chromosome One of the small bodies into which most cell nuclei break up when the cell divides.
Cochlea A part of the inner ear shaped like a snail shell which receives the sound waves.
Cretinism Slow physical and mental development due to absence or poor function of the thyroid gland.
'Cri du chat' syndrome Physical deformity and mental retardation due to absence of part of one of the fifth pair of chromosomes.
Cytomegalic virus An organism causing a common infectious disease which occasionally damages the brain of the unborn baby.
Dementia Decay of the intellect as a result of progressive brain disease.
Depression A state of unhappiness, grief or despair which may be due to misfortune or be without good reason.
Dominant inheritance Transmission of a trait; e.g., positive Rhesus group *direct* from parent to child.
Down's syndrome (mongolism) A distinctive form of physical and mental dwarfing due to the presence of an additional small chromosome (21).
Dystrophia myotonica A slowly progressive familial nervous disorder with muscular spasm and often with mental handicap.
Edward's syndrome A rare distinctive form of physical and mental dwarfing due to the presence of an additional chromosome (17-18).
Electroencephalogram A recording of the electrical brain waves taken from different parts of the head.

Enzyme A substance which, when present in small amounts, makes possible a vital chemical process; for example, the conversion of galactose into glucose.

Epilepsy A sudden, abnormal discharge of energy from the brain resulting in a fit or the equivalent.

Epithelium The membranes lining the surface of the body and the cavities opening from the surface.

Folic acid A chemical substance, a member of the vitamin B complex essential for normal growth of the nervous system.

Fontanelle Gap between the bones of the skull present at birth; 'soft spot'.

Galactosaemia A chemical disorder of genetic origin due to a missing enzyme for converting galactose to glucose.

Gamma globulin A part of the blood protein which carries antibodies against disease, e.g. German measles.

'Gargoylism' A group of chemical disorders, including Hurler's syndrome, in which characteristic chemical substances are excreted.

Genes The units of hereditary material of which the chromosomes are composed and which determine foetal growth.

Genetics The science of heredity and study of the genesis of new organisms.

Gland A part of the body which produces a secretion, e.g. liver, pancreas, thyroid.

Glia Supporting cells in the brain which often multiply after disease or injury, producing hardening.

Grave's disease Over-activity of the thyroid gland with a rapid heart rate, tremor and bulging eyes.

Guthrie test A biological method of detecting phenylketonuria on a small sample of blood; used for mass screening.

Gyri The folds in the surface of the brain, in the cerebral cortex.

Homocystinuria A chemical disorder of genetic origin transmitted as a Mendelian recessive trait.

Hormone A 'chemical messenger' secreted by the ductless glands such as the thyroid and carried by the blood.

Hydrocephalus 'Water on the brain'. Faulty circulation of the cerebrospinal fluid, usually resulting in enlarged head.

Hypotonia Low muscle tone, 'floppiness', 'double-jointedness'.

Hypsarrythmia Unusually high voltages in brain as shown by peaks in the electroencephalogram.

Infarct Blockage of blood supply leading to shortage of oxygen and possible tissue death and scarring.

Intelligence quotient (I.Q.) The attainment on a standard test of intelligence as a percentage of the average for the age.

Jaundice Yellowness of the skin and tissues best seen in the eyes by natural light; due to excess of bile pigment.

Kinaesthetic sense The 'feedback' from muscles, tendons and joints giving information on position, weight, strength, etc.

Klinefelter syndrome Maldevelopment of the testis due to an additional female chromosome in the male; causes sterility.

Kwashiorkor Degeneration of the liver due to starvation, common in Africa: also in babies with no milk supply.

Lactose Milk sugar; is split, producing galactose in the gut.

Lipid A fat-like substance in the blood and other tissues, amount in brain increased in lipidoses, a series of genetic errors.

Little's disease Spastic, congenital cerebral palsy often with small head.

Lowe's disease A congenital disorder of eye, brain and kidney affecting only boys; carried by female.

Maple syrup urine disease An inborn chemical error recognizable by a typically aromatic urine containing aminoacids.

Marfan's syndrome A dominantly transmissible error usually with reduced intelligence, increased length of body and dislocation of lens of eye.

Masochism Taking pleasure in suffering.

Mendel's laws The basic laws of heredity discovered by Grigor Mendel, differentiating dominant and recessive inheritance.

Meninges The three layers of membrane covering the brain; pia-arachnoid and dura.

Meningitis Inflammation of the meninges usually due to infection, as in tuberculous meningitis.

Microcephaly Pathological smallness of the head in comparison with the norm for age and sex.

Mucopolysaccharidoses A group of diseases due to inborn errors of metabolism including 'gargoylism', Hurler's syndrome.

Myelin sheaths The main constituent of the white matter of the brain, surrounding the nerve fibres.

Myxoedema A disease due to inadequacy of the thyroid secretion resulting in slowness, lethargy, coldness and puffiness.

Neurology The branch of medicine concerned with disorders of the nervous system.

Neurones The nerve cells, the many millions of which are the chief functional units of the human brain.

Neurosis A 'minor' mental disorder, e.g. hysteria or anxiety state not amounting to madness.

Nystagmus Visible wobbling of the eye, side to side, up and down, or circular.

Osteomalacia Thinning of the bony substance often with deformity; due usually to malnutrition.

Paraldehyde A substance with a strong, unpleasant smell, formerly much used in mental hospitals as a sedative.

Parkinson's disease A disorder of the elderly, 'paralysis agitans', the shaking palsy, tremor and stiffness.

Patau's syndrome A rare deformity causing early death due to the presence of an extra chromosome of the 13-15 group.

Phenylalanine An aminoacid found in most proteins and essential for human life and growth; excess damages the brain.

Phenylketonuria A inborn chemical disorder due to a faulty enzyme which should convert phenylalanine to tyrosine.

Placenta The organ which nourishes the unborn baby in the middle and late stages of pregnancy.

Prosencephaly Faulty development of the forebrain; the two frontal lobes may fail to separate.

Protozoa Simple form of animal life consisting of a single, actively moving cell.

Psychopathology Disorder of the mental processes as in major mental diseases, e.g. schizophrenia.

Recessive inheritance Transmission of a trait, e.g. phenylketonuria, *indirectly* through a healthy carrier.

Rhesus blood group. A trait which divides people into Rhesus positive and negative depending on the reaction of their blood with that of the Rhesus monkey.

Rubella German measles, a virus infection usually mild after birth but serious for the unborn.

Rubinstein-Taybi syndrome A rare error of development with

broad, deformed thumbs, a characteristic face and usually limited intelligence.
Sadism Taking pleasure in inflicting pain on others.
Schilder's disease A wasting of the white matter of the brain due to a group of inborn chemical disorders.
Schizophrenia A common major mental disorder often in young people with withdrawal and loss of normal feeling.
Spasticity Found in the common form of cerebral palsy with increased muscle tone, stiffness and dribbling of saliva.
Sphincters Circular muscles which can close and open orifices, e.g. anus and urethra.
Spina bifida Open spine, a congenital deformity usually fatal unless operated. Allows a cyst of cerebrospinal fluid to form.
Syphilitic encephalitis General paralysis of the insane (GPI); inflammation of the brain due to the spirochaete of syphilis.
Tay-Sachs disease Cerebro-macular degeneration. A form of lipidosis, with progressive blindness and dementia.
Terman-Merrill test A revision of the Binet-Simon scale for assessment of intelligence standardized on an American population.
Thyroid A ductless or endocrine gland in the neck; uses iodine, produces thyroxine which regulates body metabolism.
Toxoplasmosis Infection with a micro-organism common in animals; mild effects in adults but may cause serious damage to unborn child.
Tranquillizers Drugs used to relieve symptoms of schizophrenia and other mental illnesses.
Trisomy The presence of an extra chromosome producing three of a kind instead of the usual pair.
Tuberous sclerosis A congenital disorder of the brain and skin of the face (adenoma subaceum); also known as 'epiloia'.
Turner's syndrome Ovarian agenesis, i.e. failure of development of the ovaries in the female due to the absence of one X chromosome.
Ventricles Hollow spaces, e.g. in the brain, where there are normally four such cavities.
Vineland scale A questionnaire designed to assess the social development of the child.
Vitamin Substances a small quantity of which in the diet is essential to normal health, e.g. ascorbic acid (vitamin C).
Wassermann reaction A standard test for blood and cerebrospinal

fluid used in detection of syphilis.

Wechsler scale A method of assessing intelligence which gives information about different aspects of attainment.

Wilson's disease A slowly progressive inborn chemical error with accumulation of copper in the brain.

Appendix 1
Speech development (Ad hoc scale)

Reproduced by courtesy of Miss Elspeth Stephen

Approx.
age
months

1	Throaty noises
2	Single vowels (e.g., ah, uh.)
3	Coos
6	M-m-m sound
6	Polysyllabic vowels
7	Single syllables (e.g., da, ba.)
8	2-syllable babbles (e.g., dada, googoo)
9	4-syllable babbles
9	Singing tones
9	1 clear word
12	2 clear words
13	3-4 clear words
13	Incipient jargon
15	Jargon
16	6-7 words
19	9 words
21	2-word combinations
24	3-word sentences
24	Pronouns
36	Plurals

Appendix 2
Functional assessment record

Reproduced by courtesy of Miss Elspeth Stephen

Name: Date of test:

Age: Date of birth:

1 **Locomotor attainments:**
   months
   6–9   a rolls from back to side
         b sits with slight support
   9–12 a stands against support
         b sits alone
         c pulls to standing using furniture
   12–15 a walks with aid
         b crawls on hands and knees
         c sits on the floor
   15–24 a walks alone
         b manages a chair
   24–36 a manages stairs
         b runs

2 **Feeding attainments:**
   months
   6–9   takes semi-solids
   9–12   puts hand on cup whilst drinking
   12–15 a   eats bread and biscuits alone
          b   tries to help (messily) when fed
   15–24 a   eats alone with spoon
          b   drinks from cup unaided
   24–36   begins using fork
   36–48   eats with fork and spoon
   48–60   begins to use knife

Appendix 2: Functional assessment record

3. **Dressing attainments:**
   months
   - 12–15 holds out arms and feet
   - 15–24 takes off hat, shoes and socks
   - 24–36 a pulls off simple garment
     - b tries to dress
   - 36–48 buttons coat and dress
   - 48–60 dresses self except for back buttons, laces and ties
   - 60 dresses and undresses alone

4. **Toilet training attainments:**
   months
   - 12–15 clean and dry with regular potting (occasional accidents)
   - 15–24 a bowel control
     - b asks by word or sign
     - c bladder control during day
   - 24–36 clean if lifted once a night
   - 36–48 a dry through night
     - b begins to care for self at toilet
   - 48–60 cares for self at toilet

Is there any evidence of defective vision?

Is there any evidence of defective hearing?

Is there any other obvious physical handicap (e.g. C.P. etc.)?

Index of authors

Allen, R. C., 181
Barr, M. L., 41
Barton, R., 55
Berg, J. M., 109
Binet, A., 10, 54
Birch, H., 27
Blizzard, R. M., 209
Bowlby, J., 55, 176
Brandon, M. W. G., 82, 173, 174
Buck, P., 25
Burt, Sir Cyril, 64, 66
Butler, N. R., 50, 51, 117
Carter, C. O., 25, 109
Clarke, A. D. B., 129, 130, 157, 164, 165, 168, 175, 176, 219
Clarke, A. M., 130, 157, 164, 168, 175, 176, 219
Coffey, V. P., 115
Collmann, R. D., 107
Court Brown, W. M., 108
Craft, M. J., 144
Crome, L., 28, 30, 34
Darwin, C., 25
Dickens, C., 53
Elek, S. D., 115
Evans, K., 25, 109
Fitzherbert, A., 49
Fölling, A., 208
Garfield, A., 95
Garrod, A. E., 101
Gates, R. R., 107
Ginzberg, E., 58
Grad, J. C., 77, 78, 80, 126
Gregg, N. M., 114
Griffiths, R., 97
Guggenbühl, 54
Hardy, T., 9
Harlow, H. F., 91
Hermelin, B., 129, 158, 219
Hilliard. L. T., 82, 175, 177
Ireland, W. W., 25, 57
Itard, J. M. G., 54
Jessop, W. J. E., 115
King, R. D., 134
Kipling, R., 54
Kushlick, A., 17, 24, 134

Langdon Down, J., 38, 56, 207, 208
Lawson, D. N., 207
Lewis, E. O., 168, 173
Little, W. J., 26
Lovaas, I., 165
Lyle, J. G., 129
McDonald, A., 112, 115
McKeown, T., 17
Mendel, G., 30, 36
Michelson, P., 173
Mittler, P., 218, 219
Morel, B. A., 12, 57
Morris, P., 55, 128
Mundy, L., 175
Murphy, D. P., 105
O'Connor, N., 81, 129, 158, 168, 179, 182, 186, 195, 199, 204, 219
Owen, R., 55
Pavlov, I. P., 93, 161, 163-5, 219
Penrose, L. S., 12, 70, 73, 104, 204, 208
Piaget, J., 95, 96
Pinel, P., 53, 54, 61
Porteus, S. D., 10
Raynes, N. V., 134
Raven, J. C., 98
Reed, A., 55, 56
Robertson, J., 55
Séguin, E., 54
Shakespeare, R., 95
Shakespeare, W., 48
Sheridan, M.. 126, 172
Sherrington, C. S., 163
Simon, T., 10
Skinner, B. F., 164
Stein, Z., 64, 69
Stengel, E., 177
Stephen, E., 231
Stern, H., 115
Stoller, A., 107
Stott, D. H., 112
Susser, N. W., 64, 69
Swinburne, H., 49
Thomson, G. H., 50
Tizard, J., 24, 68, 77, 78, 80, 81, 126, 127, 168, 179, 182, 186, 195, 199, 204, 219

Tredgold, A. F., 50, 57, 58, 168
Tuke, W., 61
Watson, J. B., 163

Wechsler, D., 12, 49, 50, 96, 98
Woodward, M., 72, 96, 181
Yerkes, R. M., 58

Index of subjects

Abortion, 26, 109, 114, 209
Achondroplasia, 104
Administrative prevalence of mental handicap, 13
Adoption, 152
Advisory clinics, 124, 153
Alcohol, 58
Aminoacids, 102
Amniotic puncture, 26, 37, 87, 110, 209
Amritsar, 25
Anaemia, 70
Anencephaly, 103
Ante-natal care, 112
Apert's syndrome, 85, 104
Arachnodactyly, 104
Arhinencephaly, 40
Army, 12
'Ascertainment', 19, 62, 119, 130
Assessment, 84, 88-100, 136, 150, 162
Assortative mating, 173
Athetosis, 117
Atom bombs, 105
'At risk' register, 20
Audiogram, 22, 161
Australia, 107, 114, 116
Australian aborigines, 10, 48, 49
Autism, 22
Automation, 16, 81, 187, 197
Autosomes, 38, 40

BCG vaccine, 45
Bed wetting, 91
Behaviour shaping, 162, 169, 179
Behaviour therapy, 162
Binet-Simon test, 10, 66, 99
Birth, 115
Birth order, 50, 70
Birth weight, 20, 27, 116, 117
Blindness, 30, 31, 114, 115, 157, 191
Blood groups, 120, 210
Board of Control, 60
Brain chemistry, 34
Brain, development of, 47, 218
Brain in mental retardation, 29, 33, 40, 43, 46
British Psychological Society, 81

Broadmoor, 60, 185
Brooklands experiment, 68, 129
Buccal smear, 41

Cancer, 108
Carriers, 30, 31, 102, 121
Cataract, 102, 114, 159, 215, 216
Causation of mental handicap, 101-17, 218
Cerebral palsy, 20, 47, 69, 85, 117, 162, 190, 211
Ceylon, 64
Child labour, 66
Children of mentally handicapped, 174, 175
Chromosomes, 31, 38-42, 52, 107-12
Cough reflex, 90
Civil liberty, 19, 60
Cleft lip, 85
Cleft palate, 85, 159
Colchester survey, 73
Colchicine, 106
Communication, 138, 160
Conditioned reflexes, 89, 91-3, 129, 144, 162-6, 169
Consanguinity, 30
Conscription, 12
Contraception, 177
Courts, 19, 80, 184
Cousins, 30
Cretinism, 21, 33, 205-9
'Cri du chat' syndrome, 40
Culture, 64, 68
Cytomegalic virus, 115

Darenth Park, 81, 186
Day hospitals, 133, 134, 152
Day nurseries, 78, 139, 149, 178
Deafness, 21, 114, 132, 157, 160-2
Deformities, 85
Degree of mental handicap, 14
Delinquency, 71, 72, 181, 182
Depression, parental, 76, 139
Destructiveness, 142, 143, 150, 190
Development, 88, 95-8, 137

Index of subjects 237

Diagnosis of disease associated with mental retardation, 33, 133
Discharge from hospital, 81, 150
Dominant genes, 37, 104, 216
Down's syndrome, 19, 20, 27, 38, 40, 42, 84, 92, 107-12, 124, 146, 147, 158, 174, 207, 211-13
Dressing, 233
Drugs, 51-3, 106, 112, 144, 145, 147
Dystrophia myotonica, 216

Earlswood asylum, 56
Economic considerations, 64, 66, 81, 176
Education, 58, 66, 118, 120, 130, 131, 134, 135, 154, 159, 161, 164, 169, 170
Education Act, 1944, 119
Education, compulsory, 13
Educationally subnormal children, 13, 14, 19, 166, 167
Edward's syndrome, 39, 40
Electroencephalogram, 21, 46, 86, 162
Elizabethan Poor Law, 52
Employment, 17, 19, 67, 81, 82, 186, 192-5
Encephalitis, 20, 44, 46, 117, 210
Encephalitis lethargica, 45
Environment, 51, 103, 135, 176
Enzymes, 31, 33, 102, 116, 206, 212
Epilepsy, 36, 68, 85, 146, 147, 150, 191, 211
'Epiloia', see Tuberous sclerosis
Eskimos, 48
Eugenics, 15, 59, 124
Eugenics Society, 25, 50, 57
Evolution, 103

Families of mentally handicapped, 76
Family allowances, 71
Family size, 70
Father, age of, 104
Feebleminded, the, 14, 57
Feeding, 89, 232
Female chromosome, 41, 42
Fertility, 25, 72, 112, 173, 174
Folic acid, 70, 86
Fostering, 152
France, 57, 99
French Revolution, 53
Frequency of mental handicap, 10, 49

Galactosaemia, 101, 102, 215
'Gargoylism', 31, 87, 146, 160
'General paralysis of the insane', see Syphilis
Genes, 31, 52, 102-4, 107

Genetic abnormalities of the brain, 31, 215
Genetic counselling, 33, 37, 110, 121-4, 209
Genetic risk, 102, 110-12, 121, 122, 210
Genius of Earlswood asylum, the, 57
Germ plasm, injury to, 58
Gesture, 92
Glasses, 159
Glia, 29
Griffiths scale, 97
Group for the Advancement of Psychiatry, 58, 108
Guthrie test, 87, 207, 212, 217

Hand regard, 95, 155
Head circumference, 20, 85
Head injury, 69
'Head Start' programmes, 83
Health visitors, 127
Hearing, 160, 161
Hearing aids, 132, 160-2
Heart defect, 85, 124, 147
Hepatitis, infectious, 106
Heredity, 29, 32, 36, 102, 108, 121
Hester Adrian Research Centre, 218
Histidinaemia, 87, 121
Historical changes, effect of, 47
History of mental handicap, 65
Home care, 75, 131, 135
Home teaching, 131
Homocystinuria, 73, 87, 104, 121
Hospitals, 15, 61, 79, 81, 82, 133-5, 149-52, 159, 169, 184, 187, 190-3, 195, 196, 198-200
Hostels, 62, 133, 134, 151, 177, 179, 188, 192, 194, 196
Housing, 71, 75, 176
Hurler's syndrome, 146, 160
Hydrocephalus, 20, 29, 43, 44, 69, 84, 115
Hyperuricaemia, 87
Hypsarrythmia, 36, 86

Idiot, 13, 48, 67
Idiot asylums, 56, 57
Illegitimacy, 57, 72, 119, 124, 175, 176, 210
Illiteracy, 13, 58, 65
Imbecile, 13, 67
Immigrants, 71
Incentives, 167, 189
Income, parental, 76
Incontinence, 91, 132, 147, 148
'Ineducable' children, 16, 119
Infant mortality, 27, 65, 117

Infantile spasms, 36, 86
Infections, 113-15
Influenza, 115
Inheritance, indirect, 30, 31
Institute for Research into Mental Retardation, 218
Institutional surveys, 73
Institutions, 15, 55, 61, 99, 128, 134-6, 138, 176, 186, 194, 200, 201
Intelligence, 67, 80-2, 175-7, 179, 181, 182, 187, 195
Intelligence, development of, 69, 171, 175, 176
Intelligence in autism, 22
Intelligence, national, 26, 50
Intelligence quotient (I.Q.), 10-16, 68, 94, 100, 136, 171
Intelligence, relative nature of, 10
International classification of diseases, 13
Iodine, 21
Isle of Wight study, 52

Japan, 50, 51, 105
Jaundice of the newborn, 20, 116, 160
Jobs, 16, 17

Kinaesthetic sensation, 158
Klinefelter syndrome, 41-3, 72, 107, 112
Kwashiorkor, 27

Larbert Hospital, 57
Law on mental handicap, 58
Learning in mentally handicapped, 128, 141, 144, 156, 158, 166, 167, 201, 219
Legal rights, 58, 183
Leisure, 182, 183, 189, 196, 201, 202
Leukaemia, 108
Levels of mental handicap, 67
Liberty, 53, 62, 63
Licence from hospital, 59
Life expectation, 145, 146
Local authorities, 17, 18, 20, 125-8, 130, 133, 134, 153, 187
Lodgings 16, 185, 194
London survey, 24, 126
Long-term care, 74
Lowe's syndrome, 215
LSD, 52, 106
Lunacy Act, 49, 62
Lunatics, 48

Magistrates, 58, 60
Male chromosome, 40
Malformation, 109
Management, 136

Mannerisms, 156
Maple syrup urine disease, 87
Marfan's syndrome, 104
Marriage, 58, 60, 172, 173
Maternal age, 38, 104, 108, 109
Maternal health, 27, 35, 112
Maternal love, 94
Measles, 45, 210
Memory, 141
Mendel's laws, 30
Meningitis, 20, 43, 44, 69
Menstruation, absence of, 42
Mental age, 137
Mental Deficiency Act, 1913, 13, 56, 58, 60, 62, 67
Mental Health Act, 1959, 14, 19, 62, 66, 79, 81, 119
Mental health workers, 137, 184
Mental illness, 48, 71, 176
Mercury, 51
Microcephaly, 19, 20, 25, 85, 105, 115
Middlesex survey, 24
Mild retardation, 14, 19, 24, 57, 58, 67, 81, 172, 176, 179, 181, 193, 195, 198, 201
Military standards, 12
Moderate retardation, 14
'Mongolism', see Down's syndrome
Montessori methods, 156
'Moral deficiency', 182
Moron, 14
Mortality, 25
Mosaics, 38, 110
Moss Side, 60, 184, 185
Mucopolysaccharidoses, 87
Multiple handicap, 162
'Multiplication of unfit', 57, 59
Muscle tone, 158
Mutation, 37, 49, 103, 106, 108

National Association for Mental Health, 9, 60, 128, 153, 196
'National Degeneration', 57
National Society for Mentally Handicapped Children, 9, 60, 125, 127, 153, 182, 185, 218
National Spastics Society, 132
Nazi Germany, 25
Negroes, intelligence in, 12, 58
Neurones, 29, 45
New York, 30
Non-communicating children, 22
Non-disjunction, 39, 107, 108
Number, concept of, 97
Nurseries, 18
Nursery schools, 127

Index of subjects

Nurses, 128, 135, 145, 152
Nutrition, 27
Nystagmus, 159

Observation classes, 23, 175
Operant conditioning, 129, 164
Optic atrophy, 89
Osteomalacia, 116
Overcrowding, 178, 194
Over-protection, 100, 179
Oxygen, 89

Paediatricians, 122
Pain sense, 157, 178
Paper chromatography, 87
Paralysis agitans, 45
Parent counselling, 133
Parental expectations, 65
Parish responsibility, 52
Parkinson's Disease, 45
Patau's syndrome, 39, 40
'Pathological' group, 67
Pathology of mental retardation, 28, 67, 68
Pauper lunatic, 49
Performance, 98
Permanence of objects, 95
Petit mal, 86
Phenobarbitone, 86
Phenylketonuria, 20, 33, 34, 69, 79, 86, 87, 101, 102, 121, 206, 207, 208, 212, 213, 215, 216, 220
Phenytoin, 86
Physical handicap, 132
Physical restraint, 53
Piaget scale, 96
Play, 96, 155, 156
Play groups, 18, 127
Poisons, 51
Poland, 105
Poor Law, 52, 59
Porteus mazes, 10
Post-mortem examination, 33
Poverty, 27, 64, 77, 176
Pregnancy, 35, 112-16, 212
Prematurity, 70, 116, 117
Pre-natal screening, 87
Pre-school facilities, 126
Prevention, 119, 213
Prisoners, 181
Probation, 19, 80, 119, 184
Profound retardation, 14, 94, 132, 133, 149, 156
Prosencephaly, 40
Psychiatrists, 122, 125, 151
Psychologists, 82, 98, 125, 170, 188, 190

'Psychopaths', 182
Psychotherapy, 179
Public awareness of mental handicap, 9

Radium, 195, 112
Rampton, 60, 184, 185
Raven's progressive matrices, 98
Recessive genes, 30, 102
Recognition of mental handicap, 18, 19, 21
Register of handicapped persons, 19
Regression to the mean, 174
Rehabilitation, 176
Research, 79, 120, 203ff.
Residential care, 15, 132, 134, 149, 151
Retina, 30, 31
'Retreat', the, 53
Rhesus incompatibility, 120, 160, 209, 210
Rickets, 116
Royal Commission on the Feebleminded, 57
Royal Commission on the Law, 62
Royal Eastern Counties Hospital, 56
Royal National Institute for the Blind, 162
Royal Western Counties Hospital, 57
Rubella, 26, 113, 114, 120, 121, 147, 160, 215
Rubella vaccine, 114, 115, 121
Rubinstein–Taybi syndrome, 214
Rudolf Steiner villages, 145, 196
Rural areas, intelligence in, 64

Salford, 24
Schilder's disease, 31, 34
Schizophrenia, 73
School entry, 23
Schools for educationally subnormal, 19, 194, 199
School leavers, 80, 193
School provision, 63, 66, 119, 128, 134, 135, 169
Scott Report, 128
Scottish survey, 10, 50, 70
Screening, 86, 121, 126
Segregation, policy of, 56, 58, 61
Selection, 50
Sensory deprivation, 85
Sensory dominance, 157
Sensory training, 156
Serotonin, 213
Services for mentally handicapped, 118, 121
Severe retardation, 14, 170

Severely subnormal, 14, 66, 79, 82
Sex, association with opposite, 59
Sex cells, 107, 110, 111, 213
Sex chromatin, 41
Sex-chromosomes, 38, 40-2, 214
Sex education, 177
Sex-linked disease, 32
Sexual drive, 72, 180
Sexual intercourse, frequency of, 39
Sexual intercourse, inadequacy, 42
Short-term care, 74, 150, 151
Sleepy sickness, 45
Smoking, 51, 113
Social class, 27, 50, 70, 74, 116, 117, 148, 182
Social competence, 80
Social factors, 64, 69
Social problems, 71, 72, 142
Social quotient, 94
Social responses, 90, 160, 166
Social workers, 18, 62, 80, 82, 127, 152, 176, 201
Society, evolution of, 47, 103
Sparta, 25
Spasticity, 20, 85, 146
Special care units, 131, 132, 166
Special classes, 67
Specialisation, 47
Speech, 92-4, 129, 133, 138, 139, 160, 161, 231
Speech therapists, 132, 159-61
Spina bifida, 20, 44, 84, 91, 103, 147, 216
Spitz-Holter valve, 44
Squint, 158
Standardisation of tests, 10
Stages of development, 94, 232
Stanford revision of Terman-Merrill Scale, 99
Stature, 50, 116
Status epilepticus, 146, 147
Sterility, 41
Streptomycin, 45
Sub-cultural group, 68
Subnormal, 14, 79, 81
'Superfemales', 42
Supervisors, 119, 128, 170
Surgery, 44
Surveys of mental handicap, 23
'Survival of Fittest', 25
Syphilis, 46, 113, 210
Swallowing, 89

Talking, age of, 21
Tay-Sachs Disease, 30, 146
Teachers, 66, 128-30, 166, 170, 190

Terman-Merrill test, 2, 10, 70, 99, 100
Thalidomide, 52, 160
Toilet training, 91, 148, 233
Toxoplasmosis, 115
Training centres, 17, 62, 119, 130-32, 134, 139, 144, 149, 166, 182, 193, 200, 201
Transfusion, exchange, 120
Translocation, 109
Treatment, 213
Tribunals, mental health, 63, 80
Triple X females, 42, 112
Trisomy, 39, 40
Tuberculosis, in mother, 115
Tuberculous meningitis, 44
Tuberous sclerosis, 35, 86, 104, 105, 174, 216
Turner's syndrome, 42, 72, 108, 112

Unarmed pioneers, 16
Undeveloped countries, 13
'Unemployable', the, 16
Unemployment, 28
'Unfit', the, 15, 56, 57
Union of South Africa, 180
United States of America, 12, 50, 58, 70, 72, 83, 99, 105, 165, 180, 181

Variation, 'normal', 68
Victorians, 55
Village idiot, 9, 48, 49
Vineland scale, 94
Viruses, 45, 107, 113-15
Vision, 88, 132, 158, 159
Vitamin B, 86
Vitamin B12, 70
Voluntary organisations, 60, 202
Voluntary patients, 56

Waiting lists for residential care, 16, 19, 61, 133
Walking, age of, 21, 88, 232
War, selection for military service, 12, 16, 57
Wechsler tests, 11, 49, 50, 52, 98, 171, 173, 195
Weekly boarding, 133
Wessex, 24
Wilson's Disease, 216
Wolf Boy of Aveyron, 54
Workhouses, 52, 53
Work therapy, 53

X chromosome, 41, 42
X-rays, 52, 105, 106, 112

Y chromosome, 40, 112
Youth Clubs, 182